Literature and [

Los Angeles is both the [ ]
metropolis in America, a[ ]
aestheticized city. With more than eighty-five languages being
spoken in its classrooms, and one homogenous visual
language emanating from its entertainment industry, LA
radically challenges the prospects of that archaic
representational medium: literature. In its investigation of the
work of Bret Easton Ellis, James Ellroy, Anna Deavere Smith
and others, *Literature and Race in Los Ángeles* articulates their
aesthetic preoccupations with the structures of social space in
the city. Harnessing some of the theoretical insights of Henri
Lefebvre and the 'LA school' of geographers, Murphet
demonstrates the versatility of literary production in LA and
speculates about the fortunes of literature in a predominantly
visual culture.

JULIAN MURPHET is a Junior Research Fellow at St John's
College, Oxford and Visiting Professor at the University of
California at Berkeley in 2000–2001. This is his first book.

Cultural Margins

General editor
Timothy Brennan
*Department of Cultural Studies and Comparative Literature and English,
University of Minnesota*

The series Cultural Margins originated in response to the rapidly increasing interest in postcolonial and minority discourses among literary and humanist scholars in the US, Europe, and elsewhere. The aim of the series is to present books which investigate the complex cultural zone within and through which dominant and minority societies interact and negotiate their differences. Studies in the series range from examinations of the debilitating effects of cultural marginalisation, to analyses of the forms of power found at the margins of culture, to books which map the varied and complex components involved in the relations of domination and subversion. This is an international series, addressing questions crucial to the deconstruction and reconstruction of cultural identity in the late twentieth-century world.

LITERATURE AND RACE IN LOS ANGELES

Julian Murphet

PUBLISHED BY THE PRESS SYNDICATE OF THE UNIVERSITY OF CAMBRIDGE
The Pitt Building, Trumpington Street, Cambridge, United Kingdom

CAMBRIDGE UNIVERSITY PRESS
The Edinburgh Building, Cambridge CB2 2RU, UK
40 West 20th Street, New York, NY 10011–4211, USA
10 Stamford Road, Oakleigh, Melbourne 3166, Australia
Ruiz de Alarcón 13, 28014 Madrid, Spain
Dock House, The Waterfront, Cape Town 8001, South Africa

http://www.cambridge.org

First published 2001

Printed in the United Kingdom at the University Press, Cambridge

Typeset in Palatino 9.5/12pt   System 3b2   [CE]

A catalogue record for this book is available from the British Library

ISBN 0 521 80149 4 hardback
ISBN 0 521 80535 x paperback

for Felix

Because there must be production,
nature must be replaced wherever it can be replaced by every
possible means of activity,
a major field must be found for human inertia,
the worker must be kept busy at something,
new fields of activity must be created,
where all the false manufactured products,
all the ignoble synthetic ersatzes will finally reign,
where beautiful true nature has nothing to do,
and must give up its place once and for all and shamefully to all the
triumphant replacement products

Antonin Artaud[1]

Contents

Acknowledgements

Thanks are due to Trinity College, Cambridge for both the External Research Scholarship and the Senior Rouse Ball Studentship which funded this project in its initial doctoral phase, as well as two scholarships for research trips to the USA. A Junior Research Fellowship at St John's College, Oxford has enabled its transition into book form.

I want to thank Wanda Coleman and Dennis Cooper for agreeing to be interviewed by me in Los Angeles, in 1996.

Along the way, the helpful advice of the following people has been welcome: Adrian Poole, Dean Kolbas, Ashley Tellis, Pam Thurschwell, Sarah Meer, Maud Ellman, Liz Emens, Alex Houen, and Rachel Potter. Ato Quayson, the best man to have in your corner in any situation, got the first draft out of me in under three years, for which enough thanks cannot be given. Ian Bell at Keele has been a kind and supportive critic. My editor at Cambridge University Press, Ray Ryan and the series editor, Tim Brennan, have been extremely generous with time and comments, and unflagging in their support. Three anonymous Press readers have challenged the work in ways which have made it a good deal better.

Finally, I would like to remember the role Tony Tanner played in seeing this book into print. As my doctoral examiner at Cambridge, his enthusiasm for this work could not have been more encouraging, convincing me that what I had to say was relevant and interesting to a wider public. His support was the more welcome for the extraordinary authority of its intellectual basis. He has been missed.

Introduction: on minoritization and domination

Is a situation conceivable in which minorities have become the majority? A space where what is dominant is precisely the becoming-minor of all populations? We shall proceed by agreeing that it is, and that one of the greatest challenges facing contemporary thought, not to mention practice, lies in coming to terms with this radical minoritization. For the possibility is surely nothing other than our own reality at its most extreme and tendential, reserved for special places into which we gaze as into crystal balls. Chief among these is Los Angeles, the first continental US city in which whites have fallen short of an outright majority; where the global has become local, and the major minor, in often striking ways.

> Los Angeles' status of mostly Third World cultures is well known, but needs summarizing. It has the largest Korean metropolitan district outside Korea, Mexican metropolitan area outside Mexico, Filipino district outside the Philippines and Vietnamese district outside Vietnam, and is second in such ratios with the Chinese and the Japanese populations. Beyond this, it has major concentrations of Salvadoreans, Indians, Iranians and Russians. With Latinos, Jews and WASPs the largest minorities in this minoritised place, it is more fitting to see the area as a set of countries – like Europe – than a traditional unified city.[1]

It is a shift whose nature is profoundly demographic – a quality of sheer human numbers, of heterogeneous flows, which emerges as patterns of interference on the spatial itself. One end of a street becomes 'Korean', the other 'Armenian'; in between, the 'Hispanic' offers its own intensities. Meanwhile, diverse essences such as the 'African-American', the 'Samoan' and the 'Anglo' circulate up and down the avenue and impart something of their own peculiar

1

territorialities: booming car stereos, vividly painted automobiles, the little allegories of cellular phones. So in miniature, in minor interferences and incommensurabilities, the globalization of cultures is enacted.

Yet we want to be protected here from some fantasy scenario of an achieved democratization through minoritization. Indeed, the principal challenge may rest in squaring the conceptual circle of a minoritized space in which the dominant bloc rules ever more supreme, only from the outside, from the suburban hinterlands, tax-rich white edge cities and eerily insubstantial multinational corporations. The concept of the 'minor' only makes sense in determinate relation to what excludes it: governmentality, wealth, power, hegemony, or whatever shorthand you use for the concentration of might under late capitalism. So while it may be the case demographically that the Euro-ethnic population of Los Angeles has fallen to under 40 per cent of the total, that there has been a popular black mayor, and that various kinds of local political organization have increased the representation of other minorities, this is not to say that urban space is here free from the structures of power which elsewhere curtail popular control. Indeed, what is most startling is the ratio of minoritization to economic polarization. Edward Soja, in his treatment of the six-fold geography of the city today, carefully separates the geography of Cosmopolis or Heteropolis from that of the 'Repolarized Metropolis'. Of this latter he writes that '[t]here are more millionaires than ever before in Los Angeles', while as many as eighty thousand homeless men and women look for shelter every night and 'the most severe urban housing crisis in America' affects half a million more.[2] It is true that both extremes of this economic polarity reflect the range of cultures of the minoritized 'Cosmopolis', but the top 10 per cent on the ladder of wealth is disproportionately white, as are the police force, elected officialdom, and the federal policy-makers who make the largest decisions over funding and power.

Domination would appear, then, to have increased with the influx and spread of diverse ethnic cultures; the demographic revolution goes hand in hand with an intensification of inequality and injustice. To say that this is a novel development in the history of social relations, or that some contradiction is at work here which needs patient unpacking, would be to understate gravely what is at stake in a situation such as this. As this book unfolds, it will be found again and again to turn on this central problematic of the concentration of power in a space of fragmentation and abstraction. That we will be approaching it from the discipline of literary studies has, despite its initial appearance of counterintuitive illogic (surely human geography, sociology or history would be more appropriate!), a triple advantage: that it takes as its basis the embattled interests of a minority within and across the various ethnic minorities, namely *writers*; that it approaches the central problematic from its most perplexing angle, the vexed issue of its *representation*; and that, since so much of the city's domination is bound up with visual-cultural strategies, literature has the virtue of preserving in its *verbal* textures enough by way of linguistic negativity and difference to open up critical spaces within the complex minoritization-domination, and prepare for its immanent critique.

The ensuing first chapter will tackle the second of these issues in as dialectical a fashion as seems appropriate, to introduce the historical involutions of representation and space in Los Angeles; while the rest of the book will argue through close stylistic analysis for literature's unique status in this city as a repository for the otherwise forgotten and neglected realms of inwardness, sensuousness, affect, historicity, memory and ethnic solidarity. Meanwhile, it seems reasonable to articulate some of our initial concerns through a brief resumé of a few of the difficulties faced by the writers themselves, in achieving recognition locally and at large, winning readerships and wider publication, and funding their own labours. Indeed, as a minority in Los Angeles, the fractured community of its literary writers is exemplary of the general experience of neglect, prejudice, lack of achieved solidarity and self-laceration experienced by almost all the minorities under an unremitting domination.

If there is a literary establishment in America, a pantheon of hallowed luminaries including Updike, Bellow, Wolfe, Roth, Ashbery, and DeLillo, then there is no question as to its spatial location: it is in the East and North. The two co-ordinates that are unthinkable in conjunction with it are South and West, where of course we find Los Angeles and its garish entertainment industries, now joining hands with the digital information industries in an endless loop of joyous commercial philistinism. Apart from the single, now late, exception of poet Charles Bukowski, who had fame imposed upon him at the last after a film (*Barfly* [Schroeder, 1986]) was made of his work, any moderately successful Los Angeles writer who hasn't wanted to subserve the film industry has found it virtually impossible to resist the gravitational tug of the East.

3

Beginning with Joan Didion and her husband John Gregory Dunne in the late 1980s, the exodus has continued unabated: Bret Easton Ellis, James Ellroy, Walter Mosley, Paul Beatty, all have relocated in the East after literary success. And their reasons are not unsound. For to stay in Los Angeles is to relinquish many reasonable ambitions of cultural respect, guild community, grants, deals with major publishers. It is virtually to disappear. Steve Erickson, one of the city's most adventurous writers, complains in his semi-autobiographical *Amnesiascope* (1996) that the last time he 'caught a glimpse of his career as a novelist, before it disappeared altogether in the dark, was in New York City'. He suggests that 'if you're not actually from New York it becomes, every time you go there, a greater and greater monument to what you've achieved or, more to the point, failed to achieve – the urbanology of your own particular success or failure'.[3] In a more political vein, Wanda Coleman berates the logic of arts funding in the country at large, which triply discriminates against her as a black Angelena poet:

> Poetry is the most marginalized of all the arts, yet equally subject to the whims of regional prejudice. Approximately ninety percent of the public and private sector grant money doled out to artists and writers, in these United States, goes to New York. And that wouldn't be so bad, but in Southern California our institutions barely and rarely support the local White artists, so you know what we Blacks and 'multi-ethnic others' can expect. When I began my grantsmanship chase in the early 80s I was repeatedly advised that a New York City P.O. Box address would considerably increase the odds in my favor.[4]

Why this systematic marginalization of what would, in many other urban cultures, be considered a revered and honoured profession? Doubtless it has something to do with the historical glamorization of Los Angeles as 'tinseltown', the place of movie and television production, ephemeral visual culture and trash; the home of what Mike Davis calls the 'semi-proletarianized writer' under the thumb of entertainment capital.[5] It is a myth which persists even in the literary community itself, as Kathleen Tynan once related in a piece for the *New York Times Book Review*:

> In the City of Angels, when you ask a writer you respect 'What's happening on the literary scene?' he'll say 'There isn't one'. And after you've asked the same question of Christopher Isherwood, Gore Vidal, Brooke Hayward and Neil Simon, and have had no kind of encouragement for your quest . . . , someone says, 'Of course, the Dunnes'.

Introduction: on minoritization and domination

So you go and see Joan Didion and John Gregory Dunne. And John Dunne says, 'We're here because there isn't a literary scene'. To which Miss Didion adds, 'There aren't any appreciators here. No hostesses, critics, publishers or fans'.[6]

And in confirmation of the immodest estimation of 'the Dunnes' as solitary upholders of literary value in this valley of shades, Bret Ellis has said, in excuse of his own departure East, 'Trumps closing and Joan Didion and John Dunne moving away. That was the end of LA for me.'[7] At a personal level I can attest that, almost as often as I informed questioners that I was researching Los Angeles literature, I was met with the anxious incomprehension of those who could scarcely credit that such an oxymoron was any more than a feeble jest.

So it is that authors in LA themselves constitute (at least in their own self-representation) as embattled and dogged a minority as any other, scrounging money and recognition off passersby with the churlish indignation of the misunderstood, the dispossessed. It is a minority status which is ceaselessly internalized, to the point that it assumes the classic Nietzschean hallmarks of *ressentiment*: 'The slave revolt in morality begins when *ressentiment* itself becomes creative and gives birth to values: the *ressentiment* of natures that are denied the true reaction, that of deeds, and compensate themselves with an imaginary revenge.'[8] The literary writer, subjugated both by the Eastern establishment and the movie industry at home, is then predisposed to glaring back at the world of established Letters and visual entertainment with all the menace of an underclass on a hot day. And this is precisely the value of such minor-writing, in the grumbles and disaffection of a value-producing *ressentiment*, here manifest as satire, there as denunciation. The poet-narrator of Paul Beatty's splendid comic novel *The White Boy Shuffle* (1996) expresses its satiric mode thus:

> There was a different vibrancy to 24th Street that day. The decibel level was the same, but a grating Hollywood hullaballoo replaced the normal Hillside barking dog and nigger cacophony. The newest rap phenoms, the Stoic Undertakers, were filming a video for their latest album, *Closed Casket Eulogies in F Major*. Earlier in the day I had wandered into the production tent to audition for a part as an extra. The casting director blew one expanding smoke ring in my direction and dismissed me with a curt 'Too studious. Next! I told you I want menacing or despondent and you send me these bookworm junior high larvae.'
> Moribund Videoworks was on safari through the LA jungle. A caravan of film trucks and RVs lurched through the streets

5

like sheet-metal elephants swaggering through the ghetto Serengeti. Local strong-armed youth bore the director over the crowds in a canopied sedan chair, his seconds shouting out commands through a bullhorn. 'Bwana wants to shoot this scene through an orange filter to make it seem like the sun's been stabbed and the heavens are bleeding onto the streets.' 'Special effects, can you make the flames shoot farther out from the barrel of the Uzi? Mr. Edgar Barley Burrows wants the guns to spit death. More blood! You call this carnage! More blood.' My street was a soundstage and its machinations of poverty and neglect were Congo cinema verité. 'Quiet on the set. Camera. Roll sound. Speed. Action!'[9]

To reclaim the street from the soundstage; that would be one effective way of summarizing the representational urge of the Los Angeles writer. So Beatty's improbably named black hero Gunnar Kaufman scrawls his verse on the seven-foot wall separating his ghetto from the white-populated hill community above, gesturing through syntax and poetic trope against the serial reductions of his lived space to the Congo imaginaries of crude speculators in the image.

Gilles Deleuze and Félix Guattari once issued a manifesto in the name of Franz Kafka: Towards a Minor Literature! Los Angeles is already there. It is the place where all literature is minor; and by a logic as inevitable as metastasis, its literatures split, spread, deterritorialize, leap from subdivision to subdivision on a line of flight from the Sense of vision. This is the first characteristic of 'minor literatures'. The second is that 'everything in them is political . . . [Their] cramped space forces each individual intrigue to connect immediately to politics'. And the third characteristic is that here, where actual collective consciousness is fractured and dissipated, 'literature finds itself positively charged with the role and function of collective, and even revolutionary, enunciation . . . [A]nd if the writer is in the margins or completely outside his or her fragile community, this situation allows the writer all the more possibility to express another possible community and to forge the means for another consciousness and another sensibility.'[10] In LA this possibility begins in the *ressentiment* of a writerly minority, becomes allegorized when articulated with other spatial and ethnic modes of minoritization, and finally emerges from the cracks in the vision machine as poems, novels and performance works, like weeds, 'blades of grass' waving faintly in the last breath of wind blowing from paradise. Another consciousness? Another sensibility? Perhaps. There are no masterpieces here, no great artificers; just intensities of immanence and becoming-minor. We are not at any rate in need of 'classics' or 'masters', only of sober syntactical enunciations of what goes unvoiced, the 'people's concern' in this time of an ever more purified domination.

The representation of Los Angeles

at lang's. he again praises atlantis to the ersatz skies. he sees a special lifestyle where I only see high capitalism: possible that I can't see the 'real' atlantis for the high capitalism; but he just obscures it. here you have the unadulterated version before you; development, without anything actually developing.[1]

The greatest difficulty in coming to terms with Los Angeles will always be not seeing it as such; not for a lack of representations of it, but because of their contradictory plenitude.[2] Brecht's scare-quotes spring up automatically around any mention of the 'real' LA, due to the sheer volume of incompatible definitions. According to your point of view, Los Angeles is either exhilarating or nihilistic, sundrenched or smog-enshrouded, a multicultural haven or a segregated ethnic concentration camp – Atlantis or high capitalism – and orchestrating these polarized alternatives is an urban identity thriving precisely on their interchangeability. The city (or is it a city, and not a collection of cities?) recycles an extraordinary amount of oxymoronic self-referential discourse, never cohering into anything more than a patchwork of undecidable clichés – this paragraph perhaps being just another instance of that tendency.

To suggest that all of this slippery signification is nothing but a superficial appearance beneath which squats a deeper and iniquitous essence is to lapse into the kind of moralistic dismissal of the place that is now so shop-worn as to be useless. It is the kind of strategy that plays, on the one hand, to the interests of a puritanical national anti-urbanism,[3] and on the other, to the capricious elasticity of the metropolitan identity itself, which happily converts negative tropes into touristic affirmations of native cool.[4] 'Los Angeles', both place-name and epic national myth, springs precisely from the point at which the jargon of authenticity gutters out. Surface and depth, appearance and essence, all the hoary dualisms lose their hierarchy of values here, a semantic exhaustion which poses problems not only to urban analysis and historiography, but to literary criticism as well.

Indeed, the challenge here is to think of appearance *as* essence, and vice versa: to accept the '[i]neluctable modality of the visible', as Joyce once put it, in the representation of this place;[5] but also to insist, *pace* Joyce, that today the visible is technologically administered, not phenomenologically given. The vision machines and their ubiquitous product anticipate any act of seeing in Los Angeles; the commercial-visual undergrids the perceptual. So the primary acts of selection and exclusion implicit in that 'ineluctable' advance screening of the city tend to shape the secondary acts of representation with which citizens (and artists) attempt to reclaim it. LA is in this sense the virtual birthplace of what Jean Baudrillard has called the 'precession of simulacra',[6] the coming-first of perfect fictional representations of itself, which cannot then be measured against some underlying original, but are assimilated in advance into the real and, ipso facto, its further imaginary elaborations. The 'real' of Los Angeles is always and already 'real-and-imagined', as Edward Soja phrases it.[7]

Such a subsumption of the real by representation dates back to the very origins of modern LA, from the 1880s on, as a radical experiment in real estate speculation. If the Chicago School insisted that the dominant pattern of urbanization in America was the gradual radiation of suburbs around central industrial and financial districts, then Los Angeles, a true aberration, sprang up conversely in patches, a case of urban small-pox on the sun-baked face of Southern California. And unlike New York, whose modern phenomena struck the bemused Henry James 'as having, with their immense momentum, got the start, got ahead of, in proper parlance, any possibility of poetic, of dramatic capture',[8] the modernity of Los Angeles was preceded and produced by an audacious rhetorical capture.

> Los Angeles is a city that was imagined long before it was built. It was imagined to avoid city-wide bankruptcy in the 1890s, and has stayed on a knife-edge ever since, camouflaged by promotional rhetoric . . . It was the new Jerusalem, first come, first served, at the semi-arid, most westerly – and newly civilized – corner of the great frontier. However inflated the language, the strategy was simple enough. Through a consortium of local businessmen and large railroad interests, a small city would be merchandized into a metropolis.[9]

9

The 'boost', a tissue of distortions about the climate and the air, the Mediterranean fragrance and luxuriance of the region,[10] was inexorably *there* ahead of any objective attempt to represent the city's actual social and natural configuration. And this was enough to distinguish the city from all previous urban forms.

Los Angeles' exceptionalism *vis-à-vis* the rest of America, itself a notable and recurrent trope in discourse about California,[11] must be properly understood in order to clarify more recent celebrations of the city as the first 'postmodern' metropolis.[12] The critic's standard optic for seeing Los Angeles was polished classically, in Louis Adamic's colourful prose, in 1929:

> Los Angeles is America. A jungle. Los Angeles grew up suddenly, *planlessly*, under the stimuli of the adventurous spirit of millions of people and the profit motive. It is still growing. Here everything has the chance to thrive – for a while – as a rule, only a brief while. Inferior as well as superior plants and trees flourish for a time, then both succumb to chaos and decay. They must give way to new plants pushing up from below, and so on. This is freedom under democracy. Jungle Democracy . . . [I]t is a bad place . . . full of . . . wildcat enterprises, which, with their aim for quick profit, are doomed to collapse and drag down multitudes of people . . .[13]

Adamic's vision of urban anarchy and the free reign of unplanned development has been immensely influential, and contains a great deal of truth (Brecht's 'development without anything actually developing'). As long ago as 1929, intimations of a vulgar 'postmodernity' hovered over the city in the sun; Adamic's clear distaste for this experiment in unfettered modernity finding its echo in the dismissive reflections of no less a figure than Frank Lloyd Wright:

> Despite the elaborate effort that went into the scheming to make these houses 'original' or 'different', they all looked exactly alike. 'The same thought, or lack of thought', wrote Mr. Wright, 'was to be seen everywhere. "Taste" – the usual matter of ignorance – had moved toward simplicity a little, but thought or feeling for integrity had not entered into this architecture. All was flatulent or fraudulent with a cheap opulent taste for tawdry Spanish Medievalism.'[14]

The offended eye of the civilized East was unable to approve of this newer visual logic of mass-reproducibility and fraudulence. Refusing to submit to aesthetic standards established elsewhere, Los Angeles architects and designers catered to transient and jumbled fashions of style, debasing architectural 'taste' with flyweight buildings that could be erected and demolished with minimum disturbance. The argument logically followed that nothing in Los Angeles's urban fabric had had the benefit of any foresight or considered administrative sanction. The city was an appalling object-lesson in the grim costs of anything goes, *laissez-faire* urban planning. Or was it?

Some recent scholarship suggests otherwise. Evidence gathered by Michael Dear and others demonstrates that planners, architects, visionaries and the Los Angeles Board of Supervisors itself, in the early years of the twentieth century, actively promoted the notion of a 'new urban configuration' in Southern California.[15] The vast spaces available, the absence of any large, built-up urban core, and the emerging culture of the motor car, all contributed to a conscious attempt to rethink urban life on a horizontal, suburban frame: a proliferation of separate communities, 'satellite sub-centers' stocked with detached houses situated near workplaces and with shopping nearby.[16] Contrary to popular opinion, the dispersed, fragmented space of Los Angeles was in place well before the advent of the freeways, and it was a space that had been allowed and encouraged to develop by public authorities.[17]

None of which is to belittle the dominant role of Adamic's 'wildcat' private speculation and real-estate profiteering on urban form in Los Angeles; it is merely to underline the contribution of official planning imaginaries (of 'satellite sub-centers' and so forth) to the evolving shape of the city, in a direction quite distinct from previously existing models of urban form. What I am reaching towards is a qualified paradigm of Los Angeles as a new urban type, in which civic and commercial appearance *is* urban essence: beginning with the promotion of a township before it has been built, the imagination of a spread of urban centers prior to incorporation, the elaboration of a rhetoric of locality before the locality itself existed. 'By the end of 1925, LA had no less than 600,000 subdivided lots standing vacant; the city had already parcelled out enough land to accommodate seven million people, fifty years before the reality of demographic growth would catch up with the realtors' speculative appetite.'[18] Such is the logic of urban growth in Los Angeles, an ambitious intertwining of artifice, sensation, division and diffusion which became a great city, almost by happenstance; but with the combined wills of private businesses and public bodies to abstract it into existence.

The two most significant points for our purposes in this West Coast departure from classical and 'modern' urbanism are representational. First, there is the fundamental role of culture in LA's production and reproduction; and second, there is the question of totality and integration in a fragmented metropolis. Well before the emergence of the Culture Industry proper in Los Angeles,[19] the techniques of aestheticization were as basic to urban production in the city as bitumen and stucco. With the rhetoric of the boost and opportune advertising imagery, entire townships were sold, and entire town populations voluntarily imported from the Mid-West, before the first plank of timber had been erected. As I have been arguing, representation has had a seminal place in the production of Los Angeles from the outset – a fact which poses a serious conundrum to the most venerable form of the essence/appearance opposition in progressive cultural theory, between base and superstructure. For in Los Angeles, the superstructure is, in many senses, coterminous with the base. Representation is a means of production; and the division of labour is unabashedly represented. The bourgeoisie perches on the hills and edges westward, the ethnic working class crowds out segregated flatland slums and spreads east; the glittering spires of multinational capital soar up out of downtown while nearby sweatshops hum and factories are bulldozed; police haunt the skies, homeless people wander the streets – everything is on the surface. And the most innocent everyday object cajoles you into sharing the mythology of place, so that the economic banality of, say, buying lunch cannot be permitted to rest outside the ceaseless representation of 'Los Angelesness'.

In classical materialist theories of culture, this latter is in some sense presented as the delayed expression of an existing economic and physical structure of social being.[20] Los Angeles seems to call out for some other conception. Here, the ideal of a clear distinction between 'real' social life on the one hand and cultural figuration on the other is more or less untenable. Any notion of a straightforward correspondence between culture and place (or 'realism') is imperilled by the infrastructural nature of the city's cultural enactments: the precession of simulacra, the priority in a causal sense of rhetoric and visuality itself, and not merely stable visible icons or landmarks, or forms of social relation. Mike Davis writes, 'Compared to other great cities, Los Angeles may be *planned* or *designed* in a very fragmentary sense . . . but it is infinitely *envisioned*.'[21] 'The film industry has never portrayed California', says David Hockney. 'For good reason, probably. Even today I don't think there's one building you could show in a backdrop and instantly know it's LA, as you could with New York. The city itself is not that well known.'[22] Seen, but not known; photographed, but not remembered; projected, but only preconsciously spectated. The endemic representational excess obliterates whatever confidence one might have had in the pre-cultural 'real', and actively attenuates the power of memory. What is there to look at, point to, and say 'here it is'? Nothing is reassuringly local, nothing *belongs*, not even nature itself. 'Southern California is man-made, a gigantic improvization. Virtually everything has been imported: plants, flowers, shrubs, trees, people, water, electrical energy, and, to some extent, even the soils.'[23] And should you wish to focus your lens on the built environment, your every effort will be compromised by the omnipresence of 'sites that were destroyed or severely altered: office towers where houses once stood; abandoned tunnels like the famous Belmont entrance to the vanished twenties subway in Los Angeles; consumer simulations of neighborhoods, like Citywalk, near the Universal Tours.'[24]

The pervasive irreality of an arbitrarily introduced and always shifting *mélange* of appearances bedevils the city's representation, since, in that sense, it is already its own best representation. Culture has long been, in Los Angeles, a form of fixed capital, a matter of political economy in the basest sense, something every industry and municipal body has 'factored in' from the blueprint up. And to pretend to offer further acts of cultural reflection without working through this miasma of representations, to offer to put aside the crude patina and sheen of 'Los Angelesness' and cut the beast of reality along the joints, is quite possibly an exercise in *mauvaise foi*. As Brecht worries, maybe he *is* missing Atlantis for the political economy; the point being, surely, that 'Atlantis' is part and parcel of the political economy to begin with. The division between them, in good postmodern form, is what is misleading.

There is then no 'truth' about Los Angeles that does not dismay-ingly take the form of a cliché or marketing strategy; which makes the old saw that LA is a 'series of suburbs in search of a city' both an anxious admission of the absence of an urban *Ding-an-sich*, and an allaying of any resultant existential fears with the reassurance of trite formula. Nonetheless, the 'islands' in what Carey McWilliams once called the Los Angeles 'archipelago' have never been more isolated and less interconnected than they are today.[25] Gated communities, ethnic chauvinism, specialist consumer environments, the erosion of public transport, the solipsism of private transport: what we have been calling a city lacks even the pretence of a civic character or a collective will. Media stereotypes of Venice Beach bodybuilders, South-Central 'gangstas', East LA 'homies', and movie industry 'shmoozers' are just that, failing to orient us or Angelenos with regard to their social space; and the phenomenological fact that one cannot even trace mental lines of relation between these enduring imagos is especially disabling.

Given this thoroughgoing resistance to totality in the social and geographical composition of the city, it is not surprising that, ideologically, the temptations of particularism dominate life in Los Angeles. Where you live tempers what you see, whom you relate to, your personal style, your life options and passions; it tells us more or less who you are. The ideal of an Archimedean vantage point, above and beyond the gravitational forces of group adherence and territoriality, has been more or less abandoned, for reasons we will explore later in this chapter and as the book unfolds. In a city as fragmented and polyglot as this one, to 'represent' is often to issue a manifesto of localism, of tribal identity and self-aggrandisement; and all of this appears entirely natural. Nor is it unprecedented in the history of representational forms. In a brief tally of oppositions between facets of naturalism and realism, Brecht once noted that naturalism focuses on the 'milieu', while realism goes for the 'system'; in naturalism, 'segments of society . . . are "little worlds of their own"' while realism's '"little worlds" are sectors of the front in the great struggles.'[26] The recrudescence today of naturalism's 'little worlds of their own' is a feature of the literature tracked in the pages of this book; yet what is new and unexpected about this atavism is precisely its specialized divisions within the space of a single city. So that we now no longer have the Naturalist scenography of French industrial miners, or the provincial bourgeoisie, but of the tiny LA Cuban *santeria* cult,[27] or professional black middle-class women of the West side.[28] So consistently have we been warned against evaluating this particularist tendency as a cultural regression (because the alternative of totalization leads, willy nilly, to the gulags of totalitarianism), that it seems inadvisable to complain about the losses it implies. Regression or not, it is at least sure that the social space of Los Angeles has been the foremost laboratory for the dismantling of the ideal of totality, both on the socio-spatial plane, and on the cultural plane which takes flight from it.

These representational problems – the representational *mise-en-abyme*, and a breaking apart of the concept of totality – are the fundamental co-ordinates of literature in Los Angeles today, and have historically compromised the emergence of a local literary identity. Acts of literary engagement have typically come from aliens. David Fine, introducing one of the very few critical volumes dedicated to Los Angeles literature, has made much of this. 'In fact, any discussion of the Los Angeles novel must begin with the observation that it is chiefly the work of the outsider – if not the tourist, then the newcomer. With a few exceptions, largely contemporary ones, its shapers have been men and women born elsewhere who for a time lived and worked in Southern California, frequently as script writers.'[29] Lionel Rolfe similarly, but more speculatively, suggests: 'Perhaps there was a kind of synergistic relationship between LA and writers; the combination of restless authors and an ever-changing, transitory town helped produce a new vision in American literature.'[30] That vision was essentially modernist and imported – alienated, anti-commercial, and ironic – and it assumed that the jaded eye of the newcomer alone held the power to condense the otherwise imponderable lessons of a bizarre locale into palpable aesthetic forms. If things are somewhat different today, perhaps it is because national and international trends are catching up with the latent 'postmodernism' of Los Angeles's conditions of literary possibility. Now the outsider's vocation of urban mastery – the glance from without which captures the whole – has been discredited, and it is the insider, with the city's visuality and spatial practices as embedded in her mental tissues as elemental grammar, and her own 'little world' fixed firmly as her frame of reference, who is better positioned to express the truth of a city where, if it 'all comes together', it does so only disjunctively and as an exercise in media coercion.

And if this has long been true of Los Angeles, then it is increasingly true of our New World Order itself, of which it is impossible *not* to be an insider: the global marketplace of instant information flows, industrial disarticulation and mammoth financial monopolies – a world whose logic is profoundly urban, segregated, yet encased in a media blanket of simultaneity and oneness; where existence is largely a predicate of representationality, and not vice-versa. Of our contemporary social stage it has been written that 'the very sphere of culture itself has expanded, becoming coterminous with market society in such a way that the cultural is no longer limited to its earlier, traditional or experimental forms, but is consumed throughout daily life itself, in shopping, in professional activities, in the various often televisual forms of leisure, in production for the market and in the consumption of those market products, indeed in the most secret folds and corners of the quotidian. Social space is now completely saturated with the culture of the image.'[31] In this sense, it seems quite clear, Los Angeles should be a reliable test-case for determining the role and future of literature itself on the world scene, at the moment of its greatest crisis since Homer – its marginalization. For with the written word lying prostrate under the image, where better than tinseltown to interrogate the conditions of possibility of literature's survival and chances for future renewal? All that we have been arguing about the role of cultural reproduction in Los Angeles, and the problems of literary representation it fosters, forcibly suggests the city's premonitory status with regard to what are now quite obviously global trends of cultural profligacy. Coming to terms with the place and role of literature in this city may be an indispensable step towards a proper conceptualization of its international fate.

Accordingly, some defence seems necessary at this stage of the concept of postmodernism, not as peremptory shorthand for the cynicism of the contemporary in all its forms, but as an exacting critical compass with which to navigate our way through the shoals and reefs of present-day culture. Particularly when allied with the related concept of the production of space,[32] postmodernism is arguably, of all the available conceptual personae today, best suited to coming to terms with a culture co-ordinated by cultural exorbitation on the one hand, and the splintering of totality on the other. For, as it has been analysed by its most searching critics, the postmodern is that historical and cultural condition in which the problematic of space has subsumed the problematic of time in, precisely, a logic of visualization and fragmentation. Summarizing Fredric Jameson on the matter, Perry Anderson writes: 'In the age of satellite and optical fibre . . . the spatial commands the imaginary as never before. The electronic unification of the earth, instituting the simultaneity of events across the globe as daily spectacle, has lodged a vicarious geography in the recesses of every consciousness, while the encircling networks of multinational capital that actually direct the system exceed the capacities of any perception.'[33] Postmodernity is, in this apt formulation, a double negation (of the Whole and of the Subject) which is nonetheless productive of unprecedented imaginative capacities and sensory skills, and, ironically, entails an actual intensification of the very totality (of 'multinational capital') it perceptually occludes.

Moreover, this spatialization of contemporary being has every-thing to do with a definitive urbanization of the lifeworld, a global dilation of the urban to the point where it has virtually conquered existence and ceased to mean what it once did. Better to grasp what is meant by postmodernism as an urban spatialization, consider the difference between a metropolitan culture that distinguished itself against the backdrop of a still predominantly agricultural world, and one which is prohibited from doing so by the urbanization, the modernization, of just that vanishing exterior. Raymond Williams was surely correct to focus on the antinomy between the country and the city as the very animus of modernism, structuring the codes and forms of that urban culture with the sense of rural backwardness it at once opposed and romanticized.[34] Yet it is this very antinomy which today looks antiquated, as nostalgic in its way as the various nostalgias rehearsed in the modernist canon. It was Williams himself who, in 1985, clearly stressed the historical contingency of cultural modernism and consequently of the modes of literary and urban analysis which had evolved to conceptualize it. Commenting on the anachronistic and essentially residual nature of the concept of modernism in a world governed by multinational media conglomer-ates, he emphasized the immense importance of 'contemporary analysis in a still rapidly changing world' for breaking free from that conceptual deadlock.[35] He thus urged a transcendence of the terms and frames of reference treasured by cultural historians of that now vanished era, the Modern.

Decolonization and the overnight urbanization of the Third World on the one hand, and the technological revolutions specific to the First (computerization, the mass visual media) on the other, have permanently altered the very texture of our culture. The sense specific to modernism of the absolutely new, the great leap forward into untried aesthetic and political forms, rested ultimately upon the contemporaneous existence of absolute backwardness and 'sava-gery', on the colonial contract between civilization and otherness, as on the highly volatile restructuring of an antiquated class system across Europe.[36] As Walter Benjamin was at pains to show us, the era of 'High Capitalism' produced a culture vitally preoccupied with the old-in-the-new; with archaic forms and residues interlaced with the heroic march of steel, electricity and progress. The modernist image was, Benjamin insisted, a dialectical one, caught up in the tension between still potent tradition and a dynamic melting of solids into air.[37] By contrast, Fredric Jameson has argued that, with the shift to a postmodernism of consumerism, information and simulation, 'the past itself has disappeared':

> Everything is now organized and planned; nature has been triumphantly blotted out, along with peasants, petit-bourgeois commerce, handicraft, feudal aristocracies and imperial bureaucracies. Ours is a more homogeneously modernized condition; we no longer are encumbered with the embarassment of non-simultaneities and non-synchronicities. Everything has reached the same hour on the great clock of development or rationalization . . . This is the sense in which we can affirm that modernism is characterized by a situation of incomplete *modernization*, or that postmodernism is more modern than modernism itself.[38]

To these remarkable generalizations one would want to add that development remains strikingly uneven, even today;[39] but the essential point is surely valid: that modernism expressed the exceptionalism of modernized societies, whereas postmodernism expresses their unremarkable ubiquity.

The shocks of the new have long since faded into a background hum, the very concept of 'viewpoint' has been trodden under foot by vast demographic flows, technology has entered the sanctum of the body and filters all perception, the urban extends in every direction to a limitless horizon, and commodification reifies the merest particle of daily life. The act of writing today is conditioned by these processes; and they are processes which, more irresistibly than any others in history, have managed to extend themselves across an ever more total space. If, as Kristin Ross has said, 'the reproduction of the social relations of production is the central and hidden process of capitalist society, and . . . this process is spatial',[40] then postmodernity is the perfect product of that process – a pure reproduction (with every appearance of constant change) taking place in an absolutely saturated and administered space. Henri Lefebvre's apparently simple idea that '(social) space is a (social) product'[41] is extremely useful for getting to grips with a world of this sort. For our mode of production has extended itself to the point where, now, it has virtually run out of room for expansion and must henceforth concentrate its energies on regulating and reproducing itself on the ultimate economic horizon of the planet itself.[42]

> Capitalism has not only subordinated exterior and anterior sectors to itself, it has *produced* new sectors, transforming what pre-existed and completely overthrowing the corresponding institutions and organizations. The same is true of 'art', know-

ledge, 'leisure', urban and everyday reality. It is a vast process which, as usual, is wrapped in appearances and ideological masks. For example, capitalist production loots previous *oeuvres* and styles, changes them into objects of 'cultural' production and consumption and thus recapitulates these styles in restituted and reconstituted form as 'neo' this or that, élite fashions and high-quality products.

Reproduction (of the relations of production, not just the means of production) is located not simply in society as a whole but in space as a whole. Space, occupied by neo-capitalism, sectioned, reduced to homogeneity yet fragmented, becomes the seat of power.[43]

Quite apart from its descriptive utility, this passage and the many others which support it in Lefebvre's account of the production of space, bring home precisely the representational dilemmas of postmodernism we began to address in the previous section. If today capitalism – rather than simply pushing back frontiers and rapaciously exploiting new territories – produces its space with the minutest attention to detail in order to perpetuate its productive relations, then representation is ever more intrinsic to space itself; and in order to shield its resultant homogeneity, late-capitalist social space dissimulates itself in innumerable masks and appearances, each alive with its own commodified, representational intensity. The enduring challenge of representing the existent is radicalized by this double dynamic, in which the 'real' is already a representation of the real, and represents itself to the second power in a fission of images layered directly into the urban lifeworld.

And at the level of the city, the escalating abstraction of late capitalist space first became manifest in the new urban logic of suburbanization:

> In suburban space . . . detached houses contrasted with 'housing estates' just as sharply as the earlier opulent apartments with the garrets of the poor above them. The idea of the 'bare minimum' was no less in evidence. Suburban houses and 'new towns' came close to the lowest possible *threshold of sociability* – the point beyond which survival would be impossible because all social life would have disappeared. Internal and invisible boundaries began to divide a space that nevertheless remained in thrall to a global strategy and a single power. These boundaries did not merely separate levels – local, regional, national and worldwide. They also separated zones where people were supposed to be reduced to their 'simplest expression', to their 'lowest common denominator', from zones where people could spread out in comfort and enjoy those essential luxuries, time and space, to the full. As a matter of fact

'boundaries' is too weak a word here, and it obscures the essential point; it would be more accurate to speak of fracture lines revealing the true – invisible yet highly irregular – contours of 'real' social space lying beneath its homogeneous surface.[44]

I quote at length here because even the most cursory acquaintance with Los Angeles will profit from these sentences, their clear summation of its fundamental spatial logic: a 'city of rigid cultural mappings and demarcations, none more overt than those between the fortress-like white suburbs and the impoverished black ghettos "written off" both the tourist map and the dominant image of the city broadcast by its own dream-machine.'[45] How different this is from the Paris of Benjamin's researches scarcely needs stressing. Lefebvre himself, commenting on the newer peripheries of the quintessential 'capital of the nineteenth century', remarked that 'the beginnings of the [Parisian] suburb are also the beginnings of a violently anti-urban planning approach; a singular paradox'. 'With "suburbanization" a process is set into motion which decentres the city . . . Urban consciousness will vanish.'[46] This transition between two very different urban orders, between the heroic modernism of Paris and the decentered postmodernism of Los Angeles, marks the crucial break that a modernist approach to the city cannot traverse. With geographers Edward W. Soja and Allen J. Scott, one feels 'justified in advancing the claim – with apologies to Walter Benjamin – that [Los Angeles] has now become the very capital of the late 20th century, *the paradigmatic industrial metropolis of the modern world.*'[47]

And whether it is called postmodernism, hyperrealism or the simulacrum, the new cultural plenum and the fractured social sphere which it libidinizes, dictate quite unprecedented strategies of representational capture. No longer does it seem appropriate to concentrate the critical attention on crowds, shocks, monumental verticality, the hallmarks of classical industrialism, alienation of the subject, or any other of the canonical topoi of modernist literary analysis. Rather, the suppression of all of these elements is notable in this 'paradigmatic industrial metropolis'. If Los Angeles and the postmodern culture it more or less incubated and delivered to the world have anything to teach us, it is that representations of the contemporary have broken from the Mosaic laws of the modern – make it new!, aesthetic purification, mythopoesis, the cult of consciousness, and so forth – and operate instead according to very different criteria of value: principally, I will now argue, those of a distinctive kind of use value.

The question of how to approach the present, with what interpretive and analytic machinery, as a literary critic, remains far from satisfactorily answered. Fredric Jameson made some headway in 1970, with a remarkable reading of detective writer Raymond Chandler as the 'epic poet' of LA, taking fully into account the unique and anticipatory spatial forms of the city with which Chandler had successfully engaged in the 1930s and 1940s.

> [B]y an accident of place, [Chandler's] social content anticipates the realities of the fifties and sixties. For Los Angeles is already a kind of microcosm and forecast of the country as a whole: a new centerless city, in which the various classes have lost touch with each other because each is isolated in his own geographical compartment. If the symbol of social coherence and comprehensibility was furnished by the nineteenth-century Parisian apartment house (dramatized in Zola's *Pot-Bouille*) with its shop on the ground floor, its wealthy inhabitants on the second and third, petty bourgeoisie further up, and workers' rooms on top along with the maids and servants, then Los Angeles is the opposite, a spreading out horizontally, a flowing apart of the elements of the social structure.[48]

Jameson read Chandler's version of the hard-boiled detective protagonist as a formal solution to the unique spatial problems of representation furnished by Los Angeles. In a city so divided and diffused, only the tough P.I. will have sufficient (professional) cause to stitch its separate parts together in a persuasive narrative unity. We will see in more detail the persistence of this formal device in the next chapter.

Jameson's intervention, however, whilst refreshing in its refusal of the modernist paradigm in urban literary criticism, does not exactly bequeath to us a methodology for working through what is at stake in the production of literature in a city such as this. Above all, it fails to take into account what Jameson's own notion of postmodernism would help crystallize more than a decade later: the sheer volume of cultural information already at large on Chandler's mean streets. By touring briefly the conceptual and analytic apparatus of Lefebvre's *The Production of Space*,[49] I would like to suggest some ways of harnessing its insights for literary and aesthetic criticism.[50] Indeed, the cultural critic will welcome the fact that representation is not a marginal, but the central concept in Lefebvre's account of neo-capitalist space. Rather than regarding social space as the merely physical infrastructure of built environments, Lefebvre insists upon its human and therefore imaginary and symbolic aspects. This has the advantage, for analysts of Los Angeles in particular, of predisposing his theory of social space towards the role of culture in its production. If space *is* only insofar as it is processed by knowledge and the imaginary, then the intricate dialectics of image and space in Los Angeles look less unfathomable, and need only to be patiently gauged.

Lefebvre constructed a triad of concepts with which to analyse the dynamics of social space, distinguished according to the level of abstraction to which they subject social space. First, the notion of the *representation of space* accounts for the totality of knowledges and discourses that pretend to a mastery of space. The representation of space is 'conceptualized space [*espace conçu*], the space of scientists, planners, urbanists, technocratic subdividers and social engineers . . . – all of whom identify what is lived and what is perceived with what is conceived . . . This is the dominant space in any society (or mode of production). Conceptions of space tend . . . towards a system of verbal (and therefore intellectually worked out) signs.'[51] Covering the realm of knowledge and the symbolic – official languages, sciences, statistics and theories – representations of space determine a society's administrative attitude towards its space, as well as the texture of its ideology (which Lefebvre asked us to see as consisting 'primarily in a discourse upon social space').[52] We have already suggested the *a priori* status of this representational order with regard to the production of Los Angeles.

Opposite from this field of representations, Lefebvre posits the passional sphere of *representational space*, the explicitly imaginary aspects of lived space.

> Representational spaces . . . need obey no rules of consistency or cohesiveness. Redolent with imaginary and symbolic elements, they have their source in history – in the history of a people as well as the history of each individual belonging to that people. Ethnologists, anthropologists and psychoanalysts are students of such representational spaces, whether they are aware of it or not . . . [They] have no difficulty discerning those aspects of representational spaces which interest them: childhood memories, dreams, or uterine images and symbols (holes, passages, labyrinths). Representational space is alive: it speaks. It has an affective kernel or centre: Ego, bedroom, dwelling, house; or, square, church, graveyard. It embraces the loci of

passion, of action and of lived situations, and thus immediately implies time . . . [It] is essentially qualitative, fluid, and dynamic.[53]

As the 'undominated', existential preserve of social life, this is that complex of felt intensities, attractions and temporalities with which people appropriate their environments. It is also the space of the arts, but especially of the theatre, of dance and of music, since the visual and literary arts usually involve some concession to 'representations of space'. Above all, it is presently the most endangered aspect of social space, the one most under threat of being eliminated by the sway of abstraction over our lifeworld. In Los Angeles, the persistent suspicion that the city suffers an acute case of amnesia is a symptom of the waning of representational space under advanced capitalism, the substitution of memory and affect by simulation and segregation.[54]

Here, as elsewhere, cultural practices are caught up in the tensions between these two distinct orders of space, now being dominated by 'Disneyfication'[55] and the 'carceral city',[56] now manifesting signs of popular, affective appropriation, in democratic church initiatives, festivals of multiculturalism,[57] the deliberate recovery of buried pasts,[58] or indeed the 'becoming-animal, becoming-intense' of rioting itself.[59] All of the literary works considered in this book are located on the boundary between these two representational orders, negotiating dominant representations (police superintendence, visualized space, white ethnicity, 'apocalypse') and what is obscured beneath them (the body, affectivity, memories, 'other' ethnic traditions). Nor is there anything especially remarkable about this familiar tension between a representational 'superego' and its repressed 'unconscious'. What Lefebvre makes possible, however, is a political transcendence of the merely psychological, individual implications of such negotiations. What is at stake in them is, rather, the soul of the city itself.

Nor should Lefebvre's third spatial domain be absent from this brief survey of his representational theory. This, then, is what is left over when the two representational orders are already accounted for: the grinding routine of everyday life itself, the banal *spatial practices* of production, reproduction, transit, consumption, and so on. The 'spatial practice' of Los Angeles is distinguished by the unique history of this city with regard to the automobile, namely, the early and permanent subordination of the pedestrian sphere to that of the private car.[60] In no other city is the chance meeting of strangers on the street as they go about their isolated interests, let alone the phenomenon of crowds, so attenuated by a lack of public space that is not a road, a freeway or a parking lot. 'Everyday life', which for Lefebvre meant a *mixture* of spatial practices, representations of space and representational spaces, is typically reduced in Los Angeles to looking out of a car window at billboards and traffic signs – a trope repeated *ad nauseam* in the city's literature. Here, in other words, spatial practice and the dominant representations of space effectively squeeze out what would, in other cities, be the residual intensities between people as they negotiated each others' bodies, with what Michel de Certeau called the 'rhetoric' of walking in the city.[61] David Rieff writes that 'There are few experiences more disconcerting than walking along a wide LA street without the reassuring jangle of car-keys in your pocket. These streets are largely unshaded, their sidewalks appearing wider because they are so empty.'[62] Which is not to say that there are not sections of Los Angeles where the street retains some of the connotations of Benjaminian *flânerie* (one thinks immediately of Venice Beach, the vibrant Latino street culture of East LA and Broadway, the restored downtown 'Pueblo', and other select areas), and these are important to the city's writers. Yet it wants emphasizing that the street in Los Angeles is subject to an alarmist campaign of representation by the media, such that now it most generally connotes the demonized gang-turf and drive-by shootings which supposedly define unprotected public space.

At which end-point in our quick tour of Lefebvrian theory, some idea of the function of literature in postmodern space might come uncertainly into view. The tradition in structuralist thought of presenting cultural forms as 'imaginary resolutions to real contradictions'[63] acquires a new potency when these contradictions are grasped as *spatial*. That is to say, appreciating the fact that spatial practice, representations of space, and representational space can hardly be thought of as fitting into some agreeably harmonizing palimpsest of totality, perhaps it is helpful to construe of cultural forms as the means by which human subjects endeavour to make meaning of their highly contradictory social space. Spatial practice drags thought along the treadmills of the quotidian; representations of space flatter the ego's sense of conceptual mastery; while representational space exerts its own imaginary force on the body and the senses: and only some narrative, visual or dramatic cultural vehicle can catalyse the human mind into encompassing all three orders in a simultaneous act of apprehension. Otherwise, and indeed increasingly, the three aspects of social space – like galactic swirls moving always away from one another – exist in a state of unrelieved alienation, and divide the individual against herself in an existential schizophrenia which only serves to separate her the more radically from her kind. The 'imaginary resolution' of, say, a narrative or a poetic artefact to these trials of the spatial in contemporary society remains imaginary, to be sure; but that is not to suggest that it is therefore useless. Indeed, quite to the contrary, there would seem to be the most urgent use-value in a resolution of whatever kind to the disorienting contradictions between a relentlessly subdivided urban space, the passions of localized community groups, the 'non-places' of supermodernity,[64] national and territorial identities, television and computer screens, scattered ethnic geographies, the virtual spaces of multinational financial transactions, the prepackaged affects of the leisure and heritage industries, an almost fully privatized public sphere, underdeveloped 'blind-spots' in the backwaters of overdevelopment, and crass simulations of more authentic *milieux*.

Viewed spatially, then, our postmodern world is one in which the discontinuous and incommensurate govern the existential; since it is surely impossible for any one subject or group to feel simultaneously at home in even the above-mentioned spatial nodes of the contemporary, let alone the actually existing congeries of spaces. 'Not even Einsteinian relativity, or the multiple subjective worlds of the older modernists, is capable of giving any kind of adequate figuration to this process, which in lived experience makes itself felt by the so-called death of the subject, or, more exactly, the fragmented and schizophrenic decentering and dispersion of this last.'[65] Which is why Lefebvre's triad of concepts, in its very distance from the merely individual, is particularly useful, if not for the 'figuration' of the processes of postmodern space, then at least for their emergence into thought. A useful, as well as a mediating construct, to have in place between the dizzying multidimensionality of such spatial processes, and the narrative and poetic forms with which some individuals have striven, against all odds, to 'figure' them anyway. For there is no shortage of such forms – which proliferate despite all the dire predictions to the contrary of the death of print and of literature – only of a language and value system with which to analyse and interpret them.

Bearing in mind the inauspiciousness of postmodern space as an object fit for representation, with its strong fractures, multiple dimensions, saturation by the image, and underlying homogeneity, it makes sense not to judge works of literature according to criteria that are strictly aesthetic; today, rather, the didactic moment implicit in the aesthetic contract ('to teach, to move, to delight') is gaining pre-eminence in what we have come to require of the literary work. Indeed, whatever the literary work manages to teach us about our contradictory space will delight and move us at least as much as conventional affective devices, for in a context such as ours the cognitive itself has become a source of unexpected pleasure. That context is, of course, one in which aesthetic pleasure (especially formal visual and auditory stimulation) is no longer confined to the isolated work of art, but has spilled out over and saturated social space itself. Where aesthetics 'suffuses everything, where the sphere of culture expands to the point where everything becomes in one way or another acculturated, the traditional distinctiveness or "specificity" of the aesthetic . . . is necessarily blurred or lost altogether.'[66] And in that case, where 'moving' and 'delighting' is the mission not just of autotelic artworks, but of the libidinized totality of social space, and 'teaching' is the absent moment of a cultural triumphalism, it is to the didactic that artworks resort in order to distinguish themselves against their aestheticized conditions of social possibility.

And yet, one wants to suggest reservations about Jameson's own solution to this postmodern aesthetic paradox, the concept of the 'cognitive map'. The point about this successful and often misunderstood concept is that it was issued more or less in the form of a manifesto, and a defiantly socialist one at that. It named an absent but logical possibility, one to which left-wing artists could subscribe in their efforts to overcome the merely frivolous aspects of a culturally dominant postmodernism, and was offered very much 'in terms of current possibilities for some effective cultural politics and for the construction of a genuine political culture'.[67] The possibility Jameson scented was of some sort of representational capture, in the trappings of the 'sublime', of the totality itself: such was said to be the latent truth content of postmodern culture, only realizing itself in those moments where the unrepresentable 'global system' shadowily disambiguated itself from behind the curtains of a hip consumer aesthetic. Yet, despite all that is admirable and necessary in such a conception, it remains strictly Utopian (to use another of Jameson's preferred terms) so long as it lacks a committed cadre of practitioners. As he later confessed, the notion of the 'cognitive map', in which the postmodern individual was to have discovered its bearings in the non-representable totality of late capitalism, was really nothing more than a dusted-off version of the very Lukácsian concept of 'class consciousness';[68] a means for the construction of a global collective consciousness capable of contesting late capital's stranglehold on resources and power. In the absence of an ongoing project of this nature, the hard definition of 'cognitive mapping' is surely only diluted and misconceived when it is reduced to the wet, phenomenological status of the achievement of a 'sense of belonging' in postmodern space.

Not surprisingly, then, 'cognitive maps', politico-allegorical carto-graphies of the contemporary world system, are a very scarce commodity indeed in the present-day literature of Los Angeles, or anywhere else. Without this socialist vocation, works of literature can only attain their cognitive moments in other, perhaps lesser ways: either 'unconsciously', in momentary, sublime apprehensions of the totality; or in more modest and 'minor' forms, relating the individual to spaces several notches down the scale of contemporary spatiality.[69] It is in this latter sense that works of literature today most frequently wrest a cognitive spark away from the distracting aesthetics of everyday life; and, accordingly, some less overtly political concept than Jameson's 'cognitive mapping' seems in order to account for this reduced cognitive charge. What I should like to propose in this case is a return to an older, more ethnographic concept, namely Bakhtin's *chronotope*, as a better instrument for the calibration of literary texts as mediators of the spatial.

> In the literary artistic chronotope, spatial and temporal indica-
> tors are fused into one carefully thought-out, concrete whole.
> Time, as it were, thickens, takes on flesh, becomes artistically
> visible; likewise, space becomes charged and responsive to the
> movements of time, plot and history. This intersection of axes
> and fusion of indicators characterizes the artistic chronotope.[70]

It is a concept with the immediate advantage of allowing for a mutual determination of social 'space-time', by both the social and spatial structures of an historically achieved way of life, and the literary or figurative forms in which that way of life is admitted into consciousness. This is a critical and dialectical point: literature is neither purely mimetic or secondary, nor strictly functional, but both at once, and more. If it 'mirrors' the rhythms of, say, the peasant calendar or the bourgeois pocket-watch, if it 'reproduces' the spatial practices of, say, a bus-load of commuters or a castle guard, it does so within the terms of a relatively autonomous tradition of formal inheritance and generic determination. And this literary tradition, be it oral or literate, is the medium through which a society's rhythms and spaces become cultural, conscious, reflected upon and, occasionally, acted against. Literature 'fleshes out' preconscious social rhythms and spaces in formalities of syntax, rhythm and structural organization, which it was Bakhtin's genius to have distilled down to their bare essence: *chronotopes*, images of space-time unity, without which we would have very little idea how it was that Romans, Ancient Greeks, feudal peasants, or the nascent bourgeoisie *lived* the spaces and social structures we know from the architectural, legal and political records. Aesthetic value judgements are not exactly irrelevant from the perspective opened up by a concept of this sort (for without aesthetic criteria of excellence, chronotopes would surely never prosper), but one can see readily how they are conjoined to a very practical purpose.

More mundane and workaday than the 'cognitive map', then, the chronotope may yet be a better point of entry into the representational crisis of postmodernity, for the simple reason that every literary text, no matter how abstract or generic, by virtue of its constitution by syntax, image and form, is irreducibly chronotopic; since Bakhtin presented 'the chronotope as a formally constitutive category of literature.'[71] The difficulty resides in mediating between the textual chronotope on the one hand, and the 'real-and-imagined' postmodern spaces it represents on the other. And for this purpose I have found the concepts developed by Lefebvre in his *Production of Space* immensely useful; for with his triad in place as a mediating construct between literary chronotopes and the social space-time of Los Angeles, the whole knotty dilemma of the 'real' as we have addressed it is alleviated. Lefebvre's insistence that the 'real' is always and already shot through with representationality, either abstract or passional, allows for a chronotopic analysis of texts which reads them, not as mirrors held up to nature, but as *acts of appropriation of social space*. This is exactly how the present work proposes to conduct its survey of contemporary Los Angeles literature; not as a guide to literary value in the present, or a literal guide to the city, but as a series of enactments of spatial appropriation by individuals (and their group affiliations). The chronotopes of literary acts in this city will, all of them, as we shall see, have as their principal aim the contestation of abstraction by affect, the restitution

of more humane values through more or less moralistic denuncia-
tions of the existent. To write in this visualized space is to side with
the negative and some moment of the 'tradition' which offers
security against the outright positivization of the visual, the privatization of the public sphere. We are being taught, all over again, and
from the most unlikely quarter, why and how writing matters: as a
tactic of territorial reclamation.

Turning at last to the literary works themselves, as these will be
unpackaged here, it seems worthwhile to make a few prefatory
remarks about what can be expected from them and why I have
settled upon the present sample. In the first place, for reasons
already adduced, it would seem futile to look for avatars of the
'aesthetic' among them, to predict works of determinate artistic
integrity in a social space of this sort. Whatever the merits of the
aesthetic *per se* in literature – and they are beyond measure; without
them the entire Romantic and Modernist traditions would be unthinkable – it makes little sense to expect its continuance and good
health in a social order where culture *tout court* has been folded back
into social space. If the aesthetic meant anything in modernist
literature, it meant exploiting the gap between cultural expression
and the modern market, aligning yourself with the residual, arti-
sanal, anti-commodity spirit of 'craft', or alternatively, avant-gardis-
tically, collapsing this distance and unveiling the commodity nature
of art itself. Today neither aesthetic refinement nor dadaist scandal
retain much of their force. In a world where every commodity has a
cultural aura, where representation is a prime-mover of the
economy, the aesthetic simply has no place to thrive; or, it is so
ubiquitous that it loses its distinction. Henceforth there are only
ways of being within culture, none of which is any purer or more
legitimate than any other; our very ability to cogitate upon an
individual 'artwork' seems similarly compromised by the sheer
volume of cultural information absorbed in a single day. Not that
there are not differences in value between cultural acts, but these
seem increasingly to depend on the genius they display in chronotopic intensity, rather than any obeisance to prefashioned aesthetic
criteria. The one writer considered in these pages who is determined
to extend the category of the aesthetic into the present day, Dennis
Cooper, does so precisely through the strangulated and impoverished diction of drug-addled teenagers.

If these are the fortunes of the modern aesthetic, then, still less should we expect the return of the comforting, nineteenth-century assurances of Realism; though a caveat should be appended which provides that, precisely because of the apparent impossibility of realism today, it predictably enough becomes a sort of subterranean desire, a pervasive cultural craving, which not a few of the literary works considered here will exploit – egregiously or earnestly, as you will. Thrown back, then, on the inglorious resources of the non-aesthetic and non-Realistic, literature in Los Angeles has generally declared its cultural roots in one or many of the following: the commercial, mass-market pulps, and the subliterary genres they fostered – including science fiction and detective fiction; the cultural nationalisms of the 1960s, especially black and Chicano poetry; the purified 'postmodern' white writing of Joan Didion; non-literary media such as pop music, television, video or film; the alien (French) genres of erotic decadence; and the documentary-style theatre and oral histories of the 1930s. These are the primary generic resources of writing in the city today, and from them a few stylistic generalizations can also be deduced.

At the basic level of syntax, the most predictable element of literary style in this situation will be *parataxis*, or the syntactical isolation and turning of clauses away from one another. The breaking up of the epistemological certainties of Realism had already imperilled textual integration in the age of the great Moderns; these latter had had to expend fantastic amounts of creative effort simply to keep the various sentence and paragraph blocs from flowing, like glaciers of the spirit, inexorably apart. What hope today, then, for the yoking together of heterogeneous semantic elements under the sublime hypotactical parasols of modernist syntax (Proust, Faulkner, Joyce)? With the aesthetic goes the dream and discipline of unity; far better to resign yourself to the brittle reification of speech units and play, *bricoleur*-like, with the broken parts. This stylistic trait of parataxis is at any rate best suited to charting the fragmentation-in-homogenization, the multi-dimensionality of postmodern space; the very impulse to subordinate one clause to another is checked by a lived experience in which such regulated stability is unknown.

Second, and perhaps accordingly, we might expect a preponderance of the first-person voice. Bereft of any larger vantage-point or aesthetic principle with which to anchor the dissociated clauses, we will come again and again to rely on the limited assurances of the individual social atom (and, allegorically, the larger group identity with which he or she has some elective affinity) as our perspectival frame on the city. There is an inbuilt irony to this situation, of course, since the notion of the 'Death of the Subject' within a social space dominated by technological spectacle precisely cancels the earlier, modernist authenticities of the self, its stream of consciousness, alienated inward reflection, and the uncharted urges of its unconscious. Indeed, the first-person voice serves here primarily as an empty vessel, a Lockean *tabula rasa* or generic slot in which an identity must be constructed, and not a self in the traditional manner at all.

And with this lapse of a genuine subjective depth come two important options for the writer: either to counterpoint existential one-dimensionality or schizophrenia with a robust and finely tuned demotic or argot, usually ethnically oriented; or to raise that blankness to the power of two, to square the circle of positionless positionality with a diction pared of any affect or intensity whatever. And again, this stylistic parting of the ways corresponds exactly to the fissure in social space itself, between an abstract homogenization and an apparently concrete fragmentation, between representations of space and the representational spaces of linguistic group cohesion: or, succinctly, between space and place. Each stylistic option is a mode of response to these greater social and spatial contradictions, but there does not seem to be much scope for the truly miraculous event of their reunification at a higher level.

These inauspicious features are then some of the bare conditions of writing in Los Angeles today, and with them the various works will be obliged to engage the inherited baggage of cliché through which the city is endlessly represented. Michael Sorkin has usefully drawn up a catalogue of the most typical of these representations of space, and criticized the straitjacket they have put on local imagination. As what Sorkin identifies as a rhetorical system, 'Los Angeles' tends to dictate the things that can be said about it. Running through the tropes that make this system complete, he includes *the weather* (brilliant sunshine, of course, but also bucketting rain, Santa Ana winds and earthquakes); *Disney* (the suburban plannification of kitsch); *death* (from Waugh's *The Loved One* to Charles Manson and beyond); *the Movies*; *banality*; *America in extremis*; *cars on freeways*; *the artist in a strange land*; *the beach*; the antithetical trope of *'back east'*; *the future*; and of course above all of these and somehow subsuming and orchestrating them all, the master trope of *apocalypse*.[72] It would be strictly impossible, after all we have said, to draw up chronotopes of the city without working through some of these tropes – the perplexity is precisely the degree to which these representational clichés have been assimilated into the social space of LA itself. What literary acts in Los Angeles have rather to perform is the impossible task of being 'true' to this rhetorical system while at the same time transforming it through access to representational spaces which the system omits.

From the wildly eclectic range of contemporary LA writing, I have tried as far as possible to arrive at a 'representational' cross-section of the city's literature, without succumbing to the temptations of holism or special pleading. It has been my interest to focus attention on those efforts of the last fifteen years or so which have made 'postmodern Los Angeles' the object of their chronotopic labours. It is not of particular interest in this respect whether or not the author remains (or ever was) a 'local', merely of whether or not the text performs an appropriation of LA's urban space which is distinctive and has repaid careful analysis. These final criteria must of course strike the reader as arbitrary, and I should say one or two things here about how the final sample was arrived at, and how it might ideally be extended if word limits did not curtail the requisite levels of indulgence.

The notable absences from my final list, such as Carolyn See, T. Coraghessan Boyle, Gavin Lambert, John Gregory Dunne, and the brilliant science-fiction writers Steve Erickson, Octavia Butler and Kim Stanley Robinson, for all their remarkable combined talents, would surely, had they each been considered in turn, have given this book a very conventional, white-based, liberal cast which its present form deliberately eschews. By turning instead to the sub-generic stuff of detective fiction, the multi-ethnic poets of chapter four, the hollowed-out adolescent material in the third chapter, and the final instance of a 'totalizing' black woman's performance work, it has obviously been my intent to steer clear of the marketable middle ground. The chronotopic rewards of these materials are, simply, higher (because more definitive) than those of the more obvious titles and names, though these last may tend to satisfy standard aesthetic criteria more ably and professionally. Meanwhile, the science-fictional works, while of the highest interest and possibly more stimulating chronotopically than many of the studied texts, disqualify themselves on the grounds of a radical departure from the contemporary itself (though in a way which, to be sure, is symptomatic in its contemporaneity). Perhaps it is arguable that I have

opportunistically constructed a register of contemporary letters which, by omitting the middle ground, tends towards a polarized and unnecessarily antagonistic presentation of the literary scene and its implicit politics. Alternatively, perhaps that middle ground, in its desire to attenuate division through reconciliations of form, wrongfully occludes the strength and tenacity of representational politics in Los Angeles. At any rate, some definitive word needs to be spoken here about how it is I see the field of texts here collated *vis-à-vis* the whole question of urban production and politics in Los Angeles.

Let us suggest that the ideal liberal overview of writing in Los Angeles today would want to pass attentively through each of the relevant bodies of work, in a literary critical version of 'equal time' in the news media. Such a treatment would be affirmative in its multiculturalism and yet also gravitate around its own massive core of white, middle-class professional letters. Even if only implicitly, the hierarchy of a traditional value system, of good and bad, would reimpose itself on the diversity of materials, by virtue of this inevitable weighting towards the dominant. That is, a liberal treatment of LA literature, its conscience clean due to an exhaustive comprehensiveness, would of its own momentum restore the virtues of the major over those of the minor. We can see how this cultural politics relates directly to the ideologies of space itself in the present world system. In a scathing assault on the ideology of 'multiculturalism' as a screen for liberal complacency in the face of racking economic and political injustices, Slavoj Žižek writes:

> the ideal form of ideology of this global capitalism is multiculturalism, the attitude which, from a kind of empty global position, treats *each* local culture the way the colonizer treats colonized people – as 'natives' whose mores are to be carefully studied and 'respected' . . . [T]he problematic of multiculturalism – the hybrid coexistence of diverse cultural life-worlds – which imposes itself today is the form of appearance of its opposite, of the massive presence of capitalism as *universal* world system: it bears witness to the unprecedented homogenization of the contemporary world. It is effectively as if, since the horizon of social imagination no longer allows us to entertain the idea of an eventual demise of capitalism – since, as we might put it, everybody silently accepts that *capitalism is here to stay* – critical energy has found a substitute outlet in fighting for cultural differences which leave the basic homogeneity of the capitalist world-system intact.[73]

If it appears that the methodology employed in this book tends toward a conception of urban space in Los Angeles insufficiently accommodating and sensitive, if in my hands a certain dimly familiar kind of dualism reasserts itself on the grounds of what many pundits have declared to be a haven of multicultural possibilities, then that is because the logic of the city itself mimics the logic of the world at large. It will be pointed out again and again that the delirious representational excesses and erasures of the past which characterize this city are far from innocent; that they rest, ultimately, on the 'postmodernization' of a very old-fashioned and ugly political economy. The purification of capitalism in the City of Angels entails an absolute corruption of labour relations; the flood of international financial wealth goes hand in hand with slumlordism, a booming informal sector in the deunionized garment industry, racist employment practices, spiraling homelessness, and so on.[74] What I call in chapter four the 'Third World in the First' is no mere rhetorical colour, but a fit description of the astonishing repolarization of economic haves and have-nots in this happy hunting ground of international capital. So, my interest in accentuating certain irreducible polarities in the literary sector of production is informed by what I see as an overarching socio-economic contradiction which today is manifest above all in the politics of social space. It is an interest shared by most of the writers I have chosen to examine; and it is spiritedly pro-urban, even as it passes through the most negative critique of the state of the city itself.

James Ellroy, whose international reputation as the 'bad boy' or 'mad dog' of contemporary crime fiction ensures his place in our sample, revivifies the generic conventions of hard-boiled *noir* to conduct a fevered archaeology of Los Angeles' decline into postmodernity. While seeming to promise an historically 'realist' totalization of the city, his archaeology instead mourns those essentially white, suburban fantasies of urban control whose racist paranoia was summarily dispatched by the riots of 1992. The 'LA Quartet', historical novel as pulp fiction, compulsively declares its spatial and class origins – its astonishing ethnic chauvinism – in the very movement of its chronotopic elaboration, which reaches again and again into the imaginary resources of scopophilia and Ellroy's mother's death. Meanwhile, his black crime-writing contemporary Walter Mosley, who similarly revisits in his 'Easy Rawlins' series the pivotal postwar moment of the 1950s, refuses that spurious appeal to the totality, and locates his narrative chronotope squarely within the African-American community, in an attempt to restore a representational space of black, neighbourly solidarity to the city's imaginary. In both, the appeal of the period and the representational magnet of the LAPD are seen as symptomatic and ineluctable in a city where 'law and order' is a daily substitute for democracy.

Chapter three then analyses how the city's most notorious writer, Bret Easton Ellis, tried during the 1980s and 1990s to map LA's abstraction of space. His Los Angeles, in the novels *Less Than Zero* (1985) and *The Informers* (1994), is an homogeneous plenum, presented from the point-of-view of narrators for whom the commercial sphere is their only horizon. Their prose therefore registers the eclipse of any remaining 'representational space' and pessimistically presents postmodern consciousness as a product of dominating representations of space. I suggest that Ellis's prose style is itself a kind of chronotope in its cancellation of all temporal energy and its dilation of space to a seamless repetition of the same commercial signs and practices. Alongside Ellis's pessimistic achievement, the contemporary one of Dennis Cooper points in a rather different direction from the same spatial and existential juncture. Using the allegorical vehicle of the adolescent white body, and the 'minor' community of gay men, Cooper exacts extreme demands of his reader in violently desecrating the fetish form of the commodity to see what remains underneath of the representational body itself. His exquisite attention to style acts as a redemptive measure against the necessary violence of his narratives, and altogether his texts stand as allegorical maps of abstract space which lead us to the buried treasure of its affects and love.

In chapter four, I turn to the efforts of three of the best contemporary Los Angeles poets, Wanda Coleman, Luis J. Rodriguez and Sesshu Foster. In their work I find ample evidence of palpable and powerful 'representational spaces', particularly in its mediation of black and Mexican ethnic history, of working-class history, and of survival tactics for everyday life in the ghetto. Their work serves as a perfect counterfoil for the abstract pessimism of Ellis and the hysterical power-hunger of James Ellroy, presenting Los Angeles from the point of view of the ethnic, working-class oppressed, in poetic forms both lyrical and experimental. New modes of spatial and temporal energy are reclaimed by this 'multicultural' verse, and new methods of seeing Los Angeles not as a reified fetish, but *as a product* – the product of its forgotten working class.

Finally, chapter five meditates on the possibility of 'realism' in a city such as this. The dramatic work of performance artist Anna

Deavere Smith is taken as exemplary. Her play *Twilight: Los Angeles, 1992*, was the most important work of art to arise out of the ashes of the Los Angeles riots of 1992 – amongst the most destructive and terrible in the nation's history. By turning to the specific identities of individuals caught up in the violence of that event, and representing them in succession upon the stage, Smith achieves the closest thing the city has yet known to a *total* representation: an image of Los Angeles that fully respects its vastly complex and variegated constituency. My investigation examines what is at stake in Smith's performance method, and suggests the paradoxical formulation of 'postmodern realism' to account for her aesthetics. Yet, it is impossible to rest content with a work of art whose lessons have been abandoned and forgotten by the political production of space itself in LA; so a final appeal to a more fully engaged postmodernism is then attempted.

2

Neo-noir and the archaeology of urban space

Los Angeles once enjoyed a genuine cultural resistance to its dominant representations. In his *City of Quartz*, Mike Davis portrays a
protracted war of figural stealth against the city boosters' image of
LA as utopia. While the social imagineers unveiled their successive
airbrushed visions of the city, a strange assortment of mostly émigré
intellectuals and disenchanted artists concocted a dystopian imaginary for it, a 'representational space' haunted by death, despair,
entropy, dissolution and apocalypse. For many years, these two
antithetical impulses, in what Davis has dubbed the 'master dialectic
of sunshine and *noir*', vied with each other in a Manichean struggle
over the soul of the city.[1]

Of the two antithetical alternatives, the semiology of *noir* has
exerted most influence on the city's literature. Confronted in the
1920s and 1930s by the city's slick, idyllic packaging, sham architecture, deracinated cultural tradition, civic incohesion, and the sheer
improbability of the mostly retired Mid-West populace, writers from
the East such as Nathanael West, Horace McCoy and James M. Cain
assumed the role of Cassandra in local letters. Together they assembled the *noir* semiotic matrix of Los Angeles as an urban hell, or
the Los Angeles Anti-Myth.[2] The great early phase of Los Angeles
literature, which begins with Cain's *The Postman Always Rings Twice*
(1934), sought to invert the established real-estate glamour of the
New Jerusalem. David Fine writes:

> For West, Cain, Fitzgerald, McCoy, and others, Los Angeles
> could not serve as setting for the regenerative possibilities of
> America. The dream, if it had once had potency, was behind
> them. Writing against the myth of El Dorado, they transformed
> it into its antithesis: that of the dream running out along the

California shore . . . The tension between myth and antimyth, between Southern California as the place of the fresh start and as the scene of the disastrous finish, recurs in almost all the fiction.[3]

In Davis's estimation, *'Noir* was like a transformational grammar turning each charming ingredient of the boosters' arcadia into a sinister equivalent.'[4] A body of literature built upon a reactive system such as this, converting sunshine into shade, optimism into despair, El Dorado into Hell, would logically thrive in the hothouse of hype where it took root.

Yet if this nauseated polemic gave rise to a legitimate regional literature, capable of commanding national cultural attention where previously there had been at best neglect,[5] it also tended over the years to ossify into its own, rigid semiotic fretboard, on which familiar minor chords could be strummed with dwindling critical capacity. By the late 1980s, indeed, this system of dystopian tropes had for some time been subject to an unexpected expropriation. From its original vocation as a literary pestilence on LA's bourgeois 'social imaginary',[6] it has more recently been used, ironically, to assist the marketing of the city. 'In that sense, the very popular *dark* side of LA tourism, using images of urban blight, has also sold real estate. The "noir image" has glamorized, quite unintentionally, the need to destroy downtown communities. That is the ironic genius of social imaginaries as cities, either of the sunshine variety or the shady: they always wind up selling products.'[7] Thomas Pynchon seized upon this locally typical negation of the negation in his 1990 novel, *Vineland*:

> This time they'd arranged to meet in lower Hollywood at the new Noir Center, loosely based on crime movies from around World War II and after . . . This was yuppification run to some pitch so desperate that Prairie at least had to hope the whole process was reaching the end of its cycle. She happened to like those old weird-necktie movies in black and white, . . . and she personally resented this increasingly dumb attempt to cash in on the pseudoromantic mystique of those particular olden days in this town . . .[8]

It is a perfect image of the transformation of a once-salient critical style into designer chic; the enduring, capricious logic of the image in LA. No longer the progressive instrument it once was, the more or less modernist image of Los Angeles as a suburban wasteland driven by diabolical urges had been seized for interests other than those promoted by such luminous exponents as Nathanael West,

William Faulkner, Theodor Adorno and Bertolt Brecht. In Lefebvre's terminology, what was once a critical 'representational space' had been transformed into a 'representation of space', a marketing strategy used to stimulate tourism and consumption, and demonize and destroy downtown communities.

Such a reversal in the critical fortunes of a once reliable semiotic system directly affects the status of literary works erected on its blueprint. In this chapter, we will inquire into the possibilities left to the *noir* semiotic by rampant postmodernization in Los Angeles, possibilities most openly and extensively explored by James Ellroy's 'LA Quartet' and Walter Mosley's 'Easy Rawlins' novels. The seedy semiology of the original generation of *noir* authors and film-makers evolved in the context of a progressive critique of dominant representations, and was a properly demystifying tool with which to prosecute an unconscionable measure of untruth in the boosters' rhetorical arsenal. Today, with that semiology lifted from its context and melded, as image, into the quotidian fabric of the city, its use in fiction can only be read as an ironic engagement with a henceforth inaccessible 'authenticity', long-since co-opted by the very planners, developers and city officials it had been designed to thwart. This strange afterlife, it will transpire, has less to do with a residual generic authenticity than with a certain unrecognized truth-content at the heart of the too-quickly expropriated semiotic. That James Ellroy and Walter Mosley return obsessively to the LA of the 1950s and early 1960s in their very different series of crime novels, that their combined laments for a missed moment circulate around the question of policing and segregation, has everything to do with the most potent cognitive charge of *noir* as a genre or aesthetic – what I have called elsewhere its *racial unconscious*, its uncanny tendency to map urban racial unease in terms of black and white, paranoia and violence, consumerism and the void.[9]

Is it, however, permissible to speak of any cognitive content whatever to a form of literature as cheap and generic as detective fiction? Certainly Franco Moretti has argued that the apparent alignment of formal interests with cognitive impulses in crime fiction, the way in which the pursuit of truth and revelation dictates many of the narrative conventions – usually by way of retardation – is strictly chimerical. The 'truth' of detective fiction is, precisely, the reiterated act of its reader's self-deception. 'One reads only with the purpose of remaining as one already is: innocent. Detective fiction owes its success to the fact that it teaches nothing.'[10] Its narrative structures are generic in the bad sense: repetitive, schematic, closed and consumer-oriented. What little can be said about it as a repository of literary style (with the possible exception of Raymond Chandler, as we shall see), is quickly dispelled by the slightest attention to this entirely unsatisfactory formal *reproducibility*. Unsatisfactory, that is, by the standards of literary modernism, with its cult of original style, fetishization of ambiguity and discomfort with mass culture. But what if the concept of the chronotope, by disclosing the ethnographic interests of even the most 'disinterested' forms, could redeem this genre from a residual scholarly neglect by attending to the overt ways in which it makes a certain kind of teaching pleasurable? Coincident with our own interests, detective fiction would then appear, in affirmative fashion, to be committed to teaching some conception of what David Schmid calls 'safe urban space': 'Whether it is Victorian London or 1950s Harlem, detective fiction sees urban space as chaotic and in need of order . . . the city is a problem that needs to be solved.'[11] These 'models of order' clearly pretend to the status of something like Jameson's 'cognitive maps', assured acts of co-ordination for the subject in an age of dizzying abstraction; yet, it seems equally possible to approach them as what we have been calling chronotopes. Detective fiction today, in its well-nigh obsessive quest for a heightened cognition of the urban, could thus be said to have as its actual function the production of chronotopes which offer a certain measure of protection against the threats and contradictions of contemporary urbanism. *Pace* Moretti, it does not exactly teach 'nothing', but neither may its lessons be commensurable with any clear authorial intention.

That, in any event, seems a promising avenue of approach to our first series of detective novels which, more than any of the works considered in this book, makes a virtue of necessity and promotes the notion of a 'knowledge' of Los Angeles to the single animating *telos* of narration. Perhaps it seems remarkable that this evident desire for social realism should be vehiculated in a form as mechanical and unexperimental as the mystery story; yet such are the paradoxes of contemporary culture, that we have come full circle from the great separation, under Modernism, of commercial writing from serious intent. The cultural moment of 'postmodernism' itself is nowhere better signalled than in James Ellroy's exclamation that 'I love crime fiction . . . I want to make it as real as I can. I want to expand it as a voice of social history and burn it to the ground.'[12] The availability of a once-spurned subgenre to this redemptive labour in the interests of 'social history', is ample evidence of a wholesale cultural transformation. Realism, whose very definition would once have been 'not-genre', now happily finds its vessel in the generic depths of crime fiction.

Los Angeles, of course, has its own history of relation to this genre, for which it served as something like a seed-bed during the first phase of 'hard-boiled' detective writing in the 1920s and 1930s. In 'the milieu of the American hard-boiled story, the vision of the city is almost reversed' from earlier European mystery models, and 'we find empty modernity, corruption, and death. A gleaming and deceptive facade hides a world of exploitation and criminality in which enchantment and significance must usually be sought elsewhere, in what remains of the natural world still unspoiled by the pervasive spread of the city.'[13] This, as we have been prepared to recognize, is the mythos of *noir*. Consequently, as John Cawelti notes, the detective protagonist is always at threat from this disenchanted and malevolent social space, and must evolve an exoskeleton of muscle and bitter cynicism to repel the allure and danger of his lifeworld, which is also his only source of income (unlike the dilettantish amateurs of Doyle and Christie). The crime he investigates is generally only the first in a series; his efforts of detection will usually be attended by more violence, deeper plots of corrupt intrigue, and a direct, personal confrontation with vice. There is, then, in this initial phase of the 'hard-boiled' tradition, still the strong trace of an earlier Romance tradition, in this figure of the investigator as populist hero. In Chandler's famous lines, the hard-boiled protagonist:

> . . . is the hero, he is everything. He must be a complete man and a common man and yet an unusual man. He must be . . . a man of honour, by instinct, by inevitability, without thought of it, and certainly without saying it. He must be the best man in his world and a good enough man for any world.[14]

These exceptional protagonists have been classified as latter-day Robin Hoods. 'As such they are the people's champions, who stand on the margin of the law as representatives of a higher law.'[15]

And not only of Justice, but also of Art. For the great peculiarity of Raymond Chandler was not simply his ability to reinvent a genre for a new social space, but moreover his insistence that his work ennobled a 'cheap, shoddy, and utterly lost kind of writing' by its unusual dedication to *style*,[16] 'the most durable thing in writing', 'the most valuable investment a writer can make with his time.'[17]

41

Chandler's stylistic concerns (the grotesque Chandlerian similes, the descriptive *brio*, wise-cracks and memorable evocations of squalor) indeed tended to override his attention to plot coherence and consistency, to the extent that his plots have about them an air of slap-dash *bricolage*: 'it was always a plot difficulty that held me up. I simply could not plot far enough ahead. I'd write something I liked and then I would have a hell of a time making it fit into the structure. This resulted in some rather starting [sic] oddities of construction, about which I care nothing, being fundamentally rather uninterested in plot.'[18]

With plot thereby subordinated to modest stylistic experiment, the Los Angeles detective story became more interested in space than in time, and generated within its own formal evolution new procedures of chronotopography. Fredric Jameson interpreted Chandler in 1970 as the epic poet of Los Angeles, who integrated urban sprawl and fragmentation into disjointed narratives of sequential scenic investigation.[19] As Jameson put it, 'the form of Chandler's books reflects an initial American separation of people from each other, their need to be linked by some external force (in this case the detective) if they are ever to be fitted together as part of the same picture puzzle.'[20] As a result, 'hard-boiled' literature was decisive in substituting spatial totalities for temporal ones, less interested in fluid connections than in juxtapositions and jump-cuts. Its chronotope tended towards a volatilizing of the temporal plane, madly accelerated here, aimlessly meandering there, but always 'thrown', in proper Heideggerian wise, into some spatial configuration or other, in which the activity of detection had less to do with plot development than wide-eyed perception and being *per se*.

We shall have occasion to return to Chandler later, but what remains to be said in this potted prelude is that the 1950s saw the introduction, in *noir* film and fiction, of an altogether different mode of hard-boiled crime narrative, which turned the Chandlerian model on its head, and was thus already 'post-modernist' in its abandonment of his attempted stylistic recuperations. This was the 'police procedural', a supposed inside view of the operations of police departments in major cities grappling with organized crime.[21] In opposition to the quintessentially lonely, *petit-bourgeois* crusades of the private investigators of Chandler and Dashiell Hammett, the novels – by Ed McBain and Jack Webb especially – and films of police procedure substituted teamwork for individual hunches, bland objectivity for character-laden point of view, and 'just the facts, Ma'am' for Marlowe's incomparable similes and wise-cracks. This straight-laced narrative functionalism extinguished Chandler's stylistic experiments in the genre. Jack Webb's television series, *Dragnet*, epitomized this trend towards right-wing technophile facticity. It represented and helped to facilitate the implantation of a new 'panoptical' imaginary in the social consciousness of Los Angeles which arose, as we shall see shortly, in concert with the inaugural version of its 'Carceral City',[22] under the auspices of Police Chief William Parker.

Both James Ellroy and Walter Mosley depart from this bifurcated hard-boiled tradition while remaining its heirs and most illustrious contemporary exemplars. In our first case, Ellroy discovers an elective affinity with this latter incarnation of *noir*, the police procedural, and a marked hostility to the Chandlerian individualism of style and content, marshalling his devices in the name of a redoubled attempt at law and order; meanwhile, Mosley exhumes the aesthetic legacy of Chandler, but overturns the lazy prejudices of this latter with a new and aggressive political intelligence. In each case, these variations on the theme of nostalgia are symptomatic representational reflexes to a city which, in its present dispensation, draws the colour line ever more boldly around its segregated communities, and allows the 'initial American separation of people' to develop into an ethnically patterned psychogeographical neurosis. So it is that the urban racial geography of minoritization is revealed as the deeper content of *noir* fiction today, which returns to this content like a tongue to a loose tooth.

> The fifties were the real high spot for the US ('when things were going on') and you can still feel the nostalgia for those years, for the ecstasy of power, when power held power.[23]

James Ellroy, whose mother was raped and strangled in the blue-collar, far-East LA suburb of El Monte in 1958, when Ellroy was ten years old, has made it his life's work to disinter the unholy truth of Chief William Parker's LAPD from beneath the puritanical mythology of *Dragnet*; to subject to the most unflinching scrutiny the operations and personnel of a police force whose image was enshrined in that televisual fantasy. He is perhaps uniquely qualified to do so. His unsettling autobiography *My Dark Places* (1996), is explicit in its assessment of the extent to which Ellroy's young consciousness was shaped by the authoritarian narratives of Mickey Spillane and Jack Webb, starting with Webb's 'nonfiction ode to the Los Angeles

Police Department', *The Badge*, which Ellroy first read at eleven years of age:

> *Dragnet* was the saga of dead-end lives up against authority. Suppressive police methods insured a virtuous LA. The show talked a stern game and oozed subtextual self-pity. It was the epic of isolated men in an isolating profession, deprived of conventional illusions and traumatized by their daily contact with scum. It was 50s-style male angst – alienation as a public service announcement.
>
> The book [*The Badge*] was the TV show unchained. Jack Webb detailed police procedures and whined about the LAPD's white male burden at great length. He compared criminals to Communists without irony. He served up real-life anecdotes to illustrate the terrors and prosaic satisfactions of police work. He ran down some snappy LAPD cases – free of TV censorship strictures.[24]

The similarity of one of these cases, the infamous 'Black Dahlia' rape and murder of 1945, to that of Ellroy's own mother may be said to have overdetermined the young Ellroy's excessive psychological investment in this pre-pubescent fantasy scenario of hard men dedicated to the tracking-down of criminals, yet failing to solve either of these two crimes against women. 'I read the Dahlia story a hundred times', he tells us. 'My imagination supplied the details that Jack Webb omitted'.[25] In a sense, all of Ellroy's subsequent narratives have sprung from these traumatized boyhood acts of supplementary story-telling, which tried vainly to patch the holes in the myth of a Los Angeles governed by a disinterested and incorruptible patriarchal authority, and so solve the primal scene of his mother's sexually violent death.

Such psychologizing will look less schematic when it is realized how remarkably symptomatic Ellroy's novels are, especially his masterpiece, the four-volume 'LA Quartet' (1987–92), which tracks the LAPD through the late 1940s and 1950s with an obsessive interest in its failures, corruptions and sadistic violence. In what follows, I wish to determine as clearly as possible the structural fixations of Ellroy's narrative art, a critical tactic which has the advantage of resisting the inevitable temptations to moralize about a literary accomplishment so laced with sexual violence and perversion that its surface features threaten to distract from the deeper logic of the whole. Ellroy's novels form a secure semantic microuniverse, operating within repeated categories and actions, reiterated themes, and a predictable structure of spatial semes. If Chandler had suggested that other pleasures and needs, besides efficient plotting and knowing the solution to the crime, might motivate and reward our reading of detective fiction, then Ellroy's response to this 'condescending' attitude towards the pulps cannot have been more derisory. In his Quartet, *à la* the police procedurals it salutes, individual scenes are bluntly demoted to functional status, meaningless outside the awesome regime of narrative closure which brings them all into final sense. Every textual element serves the higher interest of plot unification, which in this new ideology of form assumes the massive, extravagantly complicated cohesiveness of a genuine conspiracy theory. It should also be said that Ellroy's style, to which we will return at the end of this section, is distinctly opposed to Chandler's witty modernism: 'I go back and read Chandler now and I'm almost embarrassed by how corny and badly written a lot of it is. A lot of it is brilliant, but maybe an equal amount is clunky metaphors and bullshit similes.'[26]

We shall be interested in determining the contours of Ellroy's consistent literary chronotope. Its recurrence in each installment, independent of the various historicist events that take place during the epic narration, is evidence of a deeply symptomatic imagination, and needs careful unpacking, both to examine its claims to truth and knowledge, and to suggest some relationships with the dense psychological pressures on its production. For Ellroy himself is the prototypical human product of the urban space his fiction compulsively maps, a child born and reared in the pivotal post-war period of Los Angeles' production of space. His narrative labours are, in some as yet undetermined sense, a subjection to self-analysis of a subjectivity shattered in a suburban void by the violent death of a mother and the drift into alcoholic oblivion of a weak and negligent father.

More than any of Ellroy's themes, indeed, that of the absent or failed father is the most salient for the initiation of our critique. Its quintessential instance has to do with the historical figure of Chief of Police William Parker himself, architect of Los Angeles' new policing apparatus during the 1950s. According to Mike Davis, Parker's influence on what was to become the city's notorious regime of police power and arrogance was profound:

> As reformed in the early 1950s by the legendary Chief Parker (who admired above all the elitism of the Marines), the LAPD was intended to be incorruptible because unapproachable, a 'few good men' doing battle with a fundamentally evil city.

Dragnet's Sergeant Friday precisely captured the Parkerized LAPD's quality of prudish alienation from a citizenry composed of fools, degenerates and psychopaths.[27]

Parker haunts the whole of Ellroy's Quartet – *The Black Dahlia* (1987), *The Big Nowhere* (1988), *LA Confidential* (1990), and *White Jazz* (1992) – and appears on several occasions,[28] but given the sheer volume of police corruption and brutality these novels are destined to describe, it is remarkable that Ellroy should choose both to protect the 'idea' of Parker by never implicating him in these matters, and yet to undermine his authority by demonstrating his lack of real control over the men he supposedly inspires to 'Marine-like' dedication. This tactic of enshrining and yet disabling the most potent authority-figure available to him in his novels of 'social history' is critical to Ellroy's method of investigating the consequences of what I will come to define as a 'post-oedipal' social space: a space freed from the moral order that has traditionally descended from the patriarch. In its stead, an autonomous system of power, a bureaucracy, is left to cope with the importunings of a new civil order liberated from oedipal respect and duty. It is the clash of these two discordant forces – one, a bureaucracy seemingly dependent upon the idea of paternal authority, yet actually autonomous; and two, a society unchained from God the Father and revelling in new pleasures – which Ellroy is most interested in dramatizing.

Ellroy is content to have Parker's presence and ideology infiltrate the text more generally, however, as a constellation of semic elements without characterological guise. His spirit, as it were, enters into and informs the spatial semiotics of the novels. It is evident, for instance, that the principal binary opposition of spatial semes in Ellroy's semantic universe borrows its form explicitly from Parker's dualistic representation of urban space. The Quartet's governing structure presupposes an ideological *agon* in public space, between the Bureau as such – stronghold of the 'few good men', the downtown City Hall building, with outposts in the various LAPD Division substations – and the 'mean streets' of Downtown, East LA and South-Central (alternately called 'Niggertown and 'darktown' in the texts), spaces of ethnic alterity, endemic violence and cancerous vice. Parker himself was legendary for insisting on such a dualized conception of public space, and not averse from projecting his notion of 'good vs. evil' through a racial optic, with white and black assuming their traditional places in that Manichean agon: 'all Blacks are bad guys'.[29]

City Hall, the administrative heart of the Los Angeles Civic

Center, is then logically at the spatial and ideological core of Ellroy's novels. It symbolizes the panoptical vantage-point over the sprawl of LA, housing the mayoral administration, the LAPD's special divisions, the District Attorney's office, and other contiguous bureaucracies of power. In Edward Soja's words, City Hall can be seen as 'an aggregation of overseers, a primary locale for social control, political administration, cultural codification, [and] ideological surveillance'.[30] This busy, walled-off, white-collar, vertical space (familiar as an icon of power from many crime films) provides the official motivation and sanction for the protagonists' actions. We are first introduced to its interior in *The Black Dahlia* when ex-boxer Bucky Bleichert is promoted to Warrants Division after staging a propaganda fight for the Department. His reflections are animated by a scarcely concealeable homoerotic desire:

> The sixth floor housed the Department's elite Divisions: Homicide, Administrative Vice, Robbery and Bunco, along with Central Warrants and the Central Detective Squad. It was the domain of specialist cops, cops with political juice and up-and-comers, and it was my home now. I was wearing my best sports jacket and slacks combo, my service revolver hung from a brand new shoulder rig . . . My Departmental juice was just starting. I felt ready for anything.[31]

A rearing, phallic space (for decades the tallest building in the city), City Hall is thus revealed as the locus of homosocial power and specialized bureaucratic work. Later in the Quartet, Sergeant Edmund Exley experiences its pleasures as follows:

> The empty squadroom made him happy: . . . a big space filled with desks and filing cabinets. Official forms on the walls – empty spaces you filled in when you notched an arrest and made somebody confess. Confession could be ciphers, nothing past an admission of the crime. But if you twisted your man the right way – loved him and hated him to precisely the right degree – then he would tell you things – small details – that would create a reality to buttress your case and give you that much more intelligence to bend your next suspect with.[32]

Bureau space itself seems to command this pleasurable labour of informational extraction and inscription. Its very emptiness, like Nature itself for an earlier tradition of American fiction, stands as an imperative to fill it in. The information flows from a physical and psychological discipline of 'twisting' suspects, who are plucked from the streets and bear their exotic mysteries within. The space of City Hall is, then, *a priori* articulated with another field of space, a space of the Other, of 'fools, degenerates and psychopaths' in Chief Parker's words, in a sort of colonial contract with that region of chaotic, everyday life which it must penetrate and possess as symbolic knowledge. Authoritarian space is implicated in what might be called a dialectic of desire with that other space, the patriarchal or oedipal Subject to its inscrutable Object.

The 'other' space is of course *the street*, into which Bucky Bleichert is cast on a penitential tour of duty – here specifically Skid Row ('probably the most dangerous ten square blocks in the world'[33]) – to remember what being a policeman is all about:

> I worked East 5th Street from Main to Stanford, skid row. Blood banks, liquor stores selling half pints and short dogs exclusively, fifty-cent-a-night flophouses and derelict missions. The unspoken rule down there was that footbeat hacks worked strongarm. You broke up bottle gangs by whacking winos with your billy club; you hauled jigs out of the day labor joints when they insisted on getting hired. You rounded up drunks and ragpickers indiscriminately to meet the city quota, beating them down if they tried to run from the drunk wagon. It was attrition duty.[34]

Later he is transferred to Newton Street Division,

> southeast of downtown LA, 95 per cent slums, 95 per cent Negroes, all trouble. There were bottle gangs and crap games on every corner; liquor stores, hair-straightening parlors and poolrooms on every block, code three calls to the station twenty-four hours a day. Footbeat hacks carried metal-studded saps; squadroom dicks packed .45 automatics loaded with unregulation dum-dums . . . Newton Street Division was a war zone.[35]

This kind of evacuated parataxis is typical of the Quartet, and its use with respect to the poor, black and other ethnic areas of Los Angeles especially so. In *The Big Nowhere*, '[d]usk started coming on, rain clouds eclipsing late sunshine trying to light up Negro slums: ramshackle houses encircled by chicken wire, pool halls, liquor stores and storefront churches on every street'.[36] In this casually reductive style, description imperceptibly degenerates into ideology. Theodor Adorno once posited that paratactic language 'stands opposed to subjective expression; by virtue of its generality, it reduces what is to be expressed to something already given and known'.[37] The surveiling subjects of police power do not really see or express this rundown space of everyday life; they simply reproduce it in litanies of racist iconography, 'already given and known'. That is their work here, precisely, to reproduce for us the prevailing Parkerian representation of space which insists on segregation, containment and harrassment. Thus the chronotope has no temporal dimension apart from a non-socially 'natural' one (dusk, rainclouds, etc.), and is indeed nothing but a stereotypical, timeless *topos* plucked from the recycled imaginary of pocket-novels and television series.

So the primary spatial antinomy of these texts (Bureau vs. street) is presented as a 'masculine' opposition between two fields of cliché and stereotype, clashing remakes of outworn, apocryphal originals. Pastiche is the degree zero of this sort of postmodern textuality, and its tendency is to reduce all representation to a mockery of that concept. There is, however, a distinction between Ellroy's literary representation of public space and the historical Parkerian representation of space it echoes, and that is that he has removed (or, better, displaced) the invidious morality of Parker's ideology, the simple identification of white with good and black with evil. Instead, the police force is presented as almost uniformly corrupt, morally indistinguishable from the street it hammers and persecutes. This at least Ellroy shares with the Chandler he despises: a thoroughgoing disillusion with the established regime of power, albeit an admiring and fascinated disillusion, which yet yearns for its restitution in the absence of anything better.

Disengaged from direct correspondence to the binary opposition dividing public space, Ellroy's moral binary opposition (which he maintains) engages across it. On the 'good' side, it is increasingly Detective Ed Exley's function (as a kind of understudy for his revered Chief Parker: 'Sir, you've brought the Department back from Horrall and Worton. Your reputation is exemplary and the Department's has greatly improved'[38]) to uphold the possibility of a fitting patriarchal resolution to the aporia afflicting public space, a resolution which cannot be represented as such. Exley is the tendential Father, promising a release from the endless struggles of order, the guarantee of symbolic exchange and mastery. The problem is both that Exley himself is compromised by the lies on which his career is based, and moreover that countervailing, 'evil' forces inhibit the realization of this apotheosis in narrative space-time. Whether it is Ellis Loew ('satan'[39]) or the supremely diabolical Lieutenant Dudley Smith, what generates the very production of the Quartet's plotting, its 'problematic' in the Althusserian sense, is an egregious resistance to the Exley principle, and a pulling in the opposite direction across the fraught axis of masculinized public space.

In political terms, this opposition between 'Exley' and 'Dudley' might be plotted in terms of a certain instability in US conservative ideology. On the one hand, there is Dudley Smith's proto-fascist model of 'containment' which actively exploits the opposition of black and white:

> Lad, do you recognise the need to contain crime, to keep it south of Jefferson with the dark element?[40]

> I've long been involved in containing hard crime so that myself and a few colleagues might someday enjoy a profit dispensation, and that day will soon be arriving . . . Grand means will be in our hands, lad. Imagine the means to keep the nigger filth sedated and extrapolate from there.[41]

And on the other, Exley's and Parker's 'absolute justice',[42] an ideally distributive justice that would ultimately apply across the whole of civil society.

These incompatible responses to the 'realities of maintaining order in Negro-inhabited sectors'[43] do not admit the possibility of a Left or even liberal corrective, which would replace the emphasis on 'order' with one on participatory justice. Where the Left does appear in the Quartet (the Communists in *The Big Nowhere*, Morton Diskant and Welles Noonan in *White Jazz*), they are exposed as weak, vulnerable, ridiculous, backstabbing and ineffectual: risibly *feminine*; and femininity is in Ellroy the key to a very different spatial order, as we shall see. The Left offers no model of control, which is here the paramount concern, as Ellroy tells us:

> And that's what I want to write about. America is reaching toward greater and greater levels of dysfunction. I like writing about what happens when nothing works and everything goes wrong and there is no control. And when the heroes, the people who readers are groomed to identify with, do horrifying and shameful and brutal things. I dig that stuff .[44]

Ellroy writes about the void of authority opened up by the unresolved contradictions in American public space. From this tension springs, as he suggests, a *noir*-ish regression from the ardours of civic responsibility, when the protagonists reflexively recognize their own implication in the crimes they investigate, and detour beyond the public domain, into private horror, shame and the like.

The shift from public to private entails an obvious expansion of the Quartet's spatial semiology, and the introduction of secondary narrative materials, to motivate the detectives' withdrawal into the *noir* 'representational space' of fear, nausea, anxiety and horror. Provocations for this paranoid detour through representational space are scattered at random through urban space itself, signposts of a new spatial economy which effectively spell the end of the road for Parker's rationalized representations of space (white/black; us/them) which Ellroy's detectives carry in their heads like implants:

> The district's main drag was Crenshaw Boulevard. Broad, running north all the way to Wilshire and south to Baldwin Hills; it spelled 'postwar boom' like a neon sign. Every block from Jefferson to Leimert was lined with dilapidated, once grand houses being torn down, their facades replaced by giant billboards advertising department stores, jumbo shopping centres, kiddie parks and movie theaters . . . and it hit me that by 1950 this part of LA would be unrecognizable. Driving east, we passed vacant lot after vacant lot that would probably soon spawn houses.[45]

As Josh Cohen has argued, '[t]he drama that proceeds will be intimately bound up with this process of creative destruction that will bring the new object world of urban consumer culture (department stores, amusement parks and cinemas), predicated on the deployment of spectacle, into being'; it is a process which Cohen reads specifically in terms of a feminization of everyday life.[46] Unable to locate himself on the cusp of this transformed urban future, Bleichert signals the crisis which the 'postwar boom' of real-estate development and hegemonic consumerism has triggered in a Parkerized mental space. At the very moment that disciplinary gaze had looked poised to conquer the chaos of everyday life, everyday life now answers back with an altogether different, 'feminine' spatialization: demolition and construction, simulation and spectacle, and what I want to call the privatization of public space.

Consequently, to illustrate this new dynamic, there is at the core of each of the four novels a cryptic family melodrama which dramatizes de-oedipalization as destructive of an entire civil code. In each, a family is portrayed that has suffered a severe crisis in the oedipal structure: a terrible absenting or betrayal, usually incestuous, of the paternal function, which breeds a violent psycho-sexual drive, usually in the damaged son, and motivates a string of savage murders. These family melodramas relate explicitly, in each case, to a decisive modification in the social space of the city. In *The Black Dahlia*, this is the symbolic removal of the last four letters in the giant HOLLYWOODLAND sign on Mt. Lee, and the impending disgrace of developer Emmett Sprague once the dangerously shoddy standards of his construction empire are exposed. Sprague, who had co-built the suburb of Hollywoodland, is guilty of incest with his 'daughter'

Madeleine, and so incites the psychotic rage of his wife and Madeleine's biological father, George Tilden, actual perpetrators of the 'Black Dahlia' murder. *The Big Nowhere*'s spatial crisis is manifest in the confrontation between the UAES/Communist picketers and the LAPD/Teamster reactionaries on the street outside the movie studios. And here Reynolds Loftis, a leader of the UAES, enjoys an incestuous affair with his illegitimate son, Coleman, who in turn wreaks his displaced psycho-sexual vengeance on numerous victims. The momentous spatial adjustments represented in *LA Confidential* are nothing less than the construction of Preston Exley's LA freeway system and Raymond Dieterling's 'Dream-a-Dreamland'. In this case, Dieterling sires the sick and illegitimate David Mertens, whose murderous psychosis is triggered by Dieterling's violent 'blue' cartoons, and kills in atonement for David's sins his other son Paul – for whom the Disney-esque themepark, like a sick mausoleum, is built. And finally, *White Jazz* focuses on the mass-eviction of the Chicano community of Chavez Ravine to make way for the politically expedient Dodger Stadium. Although the family link is less explicit here, the Kafesjian and Herrick families' serial adultery and incest connects with LAPD corruption, sanctioned drug-trafficking in South-Central, and a civic regime of which the Stadium is a lynchpin.

All of which is to demonstrate the destructive effects of Los Angeles' postwar production of space on private being in the Quartet, or vice versa, and the degree to which public space has lamentably been privatized. The epochal spatial restructuring of the era – 'Hollywood', shopping centres, the freeways, Disneyland, tract housing and Dodger Stadium – is figured in Ellroy as having determinate links with a newly post-oedipal domestic scene. All of these 'deviations' within the production of urban space diminish the hold of the Father and unleash a new, delirious consumer space oriented towards 'feminine' auto-eroticism: whether it is Hollywood's spectacle, the spatial flow of freeways, shopping centres, suburbanization, or commodified leisure, these markers of the post-war order indicate the spread of a new regime of *jouissance*, which, as Joan Copjec argues, it was the duty of classic *noir* to monitor and denounce.[47]

The first spatial seme to carry significant narrative weight in the 'private sector' is, predictably enough, that of the *private residence* itself. This seme stretches to embrace a large number of private houses, rooms and mere dwellings, from the luxuriant and semi-public pimp houses of Felix Gordean (*BN*) and Pierce Patchett (*LAC*), through the narratively central homes of the Spragues (*BD*), Claire DeHaven (*BN*), and the Kafesjians and Herricks (*WJ*), down through the seedy pads of Coleman Maynard (*BD*), Marty Goines (*BN*), and Billy Dieterling (*LAC*), to the most extreme instances, George Tilden's shack and house (*BD*). Contrary to one's pre-packaged image of American domestic space in the 1950s, Ellroy's version of it knows none of those comfortable signifiers of male retreat from civil society – subservient housewives, family dinners, neighbourliness, two-door garages – with which the decade has been traditionally represented. His concern is rather to demonstrate the degree to which this private sphere has collapsed under the immense weight of consumerism and spectacle in postwar Los Angeles, and carried on as a pathological and perverted spectre of itself, as a wide-open public scene.

Here, to illustrate that collapse of private into public, is detective-voyeur Danny Upshaw in *The Big Nowhere*, outside a 'fag party' at Felix Gordean's Chateau Marmont:

> Danny pressed his face to the window and looked in.
> That close he got distortion blur . . . He pulled back so that his eyes could capture a larger frame, saw tuxedos entwined in movement, cheek-to-cheek tangos, all male. The faces were up against each other so that they couldn't be distinguished individually; Danny zoomed out, in, out, in, until he was pressed into the window glass . . . his eyes honing for mid-shots, close-ups, faces.
> . . . Then shadows killing his vision, his lens cleared by a step backward – and a perfectly framed view of two fat, ugly wallflowers tongue-kissing, all oily skin and razor-burn and hair pomade glistening.[48]

There is no mistaking Ellroy's point that private being today has to be recognized as a province of 'Hollywood', and the instance of Danny Upshaw's dizzying perceptual cinematography drives this home. The mediation of desire and knowledge by the apparatus of cinema erodes and feminizes the basis of the male subject, and results in Upshaw's desperate suicide once he knows himself to be gay. Ellroy conceives of the postwar domestic scene, and its surplus, the self, as being deeply structured by the narcissism, scopophilia and castration which dominated film theory – and Freud's theory of homosexuality – for many years.[49] The spectacle has invaded private space from the inside, transforming what was once a male sanctuary away from the imperatives of the market (produce! consume!) into its most vivid, technicolour factory, with every individual now hell-bent on producing his own pleasure and consuming it in the rapturous simultaneity of narcissism. It is the space of the individual as monad, imprisoned by the dictates of his own pleasure.

It is also the space where murder takes place, as a partial revolt against this abstract colonization of privacy; behind the closed door, where 'isolation breeds guilt',[50] and where crime mutates into art. It is here that the body of the other is transformed into an aesthetic medium for the expression of the post-oedipal subject. We visit it at the scene of the crime:

> Blood on the walls. Huge, unmistakable streaks, exemplary textbook spit marks: the killer expelling big mouthfuls, spritzing the red out through his teeth, drawing little patterns on cheap floral wallpaper. Four whole walls of it – dips and curlicues and one design that looked like an elaborate letter W [. . .] White walls covered with vertical and horizontal blood lines, perfectly straight, intersecting at right angles, the killer getting the knack[. . .] horror artwork.[51]
>
> The camera man handed the prints and negatives over an hour later, commenting, 'Them walls what you call modern art?'[52]

Such a crime-scene makes entirely different cognitive demands on the detective from those of the street, equivalent phenomenologically to an encounter with Jackson Pollock's abstract expressionism – the last Modernism, last gasp of an assimilated subjectivity. The 'expressionistic' crime-scene signals a full-scale decsent into the imaginary, into representational space, away from the professional representations of space governing the LAPD.

Meanwhile the crime's grisly product, namely the dead and mutilated *body* itself – usually discovered elsewhere, in vacant lots and storm drains, the peripheries of public space – is the last of Ellroy's cardinal spatial semes. Ellroy's excessive and presumably obsessive descriptions of these cadavers have, more than anything else, earned him the notoriety he relishes. They are designed to give nightmares, and revisit the primal scene of Ellroy's mother's death and his pre-pubescent researches into murder cases with intolerable gusto. The 'Black Dahlia' corpse, having had more than a little influence on Ellroy's career and the representation of Los Angeles itself,[53] is the first of the lavishly detailed, gruesome and appalling bodies to appear in the Quartet. Again, it is Officer Bleichert who mediates it for us:

> It was the nude, mutilated body of a young woman, cut in half

at the waist. The bottom half lay in the weeds a few feet away from the top, legs wide open. A large triangle had been gouged out of the left thigh, and there was a long, wide cut running from the bisection point down to the top of the pubic hair. The flaps of skin beside the gash were pulled back; there were no organs inside. The top half was worse: the breasts were dotted with cigarette burns, the right one hanging loose, attached to the torso only by shreds of skin, the left one slashed around the nipple. The cuts went all the way down to the bone, but the worst of the worst was the girl's face. It was one huge purpled bruise, the nose crushed deep into the facial cavity, the mouth cut ear to ear into a smile that leered up at you, somehow mocking the rest of the brutality inflicted.[54]

As the waste material of the 'representational space' of the crime scene, this clinically described body is the closest any of Ellroy's spatial semes come to attaining the status of a symbol. What we get in a cadaver such as this is not so much a mystery, though it is that, as the trace of a kind of work. The body is the lifeless end-product of a last-ditch and vain attempt to carve some meaning out of serially privatized life. Ellroy's prose here is at its most descriptive, most replete with modifiers and small details, as though to meditate upon the objective nothingness which we can now see dominating his conception of private space. The serial mutilations, torturings, abjections, and abominations to which body-space is subject in the Quartet are symptomatic, for Ellroy, of an emergent feminization of being in consumer society. The dead body is a symbolic stage for the dramas of unchained materialism; its brutal fate points to the sins of excess to which humanity is 'naturally' prone once released from the ties of a rigid and authoritarian social contract.

We have noted Joan Copjec's speculation that the original function of *film noir* was to warn postwar America against the temptations of a new consumer economy, and the importunings to private *jouissance* it incessantly made.[55] It is no surprise that Ellroy should so freely have appropriated the genre's motifs, with whose cautionary project he is entirely in sympathy – only now, ironically, after the event and with all the wisdom of hindsight. For he too wants to defend the country and his city against a certain, imaginary image of the 1960s, the decade when everything good in America 'went wrong'. We can express it this way: if we consider the first two of Ellroy's spatial semes (*bureau* and *street*) as a pastiche of Parker's masculine 'dialectic of desire' between some all-knowing subject and an irrational and uncivilized other, then the next two spaces (*private* space and the *body*) partake of a very different, 'feminized' dynamic – not of desire, but of *jouissance*: the twin 1960s imperatives, regardless of traditional social mores, to be oneself and to desublimate the body. Ultimately, this addiction to the drive is construed as a death drive, a violent and cataclysmic negativity subtending the whole Quartet in the nebulous category of 'The Big Nowhere', and anthropomorphically concentrated in the character of Dudley Smith (who is ultimately revealed as the city's ur-scopophile and pornographer).

If Ellroy imagines himself to have written a critical social history of the city of Los Angeles, we are now in a somewhat better position to analyse the claim. His putative map, or representational cross-section of the city in the 1950s, takes the form of an arrested dialectic between a dominant and authoritarian *civitas*, and an emergent and insidious consumer fetishism. His 'deep-structural' narrative form then follows logically: a subject or emissary from the Bureau is sent out to surveil and impose order on the streets, where he discovers a mutilated body. The process of investigation sends him to penetrate the new private space of postwar America, where he discovers untold appetites and oedipal dysfunction, in other families and in himself. It is not only that the narratives thus touch all the bases and so produce a compelling sense of totality and roundness; it is also that the police investigator does not remain immune to any of the spatial semes, but learns to internalize each of them in turn. The pervasive sense of corruption stems from the fact that even Chief Parker's few good men are not above the pathological tendencies of the atomized citizenry. And this is precisely what qualifies the Quartet as a *noir* epic. What is more, this closed circuit of narrative energy explains for us the peculiar temporal qualities of Ellroy's urban chronotope: its increasingly desperate acceleration, its gradual reduction to a point of instantaneity.

Consumerism should be controlled, Ellroy effectively argues, by a redoubled attempt at a broader and more embracing authority structure, which would clamp down on the growing urges of a 'human nature' that can only lead to civic decomposition. And yet, the guarantee of that older virtue of oedipal authority would seem to lie in a synthesis of the primary opposition between a dominant, white administrative centre and the streets of race and class other-ness – an opposition thriving on racism, corruption, brutality and cliché. How, then, does Ellroy resolve the crushing ideological dilemma of affirming the ongoing necessity of a white-on-black power structure, or segregation, in a minoritized late twentieth-century context where such racialized hierarchies are ideologically impermissible? The solution can in no sense be representational, since it is impossible to figure forth a persuasive and affecting image of a racist power system. My sense, then, is that the desired synthesis has been shifted from the level of *representation* to the level of *presentation*: in other words, to the plane of literary style.

Ellroy's evolving stylistic texture, over the length of the four novels, moves ever closer to a kind of experimental prose in which the two contradictory tendencies (white power, subordinate ethnic culture) are driven feverishly into each other. On the one hand, a reactionary and offensively objectifying arsenal of abusive epithets: 'nigger', 'jigaboo', 'jungle bunny', 'spic', 'wetback', 'pansy', and 'fruit', strung together in a defiantly anti-PC shock-tactic of historical verbal accuracy. And on the other hand, a considered syntactic approximation of postwar black jazz itself, with its shrill staccato riffs, uncompromising fragmentation, dizzying assaults on reified auditory habits, and anti-establishment delivery style. The bad fusion of these two forces, what Ellroy calls 'white jazz', is allegorically realized in the psychotic white jazz-man Coleman Healy, whose saxophone swan-song, 'The Big Nowhere', unleashes the wild decentring of white male subjectivity that is at all costs to be avoided.[56] It is rather in the more jarring and extreme of Ellroy's own stylistic effects where the proper fusion is evidently to be sought, a kind of post-syntactical cipher where the authoritarian and the marginal-subversive interpenetrate; as in the following distasteful fantasy of surveillance work as an improvisatory instrumental solo:

> Keyed up – glom the pervert file. Dog stuff/B and E/Peeping Tom, see what jumped:
> A German shepherd-fucking Marine. Doctor 'Dog': popped for shooting his daughter up with beagle pus. Dog killers – none fit my man's specs. Dog fuckers, dog suckers, dog beaters, dog worshippers, a geek who chopped his wife while dressed up as Pluto. Panty sniffers, sink shitters, masturbators – lingerie jackoffs only. Faggot burglars, transvestite break-ins, 'Rita Hayworth' – Gilda gown, dyed bush hair, caught blowing a chloroformed toddler. The right age – but a jocker cut his dick off, he killed himself, a full-drag San Quentin burial. Peepers: windows, skylights, roofs – the roof clowns a chink brother act. No watchdog choppers, the geeks read passive, caught holding their puds with a whimper. Darryl Wishnick, a cute MO: peep, break, enter, rape watchdogs subdued by goofball-laced meat – too bad he kicked from syph in '56. One flash: peepers played

passive, my guy killed badass canines.
No jumps.[57]

Which final phrase drives home for us the realization that this extraordinary paragraph will have no narrative consequences, but must justify itself as a formal event in its own right. The profusion of alliteration, internal rhyme and assonance, the control of the rhythmic texture, and the play with symmetry and imbalance, all turn this debased list of file entries on 'perverse' life in the post-oedipal city into an experiment with literary style itself – and, despite some affinities with Beat poetry, an original and possibly valuable one. I am suggesting, though, that this crazed and syncopated parataxis functions as a rhetorical squaring of the ideological circle. The impossible task of imagining a conservative resolution to the complex of civic failures afflicting contemporary Los Angeles, is left to a stylistic device conflating right-wing Anglo-ethnic prejudice with a tendential approximation of the black jazz aesthetic; and all couched in the febrile nostalgia of period pastiche.

Ellroy's stylistic achievement is thus decidedly more complex than his anti-1960s ideology, while his narratives affirm the improbability of the imaginary resolution promised by his style. His relentless mappings of the Quartet's period chronotope repeatedly mourn the defeat of the very vision of patriarchal authority he so cherishes: 'I believe in God. Strongly. I have a kid's belief in the Almighty. I try to lead a moral life cos I believe I'm gonna be judged', says Ellroy.[58] His fictions are less certain. They are charged with the psychological complex that it has been his fate to bear. It takes no great imaginative leap to see the depths to which Ellroy has been scarred by the violent death of his mother; in a host of displaced ways, her own abandoned body figures in each of these novels, as an irresistible 'representational space' of senseless mourning and loss. So too, Ellroy's peculiar boyhood experience of the privacy of others (he was by his own confession, and in response to his mother's death and paternal negligence, a scopophile and compulsive break-and-enter specialist), has shaped his fascination with the private spaces of Los Angeles as regions of perversity and *jouissance*. And finally, his mapping of public space is so schematic and derivative, that it could only ever have been a pastiche of the representations of space peddled by pulp literature and cheap films, to which he turned as a boy for DIY therapy. The 'authoritarian' aspect of his fiction is actually only interesting insofar as it is inextricably entangled with the more powerful 'representational spaces' which it attempts, but cannot hope, to master. In his mournings of a lost, fantasy power structure, Ellroy more effectively charts the dislocation of white individuality in a saturated consumer space.

The racial component of Ellroy's period chronotope is easily ana- lysed: on the one hand, the division of public space between centre and margin is most often explicitly a racial one, 'containing' blacks and Hispanics in segregated urban zones where white power can freely exercise its muscle; and on the other, the veritable deconstruc- tion of white subjectivity has clear and determinate links to the impossibility of maintaining the principal division. It is, then, the spatial ideology of 'whiteness' which Ellroy is committed to mapping – the ways in which a new spatial economy of *jouissance*, and the fantasy of purified white supremacy over urban space as a whole, overdetermine a crisis in this ideology, which cannot be made to straddle that faultline without stylistic prestidigitation. In this sense, although the historical trappings of the Quartet are many and often convincing, the deep structure's arrested dialectic contains the temporal energy of the chronotope in a vicious circle, a 'Big Nowhere', which like the jazz solos it mimics, must always return to an unaltered motif or theme: whiteness in crisis.

It has been the distinction of Walter Mosley, however, to have responded to Ellroy's magisterial appropriations of late *noir* as a white man's burden, with a period chronotope of his own that inverts all of the Quartet's assumptions, while very properly main- taining the question of race at the ideological frontline. What arises from the novels of Mosley's 'Easy Rawlins' series is, as we shall see, and *pace* the anti-historical 'social history' of Ellroy, an invigorated temporal moment to his chronotope, a sense of *durée* adhering to the blackness which had been violently mystified out of Ellroy's LA. How this happens, and what its implications are for the representa- tion of contemporary Los Angeles, will be the subject of what follows.

There is considerable room for speculation about the emergence of *noir* as a concept and a style in the American cinema during the 1940s and 1950s, *vis-à-vis* its parallel formation alongside the most prodigious growth of the black population in northern urban centres in American history after World War II.[59] The haunted, lower- middle-class, and very 'white' structure of feeling strung out over the dirty streets, alleyways, hotel lobbies and cheap diners of *film noir*, and projected onto the hardboiled facial landscape of *noir*'s

New White Man (Bogart, Glenn Ford, John Garfield, the Fred MacMurray of *Double Indemnity* [Billy Wilder, 1944]),[60] might be said to have more than a little to do with the sudden and irreversible influx of a large new southern black presence in Chicago, Detroit, New York, and not least Los Angeles, drawn by wartime rearmament to the shipyards, munitions factories and nascent aerospace industry.[61] While not wanting to diminish the evident roles of fervent consumerism, widespread female employment, and Communism in the construction of the original *noir* chronotope in films such as *The Blue Dahlia* (Marshall, 1946), *Farewell, My Lovely* (Dmytryk, 1944) and *The Postman Always Rings Twice* (Garnett, 1946), it is at least arguable, given the indisputable function of jazz in many of these films, the growing consciousness of race as the cycle matured (in, for example, *Kiss Me Deadly* [Aldrich, 1955] and *Odds Against Tomorrow* [Wise, 1959]), and the very exaggeration of the black-white chiaroscuro cinematography, that newly accentuated racial politics and spatial segregation had a vital part in shaping the distinctive *noir* chronotope. Nor is this speculation idle; for it is informed precisely by the reconsideration of the genre prompted by the neo-*noir* of writers such as Ellroy and Mosley, who agree with critic B. Ruby Rich in her estimation that '[r]ace may have been virtually absent from the first round of noir but it has a singular capacity to reinvigorate the noir form'.[62]

Indeed, Mosley's reading of *noir* turns on the realization that the whole white structure of feeling (dread, anxiety, placelessness, flight) generated by the *noir* film cycle can be seen as an expropriation of what is in fact the precise matrix of affects on which black subjectivity in the period was actually built.[63] If literature is seen, after the event, as the production of chronotopic evidence with which to examine and reimagine the spatio-temporal 'livedness' of a social configuration, then Chester Himes's novel *If He Hollers, Let Him Go* (1946) is ample proof that the entire circuit-board of white existential angst with which *noir* wired its effects, had simultaneously been established as a *black* structure of feeling. The persecuted sense of dread with which Himes's Bob Jones attempts to navigate the violent racial geography of postwar Los Angeles exactly matches, at least in its chronotopic parameters, the inability to hide and necessity of keeping on the move of any number of *noir* protagonists. What differentiates Himes's novel from the films is, however, its very lucid consciousness of cause, the deliberateness with which it lays blame at the feet of the white authority system, policing, employment policies, and everyday racism. If in *film noir* itself that explicit designation of cause was inadmissible due to the sheer number of analogemes its pervasive darkness was ultimately called upon to encompass (Reds, women, post-combat dislocation, homeless- and joblessness, privatization, etc.), then neo-*noir*, by returning to the scene of the crime at a historical moment in which all of the more evident indices of *noir* paranoia have been either superannuated, admitted, or co-opted, is perforce obliged to confront its most reluctant content: its racial unconscious, which Mosley restores to view by mediating *noir* through its prototypical black exemplar – namely Himes himself.

In fact, the logic of this mediation implies a reorientation of the structural and ideological features of Ellroy's fictions, away from the collective ideal of teamwork in the police procedural, and back toward the lonely crusades of the alienated Chandlerian individual. Himes, like Chandler, erected his image of Los Angeles on the disgruntled figure of the damaged male self, the better to accentuate the extent of black existential crisis. Mosley's Rawlins novels – *Devil in a Blue Dress* (1990), *A Red Death* (1991), *White Butterfly* (1992), *Black Betty* (1994), and *A Little Yellow Dog* (1996) – all depend primarily upon a carefully sustained interest, not so much in the crimes or historical details they narrate, as in the character through whom these 'mystery' features are vehiculated. The first-person voice of Ezekiel Rawlins, which carries across all five books, is the finest contemporary achievement in local letters of a characterological kind; in a situation in which, as the next chapter will argue, the conditions of possibility for the survival of character have all but vanished, this requires some analysis. We will come at this ana-chronism of character from three directions: first, as a product of the narrative voice itself, which by virtue of what I will call 'lateral realism', finds itself called upon to do much more besides tell a story; second, as a reactive formation against a battery of attacks on male, black independence; and third, as a critical mode of nego-tiation within a clearly differentiated 'minority' model of commun-ity, defined by race and ethnicity. None of these conditions applies to Ellroy's protagonists, who, absolved of the responsibility to raise themselves to the level of character, may exist instead in a state of oscillation between clichéd individualism and anonymous clan membership.

In the first place, then, the matter of a sustained first-person narrative voice over a series of what are demonstrably LA detective

stories (although, importantly, Rawlins is never defined professionally in that way) must inevitably conjure up the ghost of Chandler,
whose stylistic engagements with the genre operated precisely
within the zone of phenomenological freedom afforded by such a
voice. Indeed, it could even be said that Chandler's disregard for
narrative coherence and attention to local detail, which matches
Mosley's own predilections, sprang from his commitment to the
elaboration of Philip Marlowe's voice at the expense of plot. Chandler's experiments with the detective format as a means to another
end, namely aesthetic pleasure and style (not, to be sure, an end with
which we would readily associate Walter Mosley), passed through a
genuine, well-nigh Modernist concern with point of view and
consciousness. As a consequence of this duplicitous use of the genre,
he uncovered a highly significant aesthetic facility, which I want to
call *lateral realism*; and it is here that Mosley truly reenacts the
Chandlerian aesthetic and contributes to its development by allowing it greater range and enabling it to discover hitherto sup-
pressed practical and representational spaces.

> All I wanted to do when I began was to play with a fascinating
> new language, and trying, without anybody noticing it, to see
> what it would do as a means of expression which might remain
> at the level of unintellectual thinking and yet acquire the power
> to say things which are usually only said with a literary air.
> I obeyed the formula because I honestly liked it, but I was
> always trying to stretch it, trying to get in *bits of peripheral
> writing which were not necessary* but which I felt would have a
> subconscious effect even on the semi-literate readers; I felt
> somehow that the thing to get in this kind of story was a kind
> of richness of texture.[64]

The 'bits of peripheral writing' into which Chandler packed the
better part of his art, leaving the narrative whole to flounder the
while, are typically those arrested moments of observation where
Marlowe enters an empty space and records it as sensitively and
richly as any descriptive prose in American literature. That his
objects of attention are frequently the run-down, terminal dwelling-
spaces of the lower-middle class only adds to the value of these
passages, since such spaces are so often the unseen and unsung
recesses of American society.

And here it is that Chandler has most to offer the black writer in
Los Angeles, in these passages that are not necessary to the plot but
which, in retrospect, are seen to have been the most satisfying
moments of reading; for in them, an entire sub-culture can momenta-

rily emerge into being, mapped not so much by the rigorous plotting of all its co-ordinates, as by the lateral movements of the eye across a space it does not even know it is observing. With our narrative appetite for plot advancement suspended by descriptive reverie, the black writer can then, by a Chandlerian sleight of hand, insert a milieu, of South-Central, Watts, or what have you, which, in the event of direct attention, would reify instantly into the obnoxious clichés of Ellroy's 'street'. This delicate play of foreground and background is the crux of Mosley's achievement, and rejoins what Fredric Jameson has called the tradition of 'Proustian indirection' in which 'other, radically different kinds of perception become marginally tolerated in the decorative field around the plot or "action" proper'.[65] What is more, this aesthetic dovetails neatly with what Henry Louis Gates, Jr. calls the 'double-voicing' of African-American textuality, with its 'complex double formal antecedents, the Western and the black';[66] a notion which confirms one's growing suspicion that the entire detective format here is a ruse, an appeal to a white readership that would not otherwise have had exposure to these 'bits of peripheral writing' which it has now consumed by default.

> We drove quite a ways down Central Avenue. That was before the general decline of the neighborhood. The streets were clean and the drunks were few. I counted fifteen churches between 110th Street and Florence Boulevard. At that corner was the Goodyear Rubber Plant. It was a vast field with two giant buildings far off to the northern end. There was also the hangar for the Goodyear blimp there. Across the street sat a World gas station. World was a favorite hangout for Mexican hot-rodders and motorcycle enthusiasts who decorated their German machines with up to three hundred pounds of chrome piping and doodads.
> . . . We drove to a large asphalt parking lot where hundreds of cars were parked neatly in rows like they were on sale. There were always cars parked there, because the Goodyear plant worked twenty-four hours a day, seven days a week.[67]

While this passage may lack all of the stylistic distinction of Chandler's prose, it nevertheless, in its indifference to plot advancement, occasions a reconsideration of the very function of spatial description in the genre novel. Neither Goodyear nor World will have any further role in Mosley's narrative, yet what is urged on our attention here is the iconic status of their buildings in a spatial economy which once thrived on black and Hispanic labour. The elegiac tone and tense ('before the general decline') is typical of Mosley's treatment of postwar urban space; things may be wretched now, the prose lectures its contemporary readership, but South-Central was once alive with spatial nodes of attraction and intensity, 'full' employment, counterculture, signatures of ethnicity, which only the stiff, laconic prosody of the historical genre-writer can have any hope of recapturing in the thick of postmodern amnesia and pastiche.

Lynell George has commented that '[t]hese novels work far better as pieces of social history than as hard-boiled mysteries whose plot twists are, in retrospect, thin and forced. The turns in Easy's detective path are not nearly as compelling as the everyday mountains he must scale. The nuts-and-bolts elements of the *roman noir* are over-shadowed by Easy's small acts of survival.'[68] And overshadowed, too, by the mute spaces in which this survival takes place. Rawlins's voice, then, is claimed by an ethic of witnessing, and comes increasingly to function more as a registering apparatus for the everyday life of LA's black ghettos, than an angst-ridden self-consciousness. It is sharpened by the contrasting recollections of a very different quotidian sphere in rural Texas whence Rawlins, and his companion Mouse, have emigrated.

> I drove down to the liquor store and bought a fifth of vodka and a gallon of grapefruit soda. I positioned myself in a chair on the front window and watched the day pass.
>
> Looking out of the window is different in Los Angeles than it is in Houston. No matter where you live in a southern city . . . you see almost everybody you know by just looking out your window. Every day is a parade of relatives and old friends and lovers you once had, and maybe you'd be lovers again one day . . .
>
> Because in LA people don't have time to stop; anywhere they have to go they go there in a car. The poorest man has a car in Los Angeles; he might not have a roof over his head but he has a car. And he knows where he's going too. In Houston and Galveston, and way down in Louisiana, life was a little more aimless. People worked a little job but they couldn't make any real money no matter what they did. But in Los Angeles you could make a hundred dollars in a week if you pushed. The promise of getting rich pushed people to work two jobs in the week and do a little plumbing on the weekend. There's no time to walk down the street or make a bar-b-q when somebody's going to pay you real money to haul refrigerators.
>
> So I watched empty streets that day. Every once in a while I'd see a couple of children on bicycles or a group of young girls going to the store for candy and soda pop. I sipped vodka and napped . . .
>
> By the time the sun went down I was at peace with myself. I

had a name, an address, a hundred dollars, and the next day I'd ask for my job back. I had a house and an empty bottle of vodka that had made me feel good.[69]

What Mosley's method of lateral realism permits is precisely this bubbling up to the textual surface of daily life itself, 'spatial practice' in Lefebvre's terminology, as devoid of intrinsic aesthetic merit as the clang of a trash-can lid, yet somehow lifted above everyday inattention by the technique literary indirection. Mosley's task is partially to restitute of this practice of everyday life, salvaged from the representations of space which have erased the black ghetto from the visual register of Los Angeles. Where Ellroy sees only 'bottle gangs and crap games on every corner; liquor stores, hair-straightening parlors and poolrooms on every block', and where the postmodern media projects gangs, drive-bys and the thundering jungle-drums of hip-hop, Mosley evokes both a restless productive momentum, and a slow, quiet territory populated by women, children, old men and eccentrics.

Bearing in his synapses the traces of a more rural, communitarian ideal, a whole representational space of romanticized southern black existence, Easy's more lyrical descriptions of Los Angeles blur imperceptibly into that space:

> There was a breeze off the ocean that night. The waters must have been loaded with seaweed because you could smell the brine if you breathed deep and stood still. Granite streetlamps lined the street and the barest trace of a mist was rising from the saturated lawns. I stood still for a moment imagining a chill when I was a child. The cold tickled me when I was a boy. I used to wonder if I was crazy for being out on the bayou, laughing at nothing.[70]

The lyrical stasis of the observing subject allows for the unwonted emergence in the saturated spaces of postwar LA of both deep memory and unalienated sensuality; in a word, what is tapped is a whole phenomenological reservoir of time, where the body transcends spatial practice and resumes its participation in a childish, natural 'worldliness'. Socially produced space (the granite streetlamps) is brought to an interface with Nature, and senses other than the visual (olfactory, tactile) are stimulated into activity. If such a moment is rare in its escape from the determinations of race, it is nonetheless typical for the way in which the narrative voice assumes a position of 'betweenness' *vis-à-vis* the social and the natural. It demarcates a zone of subjective freedom best exemplified in the relatively lavish description of Easy's home.

I loved going home. Maybe it was that I was raised on a sharecropper's farm or that I never owned anything until I bought that house, but I loved my little home. There was an apple tree and an avocado in the front yard, surrounded by thick St. Augustine grass. At the side of the house I had a pomegranate tree that bore more than thirty fruit every season and a banana tree that never produced a thing. There were dahlias and wild roses in beds around the fence and African violets that I kept in a big jar on the front porch.

The house itself was small. Just a living room, a bedroom, and a kitchen. The bathroom didn't even have a shower and the backyard was no larger than a child's rubber pool. But that house meant more to me than any woman I ever knew. I loved her and I was jealous of her. . .[71]

Theodore Mason observes that 'Rawlins figures his home as a zone of safety and pastoral retreat from the urban scene of Los Angeles', which understatement scarcely captures the intensity of the attachment.[72] Yet if this virtual utopia achieves a chronotopic apotheosis in its blending of the domestic and the paradisical, it also serves as an end-point for the adventures of the autonomous narrative voice, which, even as it celebrates its emancipation from everyday drudgery in this haven, finds itself driven up against other forces by the singular logic of a racist production of space.

So it is that the second promised aspect of Rawlins as a character, his reactive value in the face of external belligerence, is typified by the degree to which his home is put at risk by the forces of governmentality and criminality themselves, between which Rawlins is obliged to eke out a living. 'I got me a home already', Easy declaims proudly to some African Migration enthusiasts. 'It might be in enemy lands, but it's mine still and all.'[73] Figuring his home-ownership in such politicized, territorial terms, Rawlins clearly recognizes the extent to which his private utopia has had to be 'represented' into being, in a kind of imaginary self-fashioning through property and domesticated nature. In occupying his house, Rawlins has invested it with a feminine, well-nigh Bachelardian 'poetics of space',[74] in the full knowledge that this is a political achievement, on 'enemy lands', whose precarious fragility can be exposed at any moment. He says at one point, resigned to the inevitable, that 'you can't hide in your own house'.[75] Here is just one of countless scenes of invasion by the enemy, which underlines the point:

At eleven forty-seven a long black sedan parked in front of my house. Four men got out. Three of them were white men in business suits of various hues . . . They all got out of the car and looked around the neighborhood. They weren't timid about being deep in Watts. That's how I knew they were all cops.

Quinten led the procession up to my door. They were all big men. The kind of white man who is successful because he towers over his peers . . .

Five big men made my living room seem like a small public toilet.[76]

The traducement of Rawlins's treasured representational space, from paradise to public toilet, by the arrival of the police, signals the limitation of the first-person voice as a value-producing zone of discourse. Confronted with masculinity, authority and whiteness, Rawlins's commentary balls up into a confession of its impotence in the face of a discriminatory regime of surveillance. That he will always be able to be found and invaded, that the blanket of privacy he has pulled around himself can at any moment be drawn aside, exposing everything in his environment to a very public view: such is the recurrent admonition of these texts, which turn again and again on the humiliation of a narrative voice by powers capable of neutering its representational space.

Yet the reactive character of Rawlins' voice is amplified by another set of relations, not this time with power as such, but with the urban fabric of the ghetto itself. In order to distinguish itself as a singular value in its milieu, the voice and its protective domestic shell must be drawn into a series of contrasts with other, less salubrious spaces. The various, pointed object lessons in objectionable slum dwelling in black Los Angeles generally resemble the following: 'It was a small house with peeling white paint and bare brown dirt for a lawn. There was an overflowing trash can right there on the porch. The front door didn't belong to that house. It was an unfinished plyboard door meant for a temporary bungalow out on some construction site'.[77] What this contemptuous dismissal means in the context of its contrast with Rawlins's own house is the establishment of a certain irreducible value system in urban space itself. The good inheres in cultivating a zone of privacy where nurture, duration and respect might flourish; the bad in merely surrendering to the abstract pressure from a production of space whose racism, class arrogance and sexism seek to prohibit the creation of male 'representational space' in the ghetto. It is a value-system which can be revealed on the molar as well as the molecular level, for flyweight transience and civic impoverishment are observable on the plane both of urban vista and of individual domicile. As an instance of the latter, consider this description of archetypal loser Gregory Jewell's house:

> The rooms in the bungalow were like a ship's cabin. There was hardly enough room to turn around. The furniture was mismatched and the linoleum on the floor was rotted around the corners.
>
> . . . But I felt kindred to his misery. It seemed to me that my whole life had been spent walking into shabby little houses with poor people bleeding or hacking or just dying quietly under the weight of our 'liberation'. I was born in a house no larger than that one.[78]

Confined to such limits on the margins of the rental economy, black identity in Los Angeles can emerge only in a struggle against the spatial diminishment of possibility. Death, disease, violence, addiction and despair are again and again shown by Mosley to be the consequences of a spatial economy which, on the one hand, evacuates the potentialities of everyday life, and on the other deracinates the representational space of home with 'shabbiness' and a simple lack of room.

Meanwhile, on the macro-level of the ghetto, the disposability of most black housing is confirmed in the following urban landscape, where the roadways appear suggestively more durable and meaningful than the houses which pepper their flanks:

> LA down around Watts was mostly flat to the sea. The blacktop roads were wide and green sprouted up everywhere. Little houses ran in rows between the avenues. They seemed frail in comparison with the streets. It was almost as if the houses were just resting points on a forever roadway to somewhere else.[79]

Denied any kind of significant investment, public or private, the 'frail', 'shabby' houses pale into insignificance alongside the well-maintained roads.

Rawlins's ambitions as a property investor have very much to do with the protection of a certain spatial dignity and self-respect in black Los Angeles. He personally maintains his two apartment buildings, while his agent Mofass poses as their manager. The Magnolia Street building is a particular favourite, since it attracts the sun through its large windows, and Easy is often to be found there doing nothing in particular: 'Then I'd go upstairs and stand in the window, looking down into the street. Sometimes I'd stand there for an hour or more, watching the cars and clouds making their ways. There was a peaceful feeling about the streets of Los Angeles in those days';[80] the point being that this is what is being denied the prisoners of the flatland slum, this lazy contemplation of the daily life consigning them to oblivion. Rawlins's ability to enjoy it depends upon the extent to which he has merged with the middle class. His final, failed attempt to develop a black-owned, black-run shopping centre, 'Freedom's Plaza', in the centre of Watts is merely an extension of his homesteading, independent ideal through old-fashioned bourgeois means.

What remains to be said, however, is that Rawlins's embourgeoisement and feminization (he becomes an adoptive single parent twice over) inhibits his very masculine mode of insertion into the black community as a whole. This inner struggle reaches the point, in *Black Betty*, where in order to preserve his fantasy of participation in the American Dream, he must flee South-Central and the house in which he has invested so much representational passion: 'I took my kids to an anonymous place where people didn't know me; where no one asked painful questions about my wife and daughter; where no one knew enough about me to question my legal guardianship of Jesus and Feather.'[81] And it is not the white bureaucracy which is intent on asking these questions, so much as the black men and women who suspect his peculiar and voluntary single-parenthood as an abdication of his accepted social role in the ghetto, as a hard-drinking man amongst men. Easy's domesticity is, indeed, only one pole of an antinomy dividing his spatial being, whose other extremity is his addiction to 'street' culture itself, the nightlife of Central Avenue in the 1950s. This is, then, the third and last of our lines of approach to Rawlins as character, his participation in the unofficial culture of the black ghetto, responsible for the great upsurge in mid-century jazz as for the gangs, drugs and violence on its outer edges. Here, with its passwords and elaborate rituals of admission, urban space conceals blackness from view, protects its denizens from interference and enables a partial collective release in what Charles Scruggs calls an 'invisible city';[82] but only at the cost of an abandonment of the domestic sphere and a consequent devaluation of the feminine representational spaces cherished by Easy Rawlins in his workaday guise.

The evocations of Bone Street in *White Butterfly* will here stand in for Mosley's acute sensitivities to the allure and danger of 1950s black nightlife throughout the five novels. In the following passage, what begins as a celebration ends elegiacally, in a stylistically typical movement, as a lament for lost time. As always in Mosley, we arrive just too late, or anticipate immediate decline, and so find it impossible to enjoy ourselves in the present.

> Bone Street was local history. A crooked spine down the center of Watts' jazz heyday, it was four long and jagged blocks. West of Central Avenue and north of 103rd Street, Bone Street was broken and desolate to look at by day, with its two-story tenementlike apartment buildings and its mangy hotels. But by night Bones, as it was called, was a center for late-night blues, and whiskey so strong that it could grow hairs on the glass it was served in. When a man said he was going to get down to the bare Bones he meant he was going to lose himself in the music and the booze and the women down there . . .
>
> It was a bold and flashy time. But by that evening all the shine had rubbed off to expose the base metal below. The sidewalks were broken, sporting hardy weeds in their cracks. Some clubs were still there but they were quieter now. The jazzmen had found new arenas. Many had gone to Paris and New York. The blues was still with us. The blues would always be with us. The blues will always be with us.[83]

No doubt there are monitory tonalities creeping into even this description, and Easy throughout the novel series is to be found renouncing its temptations as so many lures to ruin; but neither is it possible finally to resist what remains of the 'good old days'.

Black urban street culture, its gambling, prostitution, music, narcotics and fashion, is here preserved with its contradictions intact, and it is essential that Rawlins be intimately familiar with it; since without his ability to move at will through the innumerable bars, clubs and brothels, his services would be useless to the LAPD, which comes to him for assistance with cases that stray into the officially unmapped terrain of the ghetto. Triangulated by a competing and contradictory set of responsibilities (feminine/domestic, masculine/communal, and legal/institutional), Rawlins manages his insuperable tensions in a chronotopic line of flight: constantly on the move, circulating restlessly between children at home, manual labour at work, inebriated dissipation in black bars, and the neatly furnished offices of condescending lawyers and policemen, he effectively sheds identities with each departure. Belonging to Los Angeles in this scattered spatio-temporal hopscotch consists in adaptive role-play, assuming and casting aside the masks of caring father, hard-boiled machismo, shuffling 'darky', acquisitive *bourgeois*, and so on, in an escalating, high-stakes game of chance against the system itself. What disappears from the equation, then, as the narratives steadily undermine Rawlins's various gains with a virtual schizophrenia, is the very stable sense of self we had begun by approving in Mosley's work. In retrospect, what we take from this remarkable series of novels is not the achieved solidarity of a coherent black subject in a regime of racism and abstraction, but the tendential extinction of it, the discovery of a missed opportunity, a buried chance, whose only trace is to be found in the elegiac and laconic voice of the narration itself.

It was speculated at the outset of this chapter that the appeal of the *noir* aesthetic today is at best double-edged: on the one hand, attempting to rejoin an historic moment of cultural resistance to anodyne utopianism, but on the other participating in a cynical, postmodern wave of urban 'disaster' chic. Later, it was urged that, if any authentic spark remained in the almost exhausted imaginary of *noir*, it lay in disambiguating its 'racial unconscious', and bringing to view the concealed chain of connections between a whole visual and narrative style, and a model of urban space predicated on segregation, harrassment, violence and racial fear. Mosley, like Ellroy alongside him, albeit from 'the other side', does just that. The logic of his *noir* chronotope, its spiralling escalation of spatial semes, its fatalistic attitude toward time, and the way an apparently robust and highly refined consciousness (Rawlins, it should be noted, reads Plato for pleasure) is ground down to nerve ends by it, hinges on a racial distribution of powers which, first, positions him as a 'black man' in the politico-legal apparatus and thus victimizes him mercilessly, but then, second, positions him as a 'black man' in the black community and thus fixes a chafing gender role. From this conspiracy of restrictions, from both sides of an absolute spatial divide in the city, there is no avenue of escape.

And this is why the tense and mood of Mosley's work, in its recapitulation of Chandler's voice, is surely the most serious and memorable of his experiments with the *noir* aesthetic. For with the classic *noir* narrative technique of what Gide called the *récit* in place, a very forceful sense of temporal closure imposes on the reading mind its resounding assessment of lost time. Fredric Jameson has written:

> The untranslatable generic word *récit* designates the classic tale-telling of events that are over and done with before the story begins or the narrator lifts his voice; this is signalled in French by that language's more elaborate system of tenses and in particular by the use of the preterite, whose presence is generally invisible in English, being indistinguishable from our

generalized past tense. But this – rather than the distinctions in social content or in gentility or violence – is the mark of the more fundamental generic shift from English to American (hard-boiled) detective story, namely that where the classic tradition (continued in the former) maintained a structural discontinuity and differentiation between open narrative (the detective's quest) and the closed *récit* of the crime to be reconstructed, the newer American form, as it began to emerge in the pulps, redoubled the closure of the crime with that of the surface quest itself, which it also staged, after the fact, as a completed adventure.[84]

Jameson convincingly reads this decisive modal shift in the American detective story as a symptom of radio culture generally, a new oral form which manifested itself in *film noir* as the inevitable voice-overs of the doomed protagonists. What the *récit* might mean today, in the full glare of the visual and as the various imagistic and atmospheric components of *noir* are assimilated into social space itself, is precisely the reinvigoration of the temporal against its contextual extermination. That is to say, Mosley's calm and stylistically almost neuter insistence on an American preterite, unlike Ellroy's desperate immersion in the 'presence' of the past, brings home its distance from us, the unavailability of everything the novels narrate and describe to our existential hunger for authentic consumption. His achievements with narrative voice are, in this sense, less bound up with the elaboration of a consistent character (for as we have seen, what is consistent about Rawlins is his characterological inconsistency), than they are with the realization of a preterite tense in whose stylistic closure our own historicity might be glimpsed. For literary style, and especially tense, is the one quality which our visual culture cannot reproduce, and, in the case of the production of Los Angeles' space, is determined to cancel. By re-establishing the resounding temporal closure with which hard-boiled *noir* distinguished itself from European archetypes, Mosley resists the banalization of the visual, and urges upon us a reconsideration of the past *as the past*. Thus, the doomed tone of the books accords with a sober assessment of the fortunes of black America since the heyday of full employment in the 1950s, with every civic and federal failure since then to address the needs of black Americans encoded in the brittle tone of fatalism.

Yet, it should not be concluded that this fatalism defeats its purpose and effectively participates in the closure of opportunity for black Angelenos; rather, what happens is that, with this reinvigoration of the temporal in Mosley's chronotope, traces of lost time are allowed partial reinstatement. We have already noted the lyrical stasis of the black immigrant subject, whose moments of rapture in Nature unfetter his deep temporality. So too, Easy's domesticity functions chronotopically as a non-instrumental temporality, liberated from the abstract dictates of spatial practice by a thoroughgoing representational engagement with nature and reproduction. In such ways, and against the grain, the black subject is enabled to produce 'new', temporally enriched spaces, representational spaces inaccessible to regulation because they are self-fashioned, interstitial and contingent.

> Southeast LA was palm trees and poverty; neat little lawns tended by the descendants of ex-slaves and massacred Indians. It was beautiful and wild; a place that was almost a nation, populated by lost peoples that were never talked about in the newspapers or seen on the TV. You might have read about freedom marchers; you might have heard about a botched liquor store robbery (if a white man was injured) – but you never heard about Tommy Jones growing the biggest roses in the world or how Fiona Roberts saved her neighbor by facing off three armed men with only the spirit of her God to guide her.[85]

This everyday politics of survival, a truly representational space, consists in a tissue of little narratives and tactics, whose invisibility is the price of their modest success. It takes place on the 'wild' margins of an administered society, and like all minor literatures, is bound up with a dialect and 'lost peoples' who are 'almost a nation'.[86] Most importantly, it has a history; there is a sense of depth and endurance into which the member subject can relax, a community of values and practices with durable dimensions. The slick surfaces of television cannot mediate this measureless space, for it is strung out among a collective; it is a changing set of stories and relations which never ossifies into anything so static as an image. It is, above all, what 'you never heard about'. Both Ellroy and Mosley are vehemently opposed to the rise and rise of abstract space, the colonization of everyday life by spectacles, consumerism and real estate, with its paradoxical element of division and separation, which afflicts both white authority structures and black community solidarity alike. Their detectives are on *that* case above all else, and are powerless to do anything about it.

3

Postcards from sim-city

[Contemporary cities] are made with the visible in mind: the
visibility of things, of spaces and of whatever is contained by
them. The predominance of visualization (more important than
'spectacularization', which is in any case subsumed by it)
serves to conceal repetitiveness. People look, and take sight,
take seeing, for life itself. We build on the basis of papers and
plans. We buy on the basis of images. Sight and seeing, which
in the Western tradition once epitomized intelligibility, have
turned into a trap: the means whereby, in social space,
diversity may be simulated and a trap of enlightenment and
intelligibility ensconced under the sign of transparency.[1]

Thus Lefebvre presents the urban today as one seamless mesmeriza-
tion of being by the visual. Architecture, planning, billboards, signs,
photographs, television and cinema screens, magazines, fashion,
murals, graffiti: all are produced to enhance the texture of urban life
with the promise of instant gratification. In place of substantial social
satisfactions and lived freedoms, we consume their visual hypos-
tases. Human bodies in urban space are ineluctably implicated in
what Lefebvre called a 'logic of metaphor':

Living bodes, the bodies of 'users' – are caught up not only in
the toils of parcellized space, but also in the web of what
philosophers calls 'analogons': images, signs and symbols.
These bodies are transported out of themselves, transferred
and emptied out, as it were, via the eyes: every kind of appeal,
incitement and seduction is mobilized to tempt them with
doubles of themselves in prettified, smiling and happy poses;
and this campaign to void them succeeds exactly to the degree
that the images proposed correspond to 'needs' that those same
images have helped fashion. So it is that a massive influx of
information, of messages, runs head on into an inverse flow

constituted by the evacuation from the innermost body of all
life and desire.²

Lefebvre's dynamic model of a clash of two 'flows', one visual,
abstract, and dominating, the other a last exhalation of life itself from
human beings caught in this overwhelming current, is instructive,
and one we will want to hang onto as a thread through the present
chapter. In this model we note the substitution of the category 'body'
for the more traditional 'subject'. The logic of visualization is such as
to bypass the elaborate mechanisms of consciousness and appeal
directly to the nerves, tissues and fibres of the overstimulated body.

Lefebvre's theory of the visual colonization of everyday life by
economic interests seems especially pertinent for a study of Los
Angeles. As outlined in the first chapter, the visual character of this
city, defined principally by its built space, was from an early stage
marked by impermanence, tastelessness and a strong sense of
façade. Similarly, one should take into account the degree to which
the ceaseless act of cinematic capture has itself spirited Los Angeles
and its past away from citizens who might otherwise have wished to
grasp it. Describing LA as the 'most photographed and least remembered city in the world', Norman M. Klein argues that very fact of
cinematic visualization in Los Angeles has contributed to the ubiquitous sense of placelessness and amnesia with which locals are
obliged to negotiate their city.³

It is a visualization which proceeds apace, an almost entirely
abstract process of dislocating subjects from their environment and
encasing them in Lefebvre's 'logic of metaphor', an idealized bubble
of dimensionless space, which does not cease at the city limits, but is
projected globally:

> Los Angeles became a city through the act of seeing and its
> industrial transmission all over the world. Because so many
> pictures were shot in LA, we were seeing its streets, its ocean
> and desert, its cars, trees, and light. Before ordinary people ever
> dreamed of traveling vacations, LA was the ideal of a place to
> go . . .
> There has developed a way of seeing and 'knowing' a thing
> without contact, experience, or responsibility. Being in the dark,
> and watching the light; being granted the privilege of
> voyeurism, but having to recognise the impotence and even the
> absence that go with its advantages; being there and yet having
> no presence. The voyeur has to accept nullity for what he gets
> to see. Millions abide by this alienation.⁴

As David Thomson suggests, much of the production of Los Angeles (immigration, tourism, movies) has been predicated on the alienated act of seeing. Pleasure is intensified at the cost of degrading, indeed, nullifying experience. Both at the macro- and micro-levels of its visualization, the city has de-realized itself in direct proportion as it has made itself the object of a gaze – that is, to a greater and greater extent.

In response to this intensifying visualization, geographer Edward Soja has proposed that one of the 'six geographies' of contemporary Los Angeles be called 'sim-city'. The exorbitation of the visual in social space constitutes 'a radical change in the urban imaginary', 'an inherently epistemological restructuring, one that affects our everyday life and how we make practical sense of the contemporary world':

> In the late modern world of Los Angeles, specialized entertainment centers such as Disneyland and Hollywood actively provided consumers with technologically more advanced hypersimulations and fantasy worlds. Over the past thirty years, however, these 'real fakes' have escaped from their formerly circumscribed territories and manufactories to infiltrate more deeply than ever before into the intimate everyday life of postmodern urban society, economy, polity, and culture. In these new secular sites and situations, the hypersimulations of urban reality have been blurring, more than ever before, the older distinctions between our images of the real and the reality itself, inserting into the confusion a hyperreality that is increasingly affecting where we choose to live and work, what we wear and eat, how we relate to others, who we vote for, how we shape our built environment, how we fill our leisure time – in other words, all the activities that together constitute the social construction of urban life.[5]

The speculations of Lefebvre are here confirmed by historical example. Borrowing from the formulations of Jean Baudrillard, about whom we shall have more to say below, Soja builds an image of contemporary Los Angeles as a virtual 'theme park' of simulated environments.

Let us suppose for the moment that these tendencies have been realized. How, exactly, is one to produce literature in a social space replete with its own visual connotation? By definition, what Lefebvre called 'representational spaces' are quite banished from this transparent visibility, there being scant space left for sufficient memory to keep the embers of phenomenological life glowing. Literature would in such a condition be disarmed of the very affective 'lived situations' which make it engaging to the subject. Without this latter 'space' to ground certain of its most characteristic effects (above all *interiority*: affects, dreams, intensities, etc.), literature would be entirely at the mercy of visual abstraction. Literature's non-visual syntax and narrative forms would simply succumb to the logic of commercial film. Critic Stanley Aronowitz has suggested that this is precisely what has happened:

> On the surface it was easy to effect a transformation of the novel as a form and the film. The tendency of the film to depict the outer shell of social character, left the core unrepresented.
> . . . Since the beginning of World War II, the film has come to dominate the novel rather than the other way around. Now the novel is marked by both the visual as well as the literal, and has increasingly abandoned imaginative evocation.
> Literalness, perhaps the dominant aspect of film, has come to occupy, largely because of film's popularity, a hegemonic place in all the arts. Its chief feature is the abandonment of subjectivity in the work. In place of interiority, which presupposed the individual who was distinguished from the objects outside of her- or himself by consciousness, even if socially determined or conditioned, literalism dissolves the subject-object split into object relations.[6]

Our argument about the social production of space spares us the necessity of endorsing Aronowitz's technological determinism ('largely because of film's popularity'), and facilitates a fuller understanding of this abolition of interiority in literature as a symptom of the retreat of representational space under a regime of simulation.

Fredric Jameson has dubbed this symptom the 'waning of affect', an erasure of the experiential depth of modern art, and its replacement by 'frivolous' and 'decorative' surfaces in postmodern culture.[7] The older affects of angst, alienation, loss, despair, isolation and dread, all have withered under the spatial abstractions of visualization, and leave nary a trace on the 'cool' surfaces of contemporary art and literature, other than in stereotypical quotations. What recourses are left to the contemporary writer who wants somehow to encrypt those affects – to complain about the loss of representational space – without looking sentimental and regressive in technique?

In this chapter, the work of Los Angeles writers Bret Easton Ellis and Dennis Cooper is analysed to yield two different sets of answers to these questions. In Ellis's novels *Less Than Zero* (1985) and *The*

Informers (1994), urban space is presented as being resistant to 'cognitive mapping', precisely because it is so encased in a seamless visual skin. The various 'characters' who populate it are walking footnotes to Carey McWilliams' thesis that the abstraction of a built environment contributes to its inhabitants' 'rootlessness and their feeling of unreality about the land in which they live'.[8] They are well beyond that state of affairs, too at home in their homelessness for the idea of alienation ever to arise. This spatial problematic in effect substitutes for the older existential thematics of literary modernism: Eliot's London, Joyce's Dublin, Döblin's Berlin, and Bely's Petersburg, all became demanding testing-grounds for the endurance of the *petit-bourgeois* individual in a space of pitiless heterogeneity and change. Whether this individual failed these rigours of the 'Unreal City' (Eliot) or survived them (Joyce), he was nevertheless always felt somehow to be distinct from it, a Subject to its kaleidoscopic Object. In late twentieth-century Los Angeles, the resonating depths of the individual would appear to have been absorbed by the object-sponge of the city, subsumed into space, surface and visuality.

With Cooper's *oeuvre*, meanwhile, something rather different is at stake. In these narratives of graphic sexual violence, counterpointed by a supremely honed and sinuous style, the implicit proposition is that some final frontier of the body, its anal orifice and mangled interior, has yet to be assimilated by the logic of visualization and metaphor. This taboo space of 'the abject' functions as a sublime, a representational beyond to which appeal is made in Cooper's case against the body's becoming-abstract in media culture. Moreover, this resistance to visual equivalence is advanced under the banner of a declared aestheticism, in which the redoubled attention to style and the development of a new grammar and syntax of oppositionality is the deeper formal project. The restitution of literature's critical vocation in image culture must not proceed solely at the level of content, Cooper insists, but very much at the level of form and sentence construction.

In either case, however, it must be said that 'visualization' as such refers primarily, indeed almost exclusively, to a certain minority in Los Angeles – the white middle class – and, specifically, to sexually ambivalent males as a subsector within it. This doubtless has to do with the domination of media-visuality by a persistent whiteness and class-gender specificity, meaning that spatial abstraction itself is experienced as such principally by those directly interpellated by the mechanisms of visualization. If it is the white, male middle class body which is most fully disposed to the 'logic of metaphor' of ocular postmodernism, then it is this minority to whom it falls to explore and excogitate its geography.

> The aggressive territoriality of Ellis's book suggests that geography and place, once a fictional hinterland for critics to interpret as they might, have gradually come to dictate the themes and structure of the novel, leaving emotional issues to become amorphous, to function as background . . . The novel has to be grounded somewhere and place, as one of our last realities, has started to function as character . . . [I]n *Less Than Zero*, it is the messages of the city that dictate plot development and it is ultimately the city . . . that owns and spawns the people . . .[9]

Elizabeth Young here articulates the aesthetic 'postmodernism' of Bret Easton Ellis in terms of a spatial ascendancy. The affective realm of emotions has receded to vanishing point behind the 'aggressive territoriality' of a narrative which endlessly retraces a closed network of commercial and private spaces devoted to conspicuous consumption. Beverly Hills, Westwood, Beverly Center, Century City, Studio City, the Wilshire Corridor, Bel Air, Palm Springs, Downtown, Sherman Oaks, the Valley, Mulholland Drive, Malibu: these are the specialist nodes of consumption and leisure through which the characters restlessly circulate.

A random quotation will suffice to illustrate the homogeneity of Ellis's LA, and the functional, not to say epiphenomenal, role of the young white consumers who frequent its boundless yet monolithic spaces.

> After leaving Blair I drive down Wilshire and then onto Santa Monica and then I drive onto Sunset and take Beverly Glen to Mulholland and then Mulholland to Sepulveda and then Sepulveda to Ventura and then I drive through Sherman Oaks to Encino and then into Tarzana and then Woodland Hills. I stop at a Sambo's that's open all night and sit alone in a large empty booth . . .[10]

Stepping back for a moment and holding this passage in our minds against an earlier instance of the LA 'freeway chronotope', it is interesting to see what distinguishes Ellis's prose from that of Joan Didion. Didion's undertaking with the freeway was to extend her sense that:

> . . . the freeway experience . . . is the only secular communion Los Angeles has . . . Actual participants think only about where they are. Actual participation requires a total surrender, a

concentration so intense as to seem a kind of narcosis, a rapture-of-the-freeway. The mind goes clean. The rhythm takes over. A distortion of time occurs.[11]

Her novel *Play It as It Lays* (1970) elaborates this popular appropriation of abstract space in the following passage:

> Once she was on the freeway and had maneuvered her way to a fast lane she turned on the radio at high volume and she drove. She drove the San Diego to the Harbor, the Harbor up to the Hollywood, the Hollywood to the Golden State, the Santa Monica, the Santa Ana, the Pasadena, the Ventura. She drove it as a riverman runs a river, every day more attuned to its currents, its deceptions, and just as a riverman feels the pull of the rapids in the lull between sleeping and waking, so Maria lay at night in the still of Beverly Hills and saw the great signs soar overhead at seventy miles an hour, *Normandie* $\frac{1}{4}$, *Vermont* $\frac{3}{4}$, *Harbor Fwy 1*. Again and again she returned to an intricate stretch just south of the interchange where successful passage from the Hollywood onto the Harbor required a diagonal move across four lanes of traffic. On the afternoon she finally did it without once braking or losing the beat on the radio she was exhilarated, and that night slept dreamlessly.[12]

The simile, 'as a riverman runs a river', invests the engineered space of concrete and bitumen with an archaic imaginary space: Maria's gradual initiation to the automotive ritual of interchange and fast lanes assumes the connotations of an apprenticeship in a complex naval art. What the prose is attempting to capture in these lines is the degree to which the new space of the freeways is making entirely new demands on the human cerebral cortex; and the success of that cortex in adapting.

The tone of Ellis's passage is so disengaged from the vestigial romanticism of Didion's as to occupy a different literary field: it is a chronotope in its own right. Whereas Maria Wyeth brings the freeway system home with her at night, and admits it into her dreams, Ellis's protagonist, 'Clay', is utterly inured to its rhythms. He is a function of the freeways, and not their 'riverman'. In this flattened chronotope, space dominates to the degree that time fails to register on the verbal geiger-counter at all. There are no temporal references, except the 'open all night' of a shop sign. Nor is Clay going anywhere; the chain-store where he stops to sit alone is merely a blank receptacle, with no greater claim on his person than the disaffected list of freeways and place names just incanted. Directionless, vapid, undescribed because unexperienced, this journey

appears in the novel only to underscore the absence of any characterological 'experience' or 'purpose' in the social space it traces.

Even when deserted by the daily mill of consumers, this space
exerts its powerful hold on the bodies of those who traverse it:

> We park and then walk through the empty, bright Beverly
> Center. All the stores are closed and as we walk up to the top
> floor, where the movies are playing, the whiteness of the floors
> and the ceilings and the walls is overpowering and we walk
> quickly through the empty mall and don't see one other person
> until we get to the theaters.[13]

The adverb 'quickly' is one of the rare markers of temporal intensity
in the novel, and it proceeds from this rather uncanny encounter
with an 'overpowering' commercial space whose unwonted emptiness and symbolically purified whiteness seem to betoken some
superhuman agency. Here the market itself is disambiguated as LA's
Higher Power, whose commandments, embedded transparently in
commercial space, dictate the movements of bodies along its pre-
scribed paths of exchange and social reproduction.

By the time of his more recent novel, the thirteen-part *The Informers*, Ellis has perfected this literary evocation of a space so controlled by the forces of consumerism, that the best it can offer is
'illusion', the worst, an extinction of human being. In the following
interminable sentence, the (feminine) first person haunts commercial
space in a frantic quest for experience and excitement which will
never come:

> I park and walk over to the American Airlines terminal and go
> to a coffee shop, making sure I get a seat by the window, and I
> order coffee and watch planes take off, occasionally glancing at
> a copy of the *LA Weekly* I brought with me from the car, and
> then I do some of the cocaine Simon gave me this afternoon and
> get diarrhea and then I roam the airport and hope someone will
> follow me and I walk from one end of the terminal to the other,
> looking over my shoulder expectantly, and I leave the Amer-
> ican Airlines terminal and walk out to the parking lot and
> approach my car, the windows tinted black, two stubs leaning
> against the windshield where the wipers used to be, and I get
> the feeling that there's someone waiting, crouched in the back-
> seat, and I move toward the car, peer in, and though it's hard to
> tell, I'm pretty sure there's no one in there and I get in and
> drive out of the airport and as I move past motels that line
> Century Boulevard leading to LAX I'm tempted, briefly, to
> check into one of them, just to get the effect, to give off the
> illusion of being someplace else, and the Go-Go's are singing
> 'Head Over Heels' on the radio and from LAX I drive to West

Hollywood and find myself at a revival theater on Beverly Boulevard that's playing an old Robert Altman movie and I park the Jaguar in a towaway zone, pay for a ticket and walk into a small, empty theater, the entire room bathed in red light, and I sit alone up front, flip through the *LA Weekly* and it's quiet in the theater except for an Eagles album that's playing somewhere and someone lights a joint and the sweet, strong smell of marijuana distracts me from the *LA Weekly*, which drops to the floor anyway after I see an advertisement for Danny's Okie Dog, a hot dog stand on Santa Monica Boulevard, and the lights dim and someone in back yawns and the Eagles fade, a tattered black curtain rises and after the movie ends I walk back outside and get in the car and when the car stalls in front of a gay bar on Santa Monica I decide not to go to the station for the eleven o'clock newscast and I keep turning the key and when the engine starts up again I drive away from the bar and past two young guys yelling at each other in a doorway.[14]

Obvious here is the meandering flow of clauses into one another without any sentence break, as though to lull us into a vicarious 'non-experience' of Los Angeles through the lens of a conspicuous consumer – from airport to parking lot to boulevard to motel to cinema to gay bar. Separate places thus blur into one another, uninterrupted by traditional grammatical stops and starts; the syntax itself performs the kind of abstraction we have been addressing. Meanwhile, several little ironies prepare us for what we will come to see more fully below as Ellis's tactic of distanciation through immanence: the way in which the first person voice is trapped into showing us the insight of its own blindness. The *LA Weekly* which Cheryl, our vacuous newscaster narrator, tries vainly to read, is a rebarbative Left-ish newssheet; it 'drops to the floor' after Cheryl reads an advertisement. And the Robert Altman film for which she waits in the cinema is over and done with, in the most radical ellipsis imaginable, before it can register a single word in the flow of clauses. Of course, Altman, like the *Weekly*, is a critical figure in the national culture, skeptical of Hollywood myths. Cheryl cannot 'see' his film for the same reason she cannot read the *Weekly* or see another human being in this entire paragraph, until the 'two young guys yelling at each other' suddenly disturb her reverie, return her partially to the world, and abruptly end the sentence – she is incapable of critical reflection. As a literary representation of abstract space, this passage is exemplary: a litany of brand-names, abstract place names and a simulated audio-visual sensorium, in which desire cannot prosper and 'diarrhea' is the only bodily event.

The problem for Ellis is very much one of how, as a writer, to disturb this unbroken surface of consumer space and insert some moment of negativity in order to protest its outright domination of everyday life. Ellis is masterful at transcoding this space into literary form, as a monstrous dilation of spatial and symbolic elements, at the expense of time, experience and the imaginary, and a collapse of the distinguishing features of subjective interiority with which to resist the belittling exterior of Los Angeles. His early strategies for suggesting an 'outside' to it, a critical distance which would somehow call into question its implacable dominion over social being, take several forms: characterological, in the moral 'growth' of Clay the narrator of *Less Than Zero*; narratological, in the increasing frequency of violent and amoral events and apocalyptic portents as that novel progresses; spatial, in the unrepresented, though frequently alluded to, place of the East, and Camden College from which Clay is on holiday; totemic, in the poster-icon of Elvis Costello stuck over Clay's bed, and the title *Less Than Zero* itself; and immanent, in the very texture of the sentences which tell the tale.

In what follows, I am uninterested in all but the last of these devices, not only because they have been dealt with by other critics – the first by Sahlin,[15] the second by Caveney and Freese,[16] the third by Young,[17] and the fourth admirably by Thurschwell[18] – but primarily because they are the signs of Ellis's relative artistic immaturity, contradicting as they do the overriding aesthetic principle of his work: that this is a social space strictly unsupportive of character, of morality, development or any idea of elsewhere. Despite Ellis's recourse to one of the oldest traditions in American letters, what Peter Freese calls 'the genuinely American tradition of vernacular first-person narration' which we recall from *Huckleberry Finn* and *Catcher in the Rye*,[19] according to Elizabeth Young, Ellis 'could never create a Jay Gatsby, a Holden Caulfield or a Dean Moriarty. The characters in his books, by very dint of their lack of individuality in a homogenized society, cannot be "created," cannot be born as personalities in the old sense, because as Ellis suggests, personality in the manner of individuals can no longer exist.'[20] To this extent, the whole artistic paradox of a central character who, on the one hand, is 'Clay' to the city's abstract visuality, and on the other can learn to condemn its amoral effects and finally choose to leave, is a sign of genuine indecision on Ellis's part. One is inclined to agree with an early review of *Less Than Zero* in *Time*, that Ellis's 'efforts to distance Clay, the narrator, from all the other zombies is unsuccessful . . . [U]ltimately, Ellis's novel is anchored to a hero who stands for nothing';[21] though I am tempted to add that this is what makes it as powerful as it is. *Less Than Zero*'s narrative form uneasily tolerates the coexistence of two distinct aesthetics: one 'existential' in the manner of a Camus, a Hemingway, or indeed a Didion; the other properly postmodernist and unconcerned with character depth or integrity. It is this latter problematic – of the spatial domination and fetishism of the market, the absence of qualities, of time, of interiority – which can be said to be Ellis's own in a strong authorial sense, defining his enduring set of preoccupations.

Ellis's style, what we have already called his distanciation through immanence, is at any rate what leaves the strongest traces in the reading mind and most surely qualifies Ellis as a cultural pessimist of the first rank. It is one thing to shake totems of a treasured past (crucially, punk) against the imposing edifice of abstract space, but quite another to use the very techniques of that space against itself, as I hope to show his style does – employing the homeopathic strategy of a consistent depthlessness and affectlessness – to dramatize those qualities in the act of reframing them. It was Jean Baudrillard who once hypothesized about the intrinsic values of an aesthetics of 'indifference':

> In my opinion, we must make of indifference a stake, a strategy: dramatize it. Why not consider indifference as the 'damned portion'? Be that as it may, I do not believe that we can go to the past in search of lost values. Postmodernism registers the present situation, the loss of meaning and of desire, the mosaic-like aspect of things, but it does not make of decadence a grandiose event. To do that, one would need a mediator, in writing perhaps: an object which would be provoking in its very indifference.[22]

If I claim for Ellis something of the status of Baudrillard's 'mediator', then that is because the nature of his verbal practice is such as to refuse any external moralistic standpoint, and yet, through a provocative indifference, to 'make of decadence a grandiose event': something larger than the little fragments of nothingness it actually presents.

The immanence of Ellis's method rests in a dogged stylistic consistency, running through all five novels, in the matter of person, tense and mood – interrupted intermittently only in the first novel by unnecessary and unconvincing slabs of an italicized past tense.

Otherwise, indeed, the entirety of Ellis's work is transmitted in the uniformly blank register of a first-person voice, and present-tense indicative mood, varying negligibly from character to character according to who is speaking. 'Indifference' is precisely the word that springs to mind when reading sentences such as the following, pared down to an absolute minimum of rhetorical effort:

> Dimitri, drunk and mumbling incoherently, shambles over to the two of us, and I think he's going to say something to Kim, but instead he sticks his hand through the window, getting the skin stuck on the glass, and as he tries to pull his hand away, it becomes all cut up, mutilated, and blood starts to spurt out unevenly, splashing thickly onto the glass. After taking him to some emergency room at some hospital, we go to a coffee shop on Wilshire and sit there until about four and then we go home.[23]

Perhaps the first thing to strike a reader of these two sentences is their formal imbalance: a long, clausally cluttered sentence narrating a moment's action, and a brief, vapid one narrating hours of it. The subject of the first sentence changes no less than four times, from Dimitri to I to Dimitri again to his hand to the blood, their respective paratactic clauses connected by pointless ands and buts. In case we are tempted to think that some genuine event has transpired to puncture the flattened blankness of the prose, however, it is soon made clear that Dimitri's 'mutilation' is only a pastiche of the cheapest pocket-novel style; phrases like 'spurt out' and 'splashing thickly' confirming one's suspicion that this is not 'happening' at all, but only suggesting another textual space adjacent to this one. The second sentence is then marked by a petulant shrug of the grammatical shoulders, a return to the lowest limits of stylistic distinction from those sub-generic heights. Its lack of objective definition is shown in the repeated indefinite articles 'some' and 'a' and the preposition 'about', and the subjective vagueness of the unidentified 'we'. Of course, this is arguably irony in the strong sense, since the subject of this passage concerns the wounding of a friend and his subsequent hospitalization. Yet if it is irony, or indeed satire, as one is tempted to conclude, it is achieved entirely at the level of style, with no further consequences, narrative or otherwise, to confirm its lethal sting in satisfying amplifications. All its force inheres in the unbroken formal law that this first-person, present-tense voice will never buckle under the satiric censure of its author.

Such stylistic immanence is itself, I want to argue, a form of chronotope. It projects the phenomenological being of a certain social sector of Los Angeles (the wealthy white middle-class) as an unqualified immediacy of time in an unqualified immediacy of space. More in this respect needs to be said about the consistency of the present tense. Ernst Bloch once wrote that the most important project for any political art worth its name is to represent the present; yet, he stressed, the present *as immediately lived* is steeped in the 'darkness of the moment'.[24] Bloch's point was that the novelist had as his duty the task of somehow putting immediacy at a distance, and showing contemporaneity from the outside, as a process, a moving totality. He acknowledged that this task was especially complicated at historic periods of social and cultural inertia:

> Times that are socially and culturally dull crawl along . . . in their now-proximity, which is then paralyzed, or even suffocated. The subjective reaction to that is boredom, the objective finding is emptiness *in actu*, seemingly immobile and without history.[25]

The emptiness of Los Angeles' 'now-proximity' as it crawls along through abstract space: such would amount to a statement of Ellis's theme. Rather than put himself outside it, however, which would foster the illusion of some escape or objectivity in a world without history, he has opted to present this suffocation from the inside, as a lived vacuity, a chronotope of blank infinities and serial points. Thus, his very style is an attempt to represent the unrepresentable void of experience opened by postmodernity. It is, in other words, a paradoxical experiment in stringing words and clauses together to create a sense of paralysis.

All of which signals the advent of some novel and unexpected use-value in what Roland Barthes called *le degré zéro de l'écriture*. The label was invented, under the shadow of Sartre in the 1950s, to promulgate the notion of a writing from which all traces of political allegiance and ideology had been erased, a 'white writing' which would thus absolve literature of its guilty implication in history. Barthes wrote:

> . . . writing at the zero degree is basically in the indicative mood, or if you like, amodal; it would be accurate to say that it is a journalist's writing, if it were not precisely the case that journalism develops, in general, optative or imperative (that is, emotive) forms. The new neutral writing takes its place in the midst of all those ejaculations and judgments, without becoming involved in any of them; it consists precisely in their absence . . . This transparent form of speech, initiated by Camus's *Outsider*, achieves a style of absence which is almost

an ideal absence of style; writing is then reduced to a sort of negative mood in which the social or mythical characters of a language are abolished in favour of a neutral and inert state of form.[26]

To which one or two things must be added. First, what might once have appeared to be the 'ideal absence of style' in Camus, probably strikes us today as being every bit as dated and stylized as any other historical form: one option among many in the shopping-mall of styles available to postmodern pastiche. And second, Camus had drawn most of his stylistic lessons from an American textual source, namely the hard-boiled prose of James M. Cain's *The Postman Always Rings Twice* (1934) – not coincidentally the first Los Angeles *noir* novel. Barthes's scholarly solecism is typically Francocentric, overlooking the immense example, too, of Hemingway, without question the originator of a modern 'white writing'; which had thus been a venerable tradition in American letters since the 1920s and would, for a college student of literature in the 1980s, have looked about as fresh and non-ideological as full-blown Dickensian rhetoric.

Yet Ellis's recovery of this 'writing degree zero' is mediated by the auspicious local presence in Los Angeles literature of perhaps its greatest and most limpid exponent, namely Joan Didion herself. Much as Barthes could have wished, Didion was novelist and journalist both, inventing for the America and more specifically the California of the 1970s a supremely economical and 'post-ideological' sentence style, adequate in every sense to the demise of the larger ideological ambitions of the 1960s. Moreover, Didion was the forerunner of an important trend in American literature, in her production of chronotopes for what Marc Augé calls the 'non-places' of 'supermodernity': the indistinct freeways, hotel rooms, resorts, airports and cocktail lounges in which the contemporary body is drained of subjective identity and forced to adopt new forms of disengaged spatial practice.[27] Didion obligingly mapped this process of deterritorialization by effacing herself and any hint of moral judgement from the very grain of her language. Quoting from the sixty-fifth chapter of *Play It as It Lays*, the following passage illustrates what is involved:

> Two or three times a day she walked in and out of all the hotels on the [Las Vegas] Strip and several downtown. She began to crave the physical flash of walking in and out of places, the temperature shock, the hot wind blowing outside, the heavy frigid air inside. She thought about nothing. Her mind was a blank tape, imprinted daily with snatches of things overheard,

87

fragments of dealers' patter, the beginnings of jokes and odd lines of song lyrics. When she finally lay down nights in the purple room she would play back the day's tape.[28]

The subject as a recording apparatus for the detritus of postmodern everyday life, caught up in a quest for experience whose results amount only to 'physical flashes', 'shocks' and rushes of sensation devoid of 'thought' – Didion's style helps produce this subject while seeming only to describe it. We must note that, although the passage is in the third person, there is no room for any 'free indirect discourse', since Maria very precisely *thinks about nothing*. She has no discourse of her own with which to etch an identity into the pellucid prose of a narrator at once inside her mind, and many light years outside it. It is the narrator's task, indeed, to demonstrate that the outside is inside; that technology and the free-floating symbols and sounds of mass life have substituted for thought itself.

It should already be clear how endebted Ellis has been to this mode of textual production. He has explicitly nominated Didion as his literary mentor and exemplar. Matthew Tyrnauer comments on this remarkably parasitic relationship: '*Less Than Zero* is more than influenced by the work of Didion; it is almost as if Ellis had appropriated her perspective . . . You can call this hero worship, but with Ellis and other members of his generation, identification goes beyond worship; the deity becomes ingrained. "When I got to Bennington, I was a total Didion fanatic who turned everyone on to Joan Didion," Ellis tells me.'[29] If Didion had affiliated herself with the tradition of 'white writing' by dint of her efforts as a journalist and essayist, refining herself out of existence in the sheer determination to capture things as they are, then Ellis could sidestep that laborious apprenticeship by latching onto the achieved entity of Didion herself, the very substance of her style, as a school and an end in itself. Incorporating Didion's diction, Ellis became her literary *doppelgänger*; liquidating his own identity in the conviction that it was much cooler to assume hers.

More interesting, however, are the determinate differences between Didion and Ellis, some of which might be evident from the following, quite typical passage from *Less Than Zero*:

> I drive over to Trent's house, but Trent, I remember, is in Palm Springs, so I drive to Rip's place and some blond kid answers the door only wearing a bathing suit, the sunlamp in the living room burning.[30]

This could hardly be Didion. So bereft of interest is its airless, amodal voice, that we pause to wonder what we are doing reading it at all. Much as the action it is describing, the sentence itself begins positively, moves unsurely through several reversals, and ends on a subject quite different from the one initially broached. Unsatisfying in every way – grammatically, syntactically, and in terms of narrative forward-propulsion – such a listless string of monosyllables would scarcely be thought of as 'literary', were it not for the internal resistance it builds over time, since this is precisely the dominant style of the novel. This internal resistance opens onto a second dimension of reception, where one recalls the instance of Didion, of whom this is a poor and distant shadow.

> So Rip and I go to Pages and Billy and Rod are there and so are Simon and Amos and LeDeu and Sophie and Kristy and David. Sophie sits with us and brings over LeDeu and David.[31]

By now we are not thinking of this as a failed pastiche of Didion, but something rather different: a *reductio ad absurdum*. One clearly senses the extent to which Ellis, by virtue of the social space he is mediating, has been obliged to go beyond Didion's more or less implacable humanism. For with Didion it was always a question of finding some last, inextinguishable spark of individual being in Plato's cave. Her third-person narration of Maria Wyeth's progress through the non-places of late capitalism ends precisely with an acknowledge-ment of her eventual self-discovery: 'Because you and I, we *know* something', the suicidal BZ tells her. 'Because we've been out there where nothing is'.[32] And while it is true that Ellis too, in his first novel, tries for something of this existential pathos, the truth-content of his style is the bleaker message that no such option is any longer viable.

Ellis's distanciation through immanence proceeds above all from his radicalization of Didion's postmodernism. To this extent, Ellis's stylistic practice establishes a complex historicity: on the one hand, the continuity of a literary mode of production, 'white writing', with roots and references in the past; and on the other, a decisive break from Didion's vestigial humanism and from the social space she endeavoured to map. His radicalization of Didion's 'writing degree zero', what I am tempted to call his *writing degree less-than-zero*, announces a quantum-shift in the consumer-space of which it is a chronotope: a demonstration that, while the non-places of late capitalism might once have been new and potentially exhilarating (as they were, just, for Didion's characters), now they are the ubiquitous second nature of the everyday, into which Ellis's characters were born and raised. And there is, *pace* Barthes, a great, unstated intensity of 'emotiveness' and 'judgment' in the consistency with which Ellis reduces Didion's meticulously nuanced chronotope to a lifeless, abstract cage of monosyllabic banality.

So the precious, if slight, distance between Didion's third-person voice and Maria herself – a distance in which we had heard the whisper of a promise of redemption – collapses into the hollowed-out immanence of Ellis's first-person monologues. Yet in *Less Than Zero*, the very endurance of the first-person voice throughout the duration of the novel suggests some degree of optimism that an identity might ultimately be forthcoming, if only Clay could get away from Los Angeles and recover a sense of self in less inhospitable climes; if only he could go East and become a writer, as the *finalé* of the novel seems to indicate that he will. I have already argued that this note of potential redemption for Clay is a violation of the very style in which he is fashioned, and a sign of artistic immaturity. It is, indeed, only with the *The Informers*, some decade later, that the deadlier promises of the early novel are fulfilled.

With *The Informers*, Ellis appears to have travelled full circle, and done to himself what he did to Didion in *Less Than Zero*. He would seem, that is, to have poached his own first novel as a kind of raw material for pastiche and deflation. There is an inescapable and disconcerting sense in these pages that Ellis is laughing at himself, caught constantly in the act of showing up his own characteristic, vapid style as a language game and a ruse in its own right. This is manifest above all in a new element of metafictional self-conscious-ness. Much of the prose appears on first sight to be an extension of the earlier technique. Yet the chronotope produced by this style is if anything more abstract, less 'lived', than that of *Less Than Zero*:

> I am about to walk out the door. The maid folds the paper. Graham takes off his burgundy letterman's sweater. The other boy wants to know if Graham has *Alien* on cassette. From the den the woman is singing 'circumstance beyond our control'.[33]

Each separate sentence indicates a universe all of its own; no pronouns appear to carry subjects or objects across sentence-breaks. Everything is definite, immediate and positive. We are not in a space of negativity and cross-referencing, but a paratactic series of simul-taneous positivities. Appended to this stylistically achieved separa-tion of the units of meaning, the final pop-song line comes as something of a jolt, since it names and thematizes what would otherwise have remained implicit.

A new, lowering metafictional menace is indeed felt throughout the novel, in moments such as the following:

> My mother, her skin yellow, her body thin and frail from lack of food, is dying in a large, empty house that overlooks a bay in San Francisco. The poolboy has set traps smudged with peanut butter around the edge of the pool. Randomness, surrender.[34]

Like a rerun of the Dimitri episode from *Less Than Zero*, here we have a sentence describing the fatal decline of a loved one, followed by a bathetic sentence concerning an entirely different space and time. Yet unlike that earlier episode, this flattened juxtaposition of unequivalent parts is then framed by an ejaculation from beyond, like a judgement passed on this chronotope of fragmentation and abstraction: 'Randomness, surrender'. It is unclear whether or not this unexpected metafictional moment, of which there are many in the text, is a violation of the law of the first-person voice. What is certain is that a new artistic temperament is now sternly in place, capable of interfering with the older 'writing degree less-than-zero' by inserting its own exasperation into the textual field. This effect is achieved elsewhere in the character Martin's litanous complaints to various characters:

> Martin starts to talk about his classes at UCLA and then about how his parents are irritating him, about how they came over to his apartment at Westwood unannounced, about how his stepfather wanted him to come to a dinner party he was throwing at Chasens, about how Martin did not want to go to a dinner party his stepfather was throwing at Chasens, about how tiredly words were exchanged.
>
> . . . Martin starts complaining that he hasn't finished the English Prices video yet . . . [etc., etc.], that yellow is his favorite color, that he recently made friends with a tumbleweed named Roy.[35]

The final, weird clauses in these sentences that go on without end call the bluff of white writing itself, and feed new fuel to a guttering style. The device is a properly spatial one, a game of 'what's wrong with this picture' with language itself, where the intrusive clause appears as an alien blot on the printed page; that it always appears at the sentence's end suggests that the last word belongs with Ellis, who can no longer refrain from heaping scorn on his contents.

Even the character-type of Clay and his various, mechanically reproducible clones, is not spared the newer form of censure, here written from the point-of-view of a father of one of the interchangeable teens:

The three of us stare at Tim like he's some kind of blank, exotic creature, more stunned than we should be by how inarticulate he actually is.

. . . Looking at Tim, one cannot help feeling great waves of uncertainty, an absence of aim, of purpose, as if he is a person who simply doesn't matter.

. . . Tim is so deflated it doesn't even seem like he exists.[36]

Perhaps this unwonted explicitness about Ellis's attitude toward the 'blank generation' he had previously presented only from the inside, has to do with an emergent frustration at the limitations of his subject-matter. Which is not to say that this father is any less void of identity or character than the son of which he is so 'uncertain', any less driven by the energies of consumption, or dominated by the spaces of abstraction (the episode takes place on a holiday in Hawaii). It is simply to signal the growing desperation Ellis seems to be feeling about his chosen method of immanence.

The most successful variation on that method in this novel is not the metafictional menace itself, however, so much as the revolving appearance of no fewer than twelve narrators, over roughly the same number of pages as *Less Than Zero*. This tactic interrupts and disables any identification-process which might have obtained between readers and the sustained narrative voice of Clay. It also precludes even the illusion of a narrative, as the text dissolves into so many discrete chapters, which are often set years apart, a fragmented textual space where narrative energy is dissipated as soon as it gathers. So although there is a core familial body of characters, there is no story to pull them together in any meaningful form. For they are all little more than reflections of each other in the house of mirrors that is Ellis's Los Angeles.

One narrator, Anne, a budding writer (who ends up scripting inane films), comments on the impossibility of narrative in this spatial regime of equivalence and repetition:

Each day seems exactly like the day before. Each day seems the same. It's weird. It's like watching yourself in the same film but with a different sound track each time you watched it . . . I know I should write about this place but I can't come out with a coherent story. I don't have a firm enough grasp or base to write from. There's really not a whole lot to assimilate or see.[37]

Building its own formal justification into the discursive plane is just one of the novel's many self-conscious strategies for framing its content. The larger and more abstract point, however – that none of these characters is qualified to 'write about this place' in the first place, that none of them has 'a firm enough grasp or base to write from' – affects the novel with the darkest kind of pessimism. Every one of the narrators (with one exception, a child-killer, who is lower-middle class) is white and middle class, the most privileged minority in the city, with greater spatial mobility, economic power, and political freedom than any other class- or race-faction; yet between them, and precisely because of the regime of visualization which encases them, 'there's really not a whole lot to assimilate or see'. The thirteen-part narrative resolves itself into a patchwork-quilt of constitutive blindnesses. The novel's formal insight is precisely this serial blindness, this inability to see the visual city.

How does one see the already seen? Clay's description of the Wilshire Boulevard apartment of Finn, a pimp, is an apt illustration of the abstract properties of this space, which clearly cannot be bounded, but unfolds into a mathematical infinity of reflection and visibility:

> Julian comes to a white door and opens it and the two of us walk into a totally spare, totally white room, complete with floor-to-ceiling windows and mirrors on the ceiling and this feeling of vertigo washes over me and I almost have to catch my balance. I notice that I can see my father's penthouse in Century City from this room and I get paranoid and start to wonder if my father can see me.[38]

We should note that this passage appears towards the end of *Less Than Zero*, and that Clay's symptoms of 'vertigo' and 'paranoia' are to be read as the resurgence of an existential thematic – a feeling of being out of place within such abstraction – that detracts from the scene's power. The substantial point is that no one else feels disjointed by this rarefied space, but they have all learned from birth how to comport their bodies in what Fredric Jameson called 'hyperspace':

> . . . [E]mptiness is here absolutely packed, . . . it is an element in which you are absolutely immersed, without any of that distance that formerly enabled the perception of perspective or volume. You are in this hyperspace up to your eyes and your body. . .
> . . . [T]his latest mutation in space – postmodern hyperspace – has finally succeeded in transcending the capacities of the individual human body to locate itself, to organize its immediate surroundings perceptually, and cognitively to map its position in a mappable external world.[39]

Like Jameson, Clay (the 'existential' Clay) feels unable to map this space, and his vertigo and paranoia spring from that inability of the 'modernist' subject to position itself within it. The greater lesson of Ellis's novels, however, is not this residual trope of alienation, but the more unpalatable truth that none of these characters seems to care, or feel any bewilderment at the volume-less, non-perspectival spaces in which they move. This space is *theirs*, or, better, they are *its*, in a new and disconcerting sense of which the literary style I have analysed above is the closest thing to a 'cognitive map' we can presently hope for. For that style was, we said, a considered production of indifference, an object lesson in not caring about place and time, other people, history or politics. If Jameson and even Clay feel disoriented by the unmappability of hyperspace, Ellis's other characters lack even the hint of a desire to map it. As one of them says with the utmost provocation: 'I realized that no matter where I am it's always the same. Camden, New York, LA, Palm Springs – it really doesn't seem to matter. Maybe this should be disturbing but it's really not. I find it kind of comforting.'[40] In Ellis's work, the stylistic texture itself is virtually an interminable monologue on the suffocating limits of such 'comfort' in the postmodern, whose innermost unstated desire is to find its way out, but cannot for lack of a map.

Having imagined postmodernism as an achieved surfeit of visual simulation, and charted Bret Ellis's homeopathic treatment of it, it now remains to wonder whether, within the race-class sector chosen by Ellis as a point of departure, there are not some resources left for the creation of what Lefebvre called representational space. Is being white and middle class in Los Angeles an automatic sentence to abstraction; or is there not some measure of negativity, even in this social stratum, as yet uncolonized by the machines of vision and reification? Moreover, is there not some scope for writing as a mode of intervention within this space, a possibility virtually ruled out at the start by Ellis's all but perfect stylistic mimesis of abstraction?

To preface the following reading of Dennis Cooper's Los Angeles fiction with the claim that it is such an intervention, on behalf of representational space, based not so much on 'indifference' as on the difference made by the act of literature itself, is not to wish away the colossal edifice of abstraction itself; rather, it is to suggest that that abstraction can be dismantled from within, if only the right tools are used, and handled with precision. It is to suggest that, like all codes and series, abstract space is subject to internal limits, which condition the possibility of reification as such, but which, when trans-gressed, expose the contingency and banality of the 'representations of space' which govern social life. And art has yet to discover a medium better suited than literature to the exploration of these internal boundaries of our prevailing cultural codes. George Bataille has been only the most outspoken critic to enshrine the intimate linkage of literature and evil, by which he meant not the pedestrian moralization of literary fields, but the 'hypermorality' of literature *per se* as the most intensely communicative and negative of represen-tational media.[41] In Los Angeles, where the visual reigns supreme, this negativity (of the linguistic sign, of syntactical sequence, of symbolic figuration, of self-consciousness) and its 'evil' retain a sovereign value as perhaps the sole remaining mode of intellectual and artistic resistance to the positivism of late capitalist culture.

At any rate, let us recall Lefebvre's argument that, under an urban regime of visualization, human beings are destined to inhabit a 'logic of metaphor', their passions and affects hollowed out by the entice-ments of visual culture. For Ellis, of course, this displacement and loss of integrity of the self signalled the bankruptcy of civilization; but there is a possibility inherent within this logic of metaphor, specified by Lefebvre, which Ellis's cultural pessimism overlooks. The 'evacuation from the innermost body of all life and desire' is a flow, says Lefebvre, which collides with the opposing inrush of messages and visuality. The resulting clash must have a scene, a space, in which its tensions and dramas are allegorically played out.

That space, the most intimate and ambivalent of all, is of course the body itself, which is transformed via the technologies of post-modern abstraction into the allegorical site *par excellence* of the contemporary politics of resistance. We should note again that, precisely to the extent that late capitalism functions within a racist and sexist distribution of power, the paradigmatic body upon which this allegorical politics will be inscribed is white, male, middle-class and youthful. What Baudrillard called the 'phallic exchange stan-dard' presides yet over American culture, reducing all representa-tion of the body, ultimately, to a colourless phallic norm; so that even the preponderance of female bodies in commercial photographic images is explained by the degree to which these bodies are them-selves 'phallic', denied their specific sexualities in favour of a perfect standard of equivalence: androgynous, ungendered, sexless.[42] Still less should we expect racially marked bodies to enjoy any specificity within the abstractions of the body today; what place they have is

generally that of a binary 'otherness' which instantly goes to recon-
firm the blanket hegemony of the white androgyne as the standard
of visual exchange.

The body's assumption of allegorical capability has principally
been dictated by the most extraordinary of all cultural and psychological 'developments' in postmodern society: namely, the neutrali-
zation of the unconscious.[43] If Surrealism garnered its energies from
the violation of repression and the raiding of dreams for their latent
wish-contents, then today the incessant disseminations of the
Culture Industry largely do that for us, emptying at a stroke the
unconscious of all its secret contents. The body in that earlier
moment was endowed with all the symbolic baggage of nature and
sexuality, the obscured kernel of civilized life; but now that semi-
naked bodies leer at us from every hoarding and magazine cover,
they have themselves entered into the system of visual equivalence
that is the simulacrum. Sexuality, once the very promise of alterity to
the economic, has been assimilated to the logic of commodity
production, while the unconscious is replaced by (and objectified as)
that 'discourse of the Other' that is simulation, hyperrealism, or
media culture. What this entails is a general desexualization of the
body as it enters the visual field. 'For it was only under repression
that the body had strong sexual potential: it then appeared as a
captivating demand. Abandoned to the signs of fashion, the body is
sexually disenchanted, it becomes a *mannequin*, a term whose lack of
sexual discrimination suits its meaning well.'[44]

In this context, the turn to the body in art is vexed by art's
anathema: the law of diminishing returns, the absence of any
cognitive shock in the face of even the most obscene bodily displays.
Jameson has written that, 'in the West, the corporate impoverishment of experience determines a kind of frenzy and desperation in
which the promises of the last bodily layer are sought after with a
well-nigh pathological single-mindedness. It is what can be called
the reduction to the body and observed in its more symptomatic
forms in pornography and violence porn, provided these are not
greeted with a simple-minded moralizing but rather acknowledged
historically as deeper truths of our social experience, and as characteristic of our socially specific relationship to Being'.[45] Following
on from this observation, it is clear in what sense the turn to the body
in some contemporary art is allegorical. For now the body is the last
frontier of privacy in society that has tried to collapse both 'public'
and 'private' into one another, on the Möbius strip of consumer

capitalism. It is also simultaneously the very hegemonic form of 'publicity', across the spectrum of media effects. Some of the most intense political and cultural wars today (over abortion rights, rape, representativity, sexual permissiveness, etc.) are waged on the terrain of the body, henceforth the battleground of a contest between a vast technology of domination and repetition, and the fleeting ephemera of individual experience, affect and choice. So, if the body no longer symbolizes for us the immanent forces of the unconscious or sexuality, it does concentrate many of the most serious social contradictions of our time. It is in this light that we shall approach the literature of Dennis Cooper.

Cooper, who is white, gay and writes in Los Angeles, has dedicated himself to exploring the bodily and ethical boundaries of gay sado-masochism, paedophilia, and necrophilia: the last strongholds of genuine taboo in the era of repressive desublimation.[46] His almost obsessive subject matter is thus born of an adamant resistance to the seemingly inexorable power of postmodern standardization over everyday life.[47] In this respect, he has recently commented on the unsatisfactory nature of heterosexual passion as a basis for a radical body-based art. His novel *Try* (1994), the first to involve a female character in any capacity, includes the following post-coital free-indirect discourse:

> [W]ith Nicole, make that with every girl so far, sex ends up being so . . . planned in advance, not by him obviously, but by history or whatever. So no matter how wild sex gets, he's still following this preset, like, outline, point by point, and when an experience is over, such as now with Nicole, it sort of gradually dilutes into a zillion other people's identical experiences, until Ziggy feels . . . used in a way? Or maybe it's just his rebelliousness problem. Still, gay sex seems to have this great scariness quotient, whereby no two situations are ever alike, as far as he can tell.[48]

So, in the casual verbal precision of a Los Angeles youth, Cooper condenses an extraordinary pronouncement on present-day heterosexuality. The quietly devastating evocation of a 'point by point' determination of every moment of male-female relations by 'history or whatever' could not be more damaging to that unique sense of sexual freedom evoked by any text in the grip of an ubiquitous illusion, here exposed as such. The 'zillion other people' whose identical experiences have always and already preceded one's own, describe a horizon of infinite iterability, before which no single sensation can any longer be felt as distinct or unique. Of course, the real purpose of this is not to make some extra-literary statement on 'experience', but to query the dominant representations of sexual space. 'Gay sex', especially in its darker forms, opens up relatively under-explored territory. For Cooper, only gay sex still contains the promise of the unique, and is thus innervated by the threat of the unknown and dangerous. It is a threat he has not failed to make good.[49]

Which is not to suggest that Cooper's work rests on the imagined immediacy of gay sexual practice; quite to the contrary, these novels, stories and poems seem to proceed precisely from the crisis of abstraction following from the 'mannequinization' of the body in visual culture. Through the representation of an extreme gay sexuality, which works violently on the mannequin as such, moments of affective and aesthetic truth are somehow to be won. The object of labour, both sexual and artistic, is in every case a boy-child whose body has become a *crypt*, both tomb and cipher. Cooper's central actantial category of the confused and drugged mannequin-boy is cryptic in both these senses: for each of these bodies is the site of a death (the death of the subject, the identification with image-objecti-fications of dead labour), and the form of a code to be cracked by the sexual exploitation of predatory adults.

The task for these older figures is to modify the cryptic body in such a way as to reveal its secrets, to expose the inside information of a blank bodily objectivity.[50] Cooper's predatory male adults (he generally refers to them as 'wolves') insist, at the extreme, on the reduction of that alterity to immediate identity with themselves.[51] Like the information society they inhabit, they subscribe to a fully realized, knowable, positive world, where the negativity of the real does not intrude to relativize the consuming subject; or if it does so, it is only as a spur to assimilate it to the positive. Which of course means that in their labour with it, the men must decrypt the cryptic body, force it to fit some sort of schema to yield a definite legibility. I want to argue that Cooper's mannequin-boys are collapsed by their older male 'consumers' into two distinct sets of binary oppositions: first, in the structured antinomy of inside and outside (skin and viscera, appearance and essence); and second, in the less conven-tional antinomy of face and 'ass' (which here allegorizes the anti-nomy of subjectivity and objectivity in the object itself). Through these codes, the crypt of the body is cracked, admitting the rush of information and the stench of death in one sublime and self-defeating act of sacrilege.

It is repeatedly stressed that the mannequin-boys are not seen by their consumers as such, but only within the logic of metaphor in which they are trapped. Ray Sexton, the real-life serial killer Cooper recreates in 'A Herd', realizes what is at stake in this logic:

> When he had his way, he imagined them as the kids in the teen magazines he picked up at the market. Those magazine's [sic] stars were Ray's angels, freed from the limits of I.Q.s and co-ordination, whose distant looks had a cloudy, quaalude effect. Teen stars' perfection haunted him and a vague resemblance to one or another could, more often than not, be gleaned from the face of a boy he had killed.[52]

Reification here is omnipresent, to the extent that the dead face of a boy and the mass-produced images of 'teen idols' merge into the glamour of iconic Beauty. Once the standard-bearer of dissidence and revolt, the post-punk 'teenager' is now the very medium of equivalence and exchange; alienated from its social role, the adolescent is repackaged as a fetish for the consumption of all.

Clearly enough, then, the first of the two codes superimposed on the teen as object by Cooper's older men – the skin/viscera binary – is in this context a rehearsal of the ancient problem of essence and appearance, the problem exactly of epistemology. If the Culture Industry has manufactured the current ideal of Beauty out of the photographic abstraction of adolescent bodies, then one way of getting at the essence of contemporary being might be to cut directly into one of Beauty's tokens. This is what Ray Sexton does in 'A Herd'.

> Ray loved being this close to a young body, smelling its haplessness and using it as a lover. Then, when he grew sick of this surface and needed to know how it curved so and what it could say, he'd want to destroy it and he would say loudly enough so that someone, if nearby, could hear, 'No one else will have this pleasure' . . . He had made so much love to the boy, in such depth and detail that the boy wished to die right now. No, the man wanted him to die. With a boy like this, asleep and all, it was too easy to read thoughts into his head.[53]

The illicit and profound excitation, then, is to have attempted essence through destruction of the aesthetic form of perfection. Only, as the narrator keeps insisting, this body is not a photograph and does not match the media-ideal in its pimply and imperfect physical reality: all of Ray's destructive labours with the body of Beauty (hacking off its testicles, chopping it up with an axe) depend upon a studied and self-enforced illusion. He literally places a mask over the boy's head so that his imaginative recreation of the image-ideal might go untroubled by a real negativity, a real lack of equivalence. The attainment of the 'inside' (blood and viscera), which should then yield the answer or information being sought, is attended by the following insight:

> He picked up an axe. He chopped what was beneath him until no owner could claim it. Then he sat down on the stairs. 3 a.m. No boy haunted him. Or could. There was a woe unlike any present on earth, Ray thought. He couldn't stop staring through everything. As if he were a god or were blind. More blind than a god, though he saw what he'd done.[54]

Having followed the logic of the fetish through to its limit, the subject experiences this deepest of alienations at the very moment of anticipated sublimity. The nothing glimpsed here 'through everything' finally exorcizes the 'teen idol' ghost of Sexton's imaginary; it takes the form of death. Cut away the surface of Beauty from the fabricated body of perfection and you are left with a corpse. Nothing is more scandalous to the contemporary reified imaginary. For the dead body interrupts the exchange standard – an unanswerable, unrefundable gift from our animal prehistory to consumer capitalism. Now that the living outnumber the dead, little is more important to the functioning of capital than the repression of death. 'Only the death-function cannot be programmed and localised. Strictly speaking, we no longer know what to do with them, since, today, *it is not normal to be dead*, and this is new. To be dead is an unthinkable anomaly; nothing else is as offensive as this. Death is a delinquency, and an incurable deviancy. The dead are no longer inflicted on any place or space-time, they can find no resting place; they are thrown into a radical utopia. They are no longer even packed in and shut up, but obliterated'.[55] Staring into this sublime utopia yields, however, a radical blindness, a nauseating glimpse at the nothing of death, its banality – a blind species being whose fundamental negativity it is the whole purpose of the simulacrum to obliterate beneath an excess of positive signification. Ray's ritual sacrifice represents the homeopathic cure to capitalism's abundant reifications; its only reward is a corpse, however, and not the expected sublimity of information's utopia. It is the end of all information.

Murder in Cooper is never an act of passion or profit, but a quest for total knowledge which must be forever deferred (or serialized), since the moment of attainment is simultaneously the moment of death of the object of knowledge. *Frisk's* Dennis is at least self-reflective enough to know this in advance, and such a state of arrest (which also has an ethical component) is what keeps him from the homocidal act, and makes him an artist-writer instead. Art in Cooper is the next best thing to death, the necessary deferral and compromise that has passed through the ethical moment and emerged with a reified aesthetic object that will neither decay nor solve anything at all, but stands in allegorically for the whole process. In this it is functionally equal in Cooper's semiotic system to shit, which is a similar compromise substitute-fetish for the corpse and, like the pornographic artwork, can be aestheticized by connoisseurs of the gift.[56]

Shit also enables our transition to the second of the binary codes imposed on teen bodies by their older consumers. The opposition of *face* and *'ass'* hinges on a drive to repress the subjectivity of the other during sex; in its canonical expressivity, no matter how drained and stupefied by drugs, the face carries the threat of a returning glance, which would compromise the godhead of the consumer-subject. So, the turn to the buttocks and anus is a turn towards the utter depersonalization of the other, effacement in the most literal of terms. '"No matter how many times I see one of these things," Alex leered, "it's still a shock. I mean, as hard as I try I can't look at this thing and recall the boy's face . . ."'[57] An early story, 'Dinner', dramatizes this polarity in its narrative of an adolescent's first sexual experience with an older man, who takes him out to a car for impersonal sodomy. Troubled by the look of doubt in the boy's eyes, the man turns him around and over to expose him: 'the ass was impeccable. The man would kiss here without having to worry about its opinion. Nothing would watch him or pull back or twitch beyond recognition. The boy was as distant from these moves as God from His priests down on earth'.[58] This tendency in the older aesthetes and predators to reduce the other to as blank an object as possible, by privileging the ass over the face, is given its didactic summation in *Try*, by the heavily satirized aesthete Roger: 'this little fixation [on the ass] involves an avoidance of more resolute body parts, namely the face and genitalia, both of which, while fascinating, present too much personality, thereby reinforcing my failure to penetrate the givens of people I crave'.[59]

The mention of genitalia brings to light one of the more interesting consequences of this persistent ass/face dichotomy, namely that, as Earl Jackson, Jr. notes, of the 'generally accepted erotogenic zones, the penis receives far less attention than the anus and the mouth'.[60] While Cooper seems to want this avoidance interpreted as an aversion from personality in the other, the penis does not in fact stand in a relation of equivalence with the face in his polar schema. Its effective absence from these texts can be read, therefore, as a strategic evasion of the 'phallic exchange standard', just as the absence of women evades the whole problem of what to do with reproductive organs in a semiotic system that sees the inside as death, productive only of waste and decay.

It only remains to be said that, for the most part, and certainly with greater pronouncement in the later novels, the polarization of face and 'ass' is resolved narratively in favour of the former; that is to say, in favour of a renewed attempt at intersubjectivity and (Cooper being an arch romantic) love. In *Closer*, the mannequin-boy George Miles, saved at the last minute from death at the hands of the predator Tom, emerges from his trials with his 'ass' hacked beyond recognition, so that it will henceforth be impossible to dispel the traces of his subjectivity by turning him over. With his object of predatory desire forever personalized and signatured ('His ass wasn't really an ass anymore', 'His ass looks like somebody threw a grenade at it'[61]), any sexual partner must henceforth be a lover, and take George as a subject, a not-quite-wholly objectified but internally differentiated personality. It is this difficult role that Steve comes grudgingly to accept as his own, unlearning his own predatory instincts in order to learn how to react to George as a speaking and articulate subject: i.e., to desire as such.

Again, this has manifold allegorical ramifications, since what inaugurates Steve's new ability to cope with the hideous sight of George's posterior is his simultaneous witnessing of pseudo-teen-idol David's gruesome demise under the wheels of a car. 'David's body is shredded like paper. His insides have pushed through some holes in his shirt, blue and greasy and jumbled. It looks like a flower bed. I have to imagine something else or I'll throw up'.[62] This gruesome fate realizes David's own earlier predictions, based on the cynical reasoning of post-punk materialism: 'if I get too close, do the explorer bit, I'll find the same old stuff. Blood, guts, bones, not much else. I could pick through that mess for the rest of my days without results . . .'[63] The gratuitous unpacking of David's viscera in a night-club has no point apart from underscoring the crude materialism whose ethic it allegorizes. For Steve, it finally allows for the beginning of genuine desire. Both imposed codes of the body dissolve at once in this narrative moment, and the body's representational space is finally liberated from the coded representations of its space. This representational space combines mourning and physical love: a mourning for the omnipresent 'dead teen' which does not take the form of sado-masochism, suicide or distraction,[64] but rather a hesitant, improvised contact with another.

Cooper's spatialization of the adolescent body speaks obliquely to the entire system of colonization and evacuation at work in our culture. The trials undergone by Cooper's mannequin-boys are those of visualization and commodification through the image: a reduction to legibility or simple semic systematicity which, when it approaches its internal limits crumbles and yields to the recrudescence of forgotten affects and longings. In this sense, the mannequin-boys of Cooper's novels are allegorical of nothing so much as the city about which they have nothing to say and within which they have no means of orientation or emplacement: Los Angeles. There is a way, Cooper's narratives insistently affirm, of tarrying with reified space such that the negative is reintroduced to it. With that tarrying, for all its taboo and ultimate insufficiency, some moment of the real irrupts within the hyperreal.

And let us be absolutely clear: Cooper's intervention is not one of 'violence' or sexual extremism as such, but a literary methodology and an aesthetic. That is, the intervention is not that of the predator-aesthetes who pervade his fiction, but the very fashioning forth of their acts of extremity in the stylistic assurance of a literary act with deep roots in tradition itself (de Sade, Genet, Lautreamont, Rimbaud, Bataille, Pinget). It is writing, a very *writerly* writing, which will reintroduce the negative to the existent. Style here reassumes its earlier, 'modernist' distance between the act of enunciation and what it enunciates, a gap which in the postmodern has often been felt lacking, as it is lacking in Ellis (and consciously, deliberately so). For Cooper, the reactivation of a certain spiritual moment comes through allegorical narrative, to be sure, but only insofar as it is vehiculated in a language which stands resolutely apart from its message. And it is this, precisely, which gives it the status of allegory in the first place, this interval between story and style; between a story whose graphic violence demands a swift forward propulsion, and a style which, almost mannered, even perfectionist, retards and diffuses the 'sensationalism' through a drawn screen of lapidary prose gestures.

Our reading minds thus caught between two quite different

textual registers, we are obligated by that unremitting dualism to approach 'what happens' allegorically. Not to do so, as the bulk of Cooper's critics have done, is to fail the most basic of interpretive tests: to account for the nature of his representation, rather than its object. His erudite mastery of the history of dissident erotica, as well as of the post-literate demotic of the white suburban youths with whom he identifies, make his precise verbal art a transubstantiation of Los Angeles' abstraction into a string of minor literary masterpieces. No one is more conscious of this paradox and the emotional complex it echoes than Cooper himself. 'I shove the knot of my feelings as deep as they'll go into as compact and smoothed-out a prose style as I can build out of what I know. But they don't belong there, any more than a man's fist belongs in a boy's ass'.[65]

The meticulously measured syntactical periods suggest a subliminal spatial figuration which is resistant to any outright description of Los Angeles as a city, preferring to mediate incompatible viewpoints on the body in order to suggest a vaster and more elaborate reality. Consider the multilayered perspectival complexity and impeccably wrought character of the following paragraph from 'A Herd':

> God wanted to cover this city with ice but thought better of it. Slow down, He told Himself. God lifted the roof off the man's house while he was busy over his victim. There was the man rummaging through a drawer full of tiny sharp objects. God barely understood them. There was the boy covered with blood. There they were together making love. God lowered the roof in its niche. He leaned back until the house, then its city became a small dot on the earth. Less than a dot. The earth was a dot, the most interesting one of the planets. God was flying backward through space, arms and legs stretched out before him like streamers. He looked a little like Martin Balsam when he flailed the front stairs in *Psycho*. But God was laughing, not shrieking. And that was how he would stay.[66]

The sentences here undertake the complex task of simultaneously realizing the point of view of Ray Sexton as he attains godhead through murder, and superadding the perspective of some greater entity whose presence relativizes and contains the unholy practices of Sexton in some total and more comprehensive spatio-ethical order. If Cooper's novels rarely venture out of doors, preferring the claustrophobic enclosure of bedrooms and basements to any objective representation of the city, it may be because his style sees through the eyes of this deity of abstraction. Into his small rooms and the bodies that occupy them, he has condensed the largest lessons about the hyperreality desiccating white, middle-class life in Los Angeles, and America at large. To suggest, as Matias Viegener does, that Cooper 'avoid[s] the temptations of allegory',[67] not only misses the point of this spatial reduction to the body, it does a disservice to a language style that has put the narrative at such a distance. 'It's the idea', Cooper contends, 'that, if you organise something well enough, somehow it will have within it *that thing*. Organising something really carefully or elaborately is all you can do'.[68]

Overcoming the abstract logic of metaphor through this meticulous attention to style is then, at the same time, an emancipation of particularity, difference and quality by literature. It is a process of liberation through precise syntactical distinction with an estimable heritage in American letters, dating back to Melville's astonishing powers of concretion, but receiving its purest statement in the critical prose of William Carlos Williams. Dismissing the facilities of simile and metaphor as a 'vegetable' acquiescence in the face of mere coincidence, Williams went on to praise 'that power which discovers in things those inimitable particles of dissimilarity to all other things which are the peculiar perfections of the thing in question'.[69] Of course, what distinguishes Cooper's allegorical method from the immediate modernist 'things' in Williams is the necessity of arriving at them by a laborious passage through the abstractions of metaphor which govern postmodern life. But there, at the end of a quest presided over by violence and abjection, it is: *'that thing'*, the body which has become affect, shimmering all over with those 'inimitable particles of dissimilarity'; a face, or close-up, in which affect is immanent, and fetishism vanquished. 'Now that the kid was a dork it felt totally different to be around him. Boring, even. That haunted look wasn't otherworldly after all, just some weird form of misery trying to hide in the nooks of an okay face'.[70] Dennis Cooper's latter-day romanticism achieves, miraculously, the banal sublimity of the true particular, the unassimilable, in an age of purified equivalence. Abstract space cannot hide it from the disciplined technique of literary discovery.

4

Cities within the city: Third World in the First

What space is there in a city dominated by spectacle for the necessary privacy and inward reflection of poetic production? David E. James's critique of the extant poetic forms and personalities of the city dwells on the hostility any LA poetry must adopt towards its mesmerizing nemesis, Hollywood:

> Poetry . . . of all the arts the least useful to the film industry and in its recent forms least compatible with its ethos, has, as if in recognition of the unavailability of its present forms to profitable marketing, constructed itself in antithesis to everything assumed by Hollywood.[1]

James unpacks a mixed bag of poetic styles emerging in response to this situation: the 'lumpen' poetry of Charles Bukowski; the tail-end of late modernism, represented by Clayton Eschelman and Dick Barnes; the aestheticized punk of Dennis Cooper and *Little Ceasar* magazine; and straightforward punk writing in a plethora of underground fanzines. This catalogue is no doubt interesting and useful, but what is most surprising about it is its omission of the most outstanding of all the poetic movements to emerge in the mid-1980s, so-called 'multicultural poetry'. For it is arguably with the work of black, Chicano, and Asian men and women that the future of Los Angeles poetry now stands or falls. The answer to our initial question, then, might well have something to do with the ethnicity of urban space, its parcellization into racialized zones somehow beyond the hypnotic reach of Hollywood.

Throughout the 1980s the journals *Poetry LA* and *The Southern California Anthology* served as springboards for the poetic careers of not a few of these multiethnic poets. Naomi Quiñonez, Michelle Clinton, Luis J. Rodriguez, Amy Uyematsu, Sumio Matsuda all began publishing in these pages.[2] And the progressive poetry workshop of Beyond Baroque, located in Venice and directed for many years by Dennis Cooper, was another basis for the dissemination of this poetry. It was not, however, until the American Book Award-winning *Invocation LA: Urban Multicultural Poetry* (1989), edited by Michelle T. Clinton, Sesshu Foster and Naomi Quiñonez, that the streets of African Americans, Chicanos and Asians were finally emblazoned in the city's imaginary. With this excellent collection, a 'minor' canon was created which dislodged the notion that poetry in LA was a white privilege, and fostered an appreciation of the city's dynamic, multiple cultural constitution. The editorial introduction focused on the ways in which the represented poets 'are the voices of the future, voices of an entirely new, Western but not Eurocentric, culture'.[3] And it is no accident that in the 1990s this future should have begun to be mapped out in earnest across the Los Angeles region. The reasons for this burgeoning interest in the multicultural scene are not hard to discern.

By the end of the 1980s, it was apparent that the city's dominant 'Anglo' bloc was experiencing the effects of one of the most significant about-turns in American urban history. This was the realization that Los Angeles had become 'the first multiracial and multiethnic metropolis in the continental United States – that is, where Whites are no longer the predominant majority'.[4] The 'LA 2000 Committee', formed in 1987 to gaze into a crystal ball and tell the demographic future, compared the city to New York at the turn of the last century, but preferred the metaphor of 'mosaic' over 'melting pot' to describe the cultural reality. Their conclusions were cautiously optimistic, advocating a strong sense of 'diversity', which acted as a 'positive force' in regional life, provided certain conditions were met: 'mutual respect', 'equality', and 'partnership'.[5] In 1990, the LA Festival sought to bring to the surface the possibilities for cross-cultural recognition implicit in the eighty-seven languages being spoken in classrooms across the city.

The recognition that Los Angeles had been irreversibly minoritized could not subsequently be denied. The overriding cultural task for Boosters and dissidents alike would henceforth be to map the city according to this newer logic of minoritization, rather than simply ignore or efface it. The poetry we are about to examine yields, I want to argue, a more authoritative social knowledge of the faultlines underlying the urban mosaic than the glib liberalism of the LA 2000 Committee. However, one unexpected obstacle has hindered critical appreciation of this work, an obstacle put in place by an understandable if somewhat naïve populism among cultural critics, who seem inclined to believe that more traditional verse forms can offer little when compared to the dynamic commercial forms of popular culture.

Indeed, not poetry, but rap music or hip-hop has received the widest approbation as the pre-eminent expressive medium for the ghettos and *barrios* of Los Angeles. George Lipsitz, who started this line of thinking back in 1986, argued, in Mike Davis's paraphrase, that 'Los Angeles's spectrum of ethnic rock musicians, muralists, breakdancers, and rappers constitute a kind of "organic intelligentsia" fomenting a cultural strategy for a "historical bloc of oppositional groups"'.[6] Brian Cross's popular book, *It's not About a Salary . . . Rap, Race and Resistance in Los Angeles* (1993), undertook a searching social history of the various hip-hop groups which had collectively mounted this 'cultural strategy'. Yet while there can be no question of the oppositional energy produced by this musical coalition, what emerges from the lyrics of their songs is often little more than puerile adolescent posturing and abuse. Repeatedly, the songs' ideology degenerates into a celebration of gun-toting gangsterism, an easy defiance of middle-American sensibilities, without attaining the kind of lyrical flexibility of even the East Coast group Public Enemy, let alone poetic modernism. This is an argument too complex to complete here. Let us simply (and provocatively) state that LA's hip-hop lyrics can withstand little serious literary-critical scrutiny, and that the city's multicultural poetry, precisely in its distance from the economic opportunism of the entertainment industry, is better suited to the kind of analysis we are pursuing in this book.

In this chapter I am interested in discharging the cognitive energies of local multi-ethnic poetry, in order to destabilize the myth of multicultural utopia fostered by the city apologists. In place of that myth, I will argue that the poetry of the city's most significant 'ethnic' poets posits a counter-image of urban decline, racist intolerance, and enduring traditional solidarities, which no amount of whitewashing can gainsay. Their grim urban chronotopes refuse any model of happy coexistence, so steeped are they in the harder lessons of history: of systematic discrimination, segregation, abuse, class partition, immigration and cheap, disposable labour. To represent the city of Los Angeles as a 'horizontal hell', a 'dripping carcass of dreams', or more simply as 'Siberian' (as the poets investigated below variously do) is not merely to work against the grain of local representations, it is rather to construct a new kind of 'representational space', inflected by ethnicity but above all by class. The poetry is a lesson not only in the persistence of the aesthetic in the least likely and least auspicious zones of capitalist underdevelopment, but also in the unconquered spirit of resistance and defiance alive in the city's ethnic spaces. To read it is to participate in the dissemination of an indominable counterculture, at times curt, crude and cynical, at times capable of the most delicate redemption, which builds on the banalities of everyday life in the ghettos and *barrios*, and rises to contest the very abstraction of 'Los Angeles' itself, by disclosing the real multiplicity of cities within the city.

At the core of the political map of Los Angeles' ethnic 'mosaic' of poverty is the suburb of Watts, in the South Central district, for many years the heart of the city's black, working-class community.[7] Following the wartime reindustrialization of Southern California during the 1940s, thousands of African-Americans from the Southern states immigrated to Los Angeles to man the new shipyards and aircraft plants. This led quickly to severe conditions of overcrowding, underfunding and constant police harrassment in South-Central LA, a legacy we have seen memorialized by Walter Mosley. Blocked from settling in other areas of the city by racist deed restrictions and general discrimination, black citizens were obliged to inhabit South-Central's dilapidated housing, and, when the wartime economic boom ended, faced spiralling unemployment.[8] In 1965, Watts became the scene of the most costly social conflict in domestic American history – to that point – since the Civil War. The riots of that year vividly demonstrated the degree to which the class and racial configurations of the great American cities had polarized along the white/black colour line. As middle-class whites retreated to secure and racially homogeneous communities at the urban periphery, the black working class reached intolerable limits of degradation and neglect in tax-poor ghettos. The costs of the resulting civil disobedience in Los Angeles (sparked by the police killing of an unarmed black motorist) were extremely high.[9] The 'rioting continued for six days, leaving 34 dead, over 1000 injured badly enough to require treatment, nearly 4000 arrested, and 1000 buildings damaged or destroyed, at a probable loss, in 1965 dollars, of $40 million'.[10]

The riots, however, had consequences other than destruction and loss. Their most constructive side-effect was the formation of a broad cultural and political alliance among progressive Angelenos to revitalize the culture of Watts, to provide it with an affirmative identity and from there to agitate against the discriminations of city and State. Thomas Pynchon, at that time a somewhat more visible intellectual, wrote a powerful portrait of Watts for the *New York Times* after the rebellion. In it he argued that, 'while the white culture is concerned with various forms of systematized folly – the economy of the area in fact depending on it – the black culture is stuck pretty much with basic realities like disease, like failure, violence and death, which the whites have mostly chosen – and can afford – to ignore'.

> The two cultures do not understand each other, though white people's values are displayed without let-up on black people's TV screens, and though the panoramic sense of black impoverishment is hard to miss from atop the Harbor Freeway, which so many whites must drive at least twice every working day. Somehow it occurs to very few of them to leave at the Imperial Highway, exit for a change, go east instead of west only a few blocks, and take a look at Watts. A quick look. The simplest kind of beginning. But Watts is country which lies, psychologically, uncounted miles further than most whites seem at present willing to travel.[11]

I am tempted to read this passage less as an exercise in critical sociology, than as the outline of a new urban aesthetic. In place of Joan Didion's rapturous freeway chronotope, Pynchon proposes its disruption: a break in the psychic flow and social blindness of the freeway's non-place. The white subject is urged to exit at the Imperial, 'for a change', and simply behold the vast, derelict plains of the black ghetto, as Easy Rawlins does at determinate points in his novels. This strategy is meant to jolt Watts out of the urban unconscious of white Angelenos, and so make a 'simple beginning' at inter-racial understanding. Pynchon duly notes that the distance between black and white that prohibits this encounter is not merely geographical, but, more important, psychogeographical. Pynchon's success in this article, I suggest, is not to be measured in terms of its sociological accuracy, but aesthetically in terms of how effectively his new model of urban vision contested the dominant image of the city as a space of distraction, and provoked new work.

The crux of his new urban aesthetic is a binary opposition for imagining Los Angeles: between the 'white' city as a space of distraction and mass media, and the 'black' city as reality itself:

Watts lies impacted in the heart of this white fantasy. It is, by contrast, a pocket of bitter reality. The only illusion Watts ever allowed itself was to believe for a long time in the white version of what a Negro was supposed to be. But with the Muslim and civil-rights movements that went, too.[12]

Watts, then, appears as the very *topos* of underprivileged 'reality', the space, perhaps, of a new Naturalism with which to confront the dominant white culture of an abstract and 'placeless' space. This can be figured in the following way:

+	−
Watts ————————	White LA
(the Real)	(fantasy/the simulacrum)

Pynchon's last nod of the head at black nationalism and Civil Rights reminds us that this new aesthetic of the 'ghetto-as-the-real' coincided with a new black political pride and militancy whose spatial springboard (outside the South) was precisely the ghettos in question. If there was a social group available to exploit the possibilities of the new aesthetic, it was black artists and poets themselves, following the lead of the likes of Amiri Baraka on the East Coast. As Manuel Castells has put it: 'ghettos were the physical basis of black revolt . . . [but] they were also their social basis: the black community emerged as a collective actor on the basis of the "space of freedom" provided by the ghetto . . . The ghetto became a city within the city, where alternative rules of an alternative society were to emerge'.[13] Mike Davis writes that, 'Most importantly, the [1965] Rebellion inspired unity and élan in South-Central Los Angeles, giving birth to a local version of the Black Arts Movement across a full spectrum of practices from Tapscott's Arkestra to the rap poetry of the Watts Prophets. Bernard Jackson and J. Alfred Cannon founded the Inter-City Cultural Center in 1966 which grew into a flourishing theater center with its own press and school. Wanda Coleman, Kamau Daaood, Quincy Troupe, K. Curtis Lyle, Emory Evans, and Ojenke established a distinctive Watts idiom in fiction and poetry'.[14] The 'distinctive' idiom (and chronotope) of this group might well be tracked in the massive corpus of the indefatigable Wanda Coleman.

Coleman herself bridles at Davis's cursory survey, feeling as she does that the male poets with whom she is grouped offered her, as a black woman, less solidarity than might have been welcomed.[15] Indeed, the poetic inspiration she more frequently cites is the rump of the original Beat movement on the West Coast: Bob Kaufman,

Clayton Eschelman, and Charles 'Hank' Bukowski. Nevertheless, she repeatedly affirms the importance for her as an artist of the August 1965 uprising, and recapitulates in her verse the aesthetic outlined by Pynchon's article: white LA as 'strange' and unreal; Watts as the real. Much of Coleman's published work, which spans the years 1968 to 2000, is an embittered reflection on the fate of the racial pride and political intelligence brought into being by collective action in the streets of Watts. Dominated by male intellectuals and activists, decimated by the FBI and other security forces, and able to sustain what she sees as only a minimal and ephemeral cultural identity, Black Power represents for Coleman the last stand of a black militancy riven by internal contradictions and doomed from the outset by an intransigent state apparatus. Its memory is as inspiring as it is disheartening for her. As she writes to the ghost of the late black counter-cultural organizer in LA, Hakim A. Jamal: 'I have kept The Faith, Jamal, but it hasn't kept me'.[16]

In place of the political 'Faith', verse has been the arena for Coleman's ongoing struggle against dominant models of identity. As she says, 'poetry has become my last stand, more or less'. Yet her poetic practice has been as fractured and occasionally desperate as the straightforward politics from which it departs. Tony Magistrale, Coleman's best critic, elucidates her aesthetic as a fatalistic urban realism, consequent upon her marginalized social situation. 'The subjects of Wanda Coleman's poetry are black oppression, female persecution, and the inequitable class structure of contemporary America. Pared of romantic illusions and academic pretensions, her poems are honest and uncompromising commentaries about those who have been excluded from the American Dream'.[17] More consciously than perhaps any other American writer, Coleman occupies a political corner beset by multiple discriminations.

> My poverty level steadily climbs. I pay blood for everything. Open my pages and read my bleed: the essence of racism is survival; the primary mechanism, economics. The power to have is the power to do. I, black worker 'womon' poet ange-lena, disadvantaged first by my skin, second by class, third by sex, fourth by craft (the MSS and juvenilia of pitiably poor poets pull down greater pissbah posthumously), fifth by regionality.[18]

What we shall be interested in determining is what this victimized and emphatically 'minor' subject-position – both enforced upon

Coleman and adopted by her – has produced in the way of literary chronotopes.

As suggested, her poetry's consistent ground note has been the presentation of Watts everyday life as *reality*:

> here are the streets
> real as real as real
> ugly
> do you see motherfucker
> do you see the ripe con
> do you see the zombies in the field
> they're after you
> it took 20 years for that nightmare to come true
> adventuress
> adventuress
> bitch, get it thru your head
> batman is a cartoon and
> you cannot fly   ('Anticipating Murder'[19])

In the line 'real as real as real', which echoes but inverts Gertrude Stein, the simile has nowhere to go but back to its beginning, circling around its own premise with a desperation provoked by the powers of local hyperreality. Similarly, 'ugliness', a familiar trope of literary and pictorial Naturalism, receives a blankly nominal incarnation, since to deck it out in images would be to fall back into the logic of the simulacrum. As if this blunt verbal insistence were not enough, the next line addresses us with the casual obscenity of 'motherfucker', a linguistic slice of the 'reality' already performatively adduced; we are requested to look upon and 'see' these streets, the poem posing as the transparent screen to a world that is presumably otherwise kept from our view. Yet the addressee is then unmistakably interpellated as a black woman who dares to walk the streets of the ghetto. She desires 'adventure', to roam and seek excitement and pleasure, but the poetic voice irresistibly calls her back to 'reality', away from Culture Industry-induced fantasies of 'batman' and flight. Unsurprisingly, the 'you / adventuress / bitch' of these lines reverts in the next stanza to an uncapitalized 'i', telescoping speaker and addressee into the same lower-case, minoritized subject.

The ephemeral and dismissive reference to 'batman' nevertheless opens an alternative space to the two-dimensional reality of the ghetto, one which we will come to see as symptomatic. There is a struggle, throughout Coleman's work, between the repetitive, dominated spatial practices of everyday life in the ghetto, and evanescent strands of utopia which occasionally take root and wither in the narrow interstices of that life. These glimpses constitute one aspect of what we will call Coleman's characteristic 'representational space', her ability to uphold some degree of sensuous optimism even in the face of the bleak everyday of postmodern urbanism. The other aspects of her representational space, her dual ethnicity, and the female body, will be returned to shortly. In the following poem about public transport in Los Angeles (which only the poor use), note how Coleman's redemptive eye endows the other passengers with a 'lyrical consciousness' otherwise denied them:

RETURNED TO THE POPULATION
the narcomic rhythm of the crosstown bus
shakes me into a trance
as the sizzling avenues of hollywood
slip past. i am lulled into the lyrical consciousness
of bodies – size, skin color, cuts of hair
faces malignant or benign
the way flesh runs to fable in spacey eyes of the wise
the way we are summoned to earth's core
i am free at last to feel without tremor. to study
scientifically the shape of thangs to cum[20]

The 'narcomic rhythm' and 'sizzling avenues' of the bus are utilized in a very particular way by the entranced lyrical subject. Against the imperatives of abstract space, the subject appropriates her everyday transfixion for a progressive hope. The atomized commuters on board the bus fuse under her gaze into a larger organism, a soup of bodies whose ethnic and stylistic differences speak no longer of social divisions, but of ultimate unity. It is the fantastic literary mediation of 'fable' and the 'earth's core' – the stuff of adolescent Romance and science fiction – which foments the final transition from banal reality to the subject's 'free' imagination and affect. Finally, the 'shape of thangs to cum' diverts H. G. Wells through a sexualized black urban register which instantly recasts that sanitized European vision of the future in an American stew of races and individuals.

The transient swerve of the everyday through a poetic space of sensuous redemption is characteristic of Coleman's technique, which seems incapable of inscribing the numbing routine of quotidian ghetto-dwelling without also notching up signs of its transcendence. The everyday flattens out into an abstract grid of determination and unfreedom ('this horizontal hell without god / endless / endless'[21]); yet the sensitivity of the poet is impressed with odd, delicate moments of natural excess and of the body's pleasure within the sterile expanses of urbanism. The verse is an attempt, then, to improvise a chronotope bridging two interpenetrating but contradictory spaces. On the one hand, it is a sober preparation for the shocks of a calculated and exploitative social space without room for individuality ('i could do with more space'[22]). On the other, it is an instruction-manual in the tactics of spatial appropriation for the body, even in extremes of impoverishment and closure.

> in the bathroom
> i rinse away illusions, brush my teeth and
> unbraid my hair
> there're the children to wake
> breakfast to conjure
> the job
> the day laid out before me
> the cold corpse of an endless grind
> so this is it, i say to the enigma in the mirror
> this is your lot/assignment/relegation
> this is your city
>
> i find my way to the picture window
> my eyes capture the purple reach of hollywood's hills
> the gold eye of sun mounting the east
> the gray anguished arms of avenue
>
> i will never leave here   ('Prisoner of Los Angeles [2]'[23])

The ghetto still functions as the imprisoning *real* (the persona 'rinses away illusions' in the bathroom), and the vast city beyond it a phantasmatic, deathly virtuality. Meanwhile, a repetition of the lowercase 'i' demands attention as the residue of subjectivity itself in this monstrous urban space. It is a graphic insigne of the belittlement of the subject wrought by the five-fold process of marginalization already described. Finally, the fourth term of Nature enters the representational fray as a 'sublime' exterior (framed by the 'picture window'), through which the subject detours each morning to attain some degree of organic integrity, so as not to succumb to the city as fate. The eye's capture of purple hills and the golden dawn counterpoints the body's agonized capitulation to an impersonal and thankless daily discipline, metaphorized here into the cadaverous embrace of death.

Nor is Nature the only representational space through which the subject is diverted in Coleman's verse to reclaim it from a twodimensional determinism. She also seeks to reappropriate urban space through the figure of female sexuality. In her best-known poem, Coleman confronts the reader, immediately, with a figuration of Watts as a black woman's genitalia.

> WHERE I LIVE
> at the lip of a big black vagina
> birthing nappy headed pickaninnies every hour on the hour
> and soul radio blasting into mindwindow
> bullets and blood
> see that helicopter up there? like
> god's eye looking down on his children
> barsandbarsandbarsandbarsandbars[24]

The startling opening figure of the ghetto-as-vagina enters into opposition with the familiar concluding trope of this section: namely, the city-as-prison, as seen from above by the panoptic eye of the Los Angeles Police Department. The white, administrative, patriarchal view from above meets the black, corporeal, maternal yield from below – mediated by the buckling 'mindwindow' of the minoritized urban subject, the 'i'. This complex of figures coheres into a distinctive urban chronotope that belongs peculiarly to Wanda Coleman. In it, regenerative time is seized for the ghetto, and lifeless space relegated to the superintendent eye of Authority.

In the poem's final movement, however, the opening section is reprised and recast to present a somewhat different personification of the ghetto-Mother.

> where i live
> at the lip of a big black vagina
> birthing nappy headed pickaninnies every hour on the hour
> the county is her pimp and she can turn a trick
> swifter than any bitch ever graced this earth
> she's the baddest piece of ass on the west coast
> named black los angeles

The difference is critical. It transforms what might otherwise have been an ambivalently political vagina-ghetto into a calculating and cynical one. Like everything else in LA, this monstrous whore of Watts is hyperbolically constructed, the swiftest and 'baddest' of her kind. Her body is the acquiescent object of an inhuman exploitation at the hands of a hitherto unmentioned agent, 'the county'. Coleman's resilient pessimism seems to contradict, in these final lines, the grotesque feminist realism proclaimed in the poem's opening movement. Ambivalence goes to the root of her chronotope. Coleman seems uncertain whether to celebrate the ghetto as mother, or repudiate her for collusion with the powers that rape and pimp her.

In a later poem, the note of despair is taken up on a bitter, epic scale, and modulates into the rhetoric of mourning. Note how in the following lines the figure of Watts-as-vagina is revisited, but in an explicitly funereal and emotionally flattened register.

> hear now this soft spoken black woman born of this cobalt
>   blue world
>   mourns silent mourns deep
> rides her sepulcher on wheels alone, for the pleasure clock of
>   romance
>   has been bashed in
> and unmercifully destroyed in the deep eternal grind of
>   machines
>   where her stinking meat
> rots wrecked at society's bottom, blessed by cool denimed
>   crew-cut
>   saints who cruise calmly
> in final rites of hungry avenue flesh and blood hunters
>
> yes. los angeles cement cunt where die all my beautiful men
>   quiet in their level beds
> of neon and holly wood. yes. and i too die here
>   give birth to babies/dreams
> this tall black child of november drives shrouded in slacks of
>   fad
>   my kinky crown tangled
> in twisted combs of glass and granite in the grasping hands of
>   5 p.m. traffic   ('Los Angeles Born and Buried'[25])

It is the *quietness* of the 'beautiful [black] men' as they go gently into the dark night of Los Angeles's 'cement cunt' that is especially disturbing here. The absence of any resistance to this glacial reification echoes in those oblique references to the black Holocaust of the Middle Passage: the speaking voice's 'stinking meat' at the bottom of society's flesh-trading vessel. This code of the Middle Passage, elsewhere expanded into a virtual metaphysic (she calls it 'African Sleeping Sickness'), serves Coleman as a properly ethnic 'representational space', a sacred text of apocalypse through which African-American history might be illuminated. Yet all of this emerges, as it were, from the rear-view mirror of a car at rush-hour, whose driver is conversant both with the physical codes of the alienated city – neon, glass and granite – and the representational codes of her history, and cannot control the fusion of the two chronotopes as they create spectacular interference patterns across her imaginary lens. 'Seeing' the city amounts for Coleman to this bifurcated mode of spatial apprehension: at once quotidian, banal and oppressive; and fantastic, epic and transgressive.

Coleman repeatedly invents allegorical mechanisms for realizing this spatial dualism in controlled metaphorical performances such as the poem 'Gonwandaland', which appropriates LA in a double movement of identification: her body with the land beneath and 'before' the city, and the land itself with the indigenous peoples who are also part of Coleman's ethnic constitution (she is ethnically both African American and Amerindian). The strength of the poem consists in its lyrical evocation of a regional space unspoiled by exploitative economics, which is also the imaginary space of her own being, that is 'lost here' in a measureless darkness (Los Angeles):

> *fortune cookie say: there will always be*
> *delicious mysteries in your life*
> firmness is kinky illusion. no stomping ground/the marriage
> of fire and water tar pits deserts earthquakes
> emotional swamps of mood. lakes of molten love. a sky of cries
> gale winds. night rains. shifting auroras of pain
> floes of anger. lusty flora, greedy fauna
> a multiplicity of reds browns blacks
> oases of crystaline thought peopled by ghosts. the ending
> forever beginning. the yawn of shadow
> struggling to burst into light
> lost here[26]

If Gondwanaland is the hypothetical supercontinent from which the various continents split off during the Jurassic Period, then 'Gonwandaland' is the vanished Southern Californian region inhabited by indigenous tribes before the invasions of Spaniards, Mexicans and Anglos devastated their land and culture, enslaved them and finally all but eradicated them. It is that region become her own body, her own affective substructure. Haunted by the ghosts of a 'multiplicity of reds browns blacks', the mythical space of her body resounds with their ethnic pastoral prehistory, and gives onto a Nature as yet undominated by instrumental reason. What this reacts against is the seamless monstrosity of late capitalist life for the disadvantaged, where nothing prospers that is gentle or good:

> *there's nothing delicate here. delicate*
> *things do not survive. they get beaten up/raped/shot/*
> *runover/knifed/poisoned or pushed into suicide*
> *they harden, become brittle, or bend*
> *baked under sun of years, adobe will not*
> *yield to crop, but brick to build –*
> *where the farmer fails, the architect prospers: a city*

(one day we will plow you under and dance the ritual of
    your passing)   ('Flight of the California Condor'[27])

Against the lyricism of her representational space abuts this crude,
malignant urban vision, which might properly be assimilable to the
tradition of satire, extending from Juvenal through Voltaire, Swift,
Hogarth, Brecht and George Grosz to Coleman's own enumeration
of the various reified urban types:

> these streets are lean, familiar faces in bitter forms that
> dot doorways, cluster at corners, weave along the walk. i know
> the pimp, the pootbutt, the whore, the worker, the blind, the
> cowboy, the ditty-bop, the gangster, the hype, the hustler, the
> young whites who visit the old whites who couldn't make
>   the flight
> exiled, the ghetto becomes home
> the adjective bank is empty
> the seer's tongue ensconces in
> a coat of cryptic truths
> her fingers/talons wet with
> blood of capture
> having plucked him from
> the desert's floor

mother of angels let me burn forever in the oven of your love

Separated by virtue of her reflexivity from the mill of the everyday,
the poet imagines herself as the endangered local species of condor,
taking a last, desperate flight above an urban 'desert' that has
destroyed its food-supply ('adjectives'). Sinking into inevitable extinction, she claims a final capture – a lover who has abandoned her
– to squeeze from his entrails blood to fill her quill this last time. Yet
the ghetto, a place of exile, for all its manifold alienations, has
become 'home', and the condor's dying wish is to be consumed in
the fire of its embrace. No doubt, some dim trace of the phoenix
myth subsists in this anguished, italicized plea; but the 'oven' door
of the ghetto swings balefully shut.

One of the ironies of Coleman's development is that, despite her
own prediction ('i will never leave here'), she has indeed moved
away from Watts, to a more affluent middle-class black community,
thus representing a wider mobility of the black middle-class in the
late-1980s, just as wide-scale factory closures and urban underinvest-
ment were bringing South-Central to the brink of yet another
rebellion. The influence of this personal history on her recent work
has been to augment her representations of Watts with sinister
intimations of apocalypse. The longer poem, 'Region of Deserts',

presents the return journey of a now dislocated Coleman (she calls
herself a 'haint') to her utterly blighted homeland, succumbing to the
semi-arid ecology it lies above.

> everywhere shards of glass
> angry fruitless shatterings of
> bottles and barred store windows
>
> protest
> the rusted scarecrow of sign designating store hours
> walls of blistered cracked peeling stucco
> twisted rust red steel corpses of
> abandoned autos
>
> mexico reclaims this desolation[28]

There is no human life left anymore. The decaying and broken
objects of a grotesquely unequal capitalism litter the ground with
trash, trash which is read as a cryptic 'protest' against the very
conditions it designates. Julian Stallabrass writes that the everyday
rubbish of major cities 'reveals the broken utopian promise of the
commodity.'[29]

> Trash, breaking with the false unity of the consumer object,
> reveals its allegorical potential by unmasking the symbolic
> pose of the commodity as a sham. Torn, dirtied or broken,
> thrown into combination with other fragmentary objects, while
> it remains itself, it becomes a broken shell, its meaning reaching
> out to its partners in a forlorn but telling narrative.[30]

Coleman's poetic treatment of Watts' trash segues into a narrative
of Mexican reclamation, as the 'American Dream' of small business,
home and automobile blasts apart into shards on the pavement. She
continues:

> where my shattered heart pines
> home to liquor stores and churches on every corner
> > to dark red and gold wall-papered holes
> > of refuge
> > to stark welcoming envelopes of
> > food stamps and government stipends
> > to mom and pop stores with their counters of
> > stinking stale meat and overripe fruit
> > to black and white armored knights
> > slaying for want of dragons
>
> home to boarded up remnants of memory
> to find them broken into/violated[31]

Memory, the vital repository of representational space and a
feeling for time, has been raped by the inexorable power of

abstract space to dominate life, flatten it to the 'everyday', the grim predictability of every element of social being arranged in order, 'on every corner'. The concept of home is itself stripped from the subject in a spatial process of alienation. Between her and home there is now an irreversible rupture; returning to the place she had once loved despite herself, she sees it for what it is, a discarded husk of community, a cluster of stereotypes and refuse from which even the illusion of the real has now departed.

Indeed, with this poem the neo-Naturalist chronotope that had structured Coleman's earlier work collapses under the weight of detritus spewed up by the real's explosion. These fragments of urban documentation no longer fuse into a critical mass of local identity. The space of which they speak is no longer 'Watts', but something on an infinitely larger scale. In a word, this shattered 'Watts' is now allegorical of a properly global phenomenon, what has variously been described as the 'Third World in the First', the 'Brazillianization' of all major cities, and the 'underdevelopment' of determinate zones within spaces of urban overdevelopment.[32] It is what Edward Soja would cite as evidence of the repolarization of the 'World City'; the impact of a global economy on backward spaces like Watts being their removal from the sphere of investment and development, their decline into slums, in a pattern that reaches around the world. It is no longer possible simply to say 'here are the streets/real as real as real', for something has prevented their recognition. That something is the fully-fledged globalization of capital, for which nothing is any longer unique or immediate. The blighted ghetto street-scene Coleman revisits now stretches over a global canvas, over the streets of Los Angeles, Mexico City, New York, London, Karachi, Berlin, *ad infinitum*, as consumer society transforms more and more of the world's surface into polarized spaces of wealth and poverty, power and powerlessness. The final apocalypse is registered as an explosion of the subject herself in the face of this erasure of the 'present', the *hic et nunc* of the real Watts that once sustained her:

> it looks worse every time i come here it looks worse
> all but closed down
> all the biz-zi-nesses goin' out of business
> all the new shine gone
> nothin' left but rust, dust
> and the cracked bones of a dream

in the eye of sun
i burst into particles of pain
scatter everywhere across the disappearing present
look close

the memory of my shadow can be found
clinging to bleached slum walls

i am a haint here

settled in the sand of its past
my skull grins[33]

This belated *memento mori* grinning up from the sand of an imponderable natural history is all that is left of affective or representational space after the atomization of the lyrical subject. The 'disappearing present' into which this subject has been scattered, in radiating 'particles of pain', retains a spatial form: the 'bleached slum walls' which outlive the transient businesses and families they once housed. The new social space bounded by these petrified walls is the netherside of postmodernity: a global ghetto, whose vista exceeds even the wildest imaginings of poetry. It is not so much, then, that Mexico has reclaimed this desolation, as that the desolation itself is subsuming Mexico, parts of America, and much of the rest of the world.

So it is that Coleman's earlier 'doubled' chronotopes, everyday and fantastic at once, have yielded in the later work to a properly allegorical map of postmodern space itself: not in its glossier abstract forms, but in its destructive and blighting abstraction. Built space here gives way, in its spectral afterlife, to the dark side of abstraction's gleaming infinitudes: to a dark trench of slums, disease, trash, and a very different kind of emptiness from that explored by Bret Easton Ellis. Yet the demise of representational space is no less stark and debilitating for Coleman's poetic practice than it was for Ellis as a novelist. It remains to be seen where she can go from here, from this confrontation with Watts as the 'not-real', if I can put it that way; for this recognition, that her own place has been deracinated by malignant new processes of spatial standardization, affects not only Coleman's habitual *penchant* for Naturalism, but equally her habit of resorting to ethnic historicity and Nature as spaces of resistance. The new abstractions of the Third-World-in-the-First present representational challenges she has yet to meet.

There is, however, another sense in which Mexico is 'reclaiming' the Los Angeles suburb of Watts. It will be recalled that between 1822 and 1848, Mexico had possession over the entire region of *Califas*, before the Mexican-American war (and a few million dollars) handed the territory to the American victor. Since 1848, the anomalous position of Mexican-Americans, or Chicanos, in Southern California society has greatly helped to define its character and culture. At once 'native', since they preceded the *gringo* settlers by many years, and outside the dominant bloc due to prevailing ethnic and linguistic chauvinism, Chicanos have never ceased to immigrate (legally and otherwise) to a land that was once their own, but which now seeks violently to exclude and marginalize them.

Zena Pearlstone suggests that in their settlement, Chicanos have by and large resisted integration into the culture of their conqueror,[34] using urban *barrios* as protective spaces of ethnic solidarity. Theirs has been both a defiantly traditionalist and an innovative *bricoleur* culture, fusing ancient Mayan iconography, Mexican murals and ballads, Latin rhythms, and the automobile fetishism of America into a distinctive assertion of identity amid the dizzying flux of late capitalist American life. In Los Angeles, the second largest Mexican city in the world, Chicanos have tended, since the 1920s, to settle and live in Boyle Heights and the massive *barrio* of East Los Angeles. Generations of Chicanos have lived in these ethnically partitioned spaces, where a remarkable degree of civic cohesion and dignity has accordingly been won. This reached its defining moment in the wide-scale Chicano Moratorium Against the War (1970), to protest the disproportionate number of Hispanic casualties during America's military intervention in Vietnam. As Chicano identity was being fashioned across the Southwestern states (*Aztlán*) from the mid-1960s onwards, one of its principal sites of articulation was East Los Angeles.

The pattern of settlement has not remained stable, however, and during the heaviest waves of immigration from south of the border in the 1980s ('the [Hispanic] population grew by 22 per cent between 1980 and 1985',[35] and by 62 per cent over the 1980s as a whole), the *barrio* spilled over into neighbouring suburbs. We have mentioned that in this period there was a significant rate of black exodus from Watts as the inequities and racism of the place became too much for sections of the black middle class to bear. The gap was largely filled by Mexicans, who had been there from the first but now began to assume fuller occupation. This recomposition of hitherto relatively unfluctuating ethnic residence patterns has had a decisive effect on the economy and politics of the city, and according to some conservative analysts was a precondition for the uprising of 1992.[36] But the specific transformation of Watts has had ramifications of a different kind as well, most importantly for us, at the level of its literary representation.

Luis J. Rodriguez's poem, 'Watts Bleeds', envisages a ghetto distinct from Coleman's portraits.

> Watts bleeds
> leaving stained reminders
> on dusty sidewalks.
>
> Here where I strut alone
> as glass lies broken at my feet
> and a blanket of darkness is slung
> across the wooden shacks
> of nuestra colonia.
>
> Watts bleeds
> dripping from carcasses of dreams:
> Where despair
> is old people
> sitting on torn patio sofas
> with empty eyes
> and children running down alleys
> with big sticks.
>
> Watts bleeds
> on vacant lots
> and burned-out buildings –
> temples desolated by a people's rage.
>
> Where fear is a deep river.
> Where hate is an overgrown weed.[37]

In the first place, the rhetoric of this presentation is noticeably more restrained than Coleman's, relying less on exorbitant metaphor and obscenity than a consistent image (blood), and balanced periods. As with Coleman, the ghetto is corporealized, only in Rodriguez's verse the analogy is sustained as a meditative litany, rather than invoked as a provocative gesture. The desolate object-world of Watts appears in snatches: the broken glass, dusty sidewalks, empty eyes, wooden shacks, torn patio sofas, vacant lots and burned-out buildings. What unites them as a single vision is the prevailing Catholic symbol of blood, which leaks from all of these objects, or stains them with the crimson residue of oppression. Interspersed throughout this constellation of everyday objects is an understated poetic space which invests it with concretized abstractions: 'despair is', 'fear is', 'hate is'. The last two of these abstractions are fleshed out in a natural representational space: the deep river subterraneously connecting a frightened populace, and the weed of animosity spreading over the city's surface. In the poem's concluding, rhapsodic prosopopoeia, Watts itself is enjoined to partake of the 'natural' representational space and so dismantle the concrete second nature stamped upon it from above.

> Oh bloom, you trampled flower!
> Come alive as once
> you tried to do from the ashes.
>
> Watts, bleeding and angry,
> you will be free.

The symbol of a bleeding flower is intended to prepare the reader's imagination for an eventual salvation of derelict urban space, through the concerted agency of the oppressed of the ghetto. Watts's incendiary past of rebellion is carried over into the future in what turns out to be a veritable prophecy of the events of May, 1992. All that is wrong with the prediction is its outcome, of course, since the 'ashes' of 1992 have smothered all attempts at civic rebirth. Memories of the urban renewal projects of 1966 sour in the memory, and Rodriguez's optimism looks childish alongside Wanda Coleman's searing pessimism.

Rodriguez's biographical note in his first published collection of poetry, *Poems Across the Pavement* (1989), usefully introduces the preoccupying concerns of his verse:

> Luis J. Rodriguez was born in El Paso, Texas in 1954, the son of Mexican immigrants. Two years later, his family settled in the Watts community of Los Angeles. Luis' teenage years were often spent in the streets of an east Los Angeles County *barrio*. He later worked several years as a blast furnace operator, carpenter, truck driver, steel worker and chemical refinery mechanic.[38]

What remains to be added to this narrative is that his poetry, so much of it concerned with Los Angeles, has been written in Chicago, a fact which is of critical importance in understanding its characteristic sense of distance and nostalgia for a childhood spent in dissipation and gang warfare – as his popular published memoir, *La Vida Loca*, attests.[39] This distance accounts for Rodriguez's presentation of the great *barrio* of East LA as a composite of past and present tenses.

> THE VILLAGE
> Aliso village. East LA
> Welfare/unemployment/teenposts.
> Brown/black villagers
> wade in a sea of stucco green

imitating cool, as 14-year-old
girls, with babies by their feet,
sling oldies from darkened porches,
here, across the LA River,

concrete border
of scrawled walls,
railroad tracks, and sweatshops,
here, where we remade revolution

in our images. Here,
where at 18 years old and dying,
I asked her to marry me.

I carry the village in tattoos
across my arms.[40]

The final image of the village written on the body transgresses the border between metaphor and metonymy; the village is not simply referred to or connoted by the indelible tattoos, but incarnated there upon his arms. Such hyperbole is surely a symptom of the distance it strives to master, since it is only in *unheimlich* Chicago that the body can become so pregnant with an urban space half a continent away. The greater the geographical distance from *el barrio*, the heavier and more potent each sign becomes with its robust and masculine essence. Meanwhile, the snapshot impressionism of the previous stanzas is reminiscent of Coleman's more satirical surveys of a comparable space; but, again, the symbolic forces itself to the foreground in a very different ethnic gesture. So that the 'concrete river' suggests itself as more than a mere content within the formal catalogue of everyday features. Indeed, what could be more semiotically loaded than a river that has become a wall, a massive 'concrete border / of scrawled walls' against which the *barrio* huddles and comes into being as such? This artificial and denaturalized river, devoid of any mud banks, vegetation or aquatic life, is Rodriguez's preferred symbol for the crushing forces of abstraction and modernization on 'representational space' *per se*, and the ethnic identity of Mexican Americans in particular.

The river, we understand from his poem 'The Concrete River', was the liminal plateau where the adolescent Rodriguez and friends would repair to inhale paint fumes and flee the fatality of *barrio* life. Before it gives way to a yawning suicidal abyss, a drug-stimulated space of the imaginary is prised open in the poem's concrete borderland:

This river, this concrete river,
Becomes a steaming, bubbling
Snake of water, pouring over
Nightmares of wakefulness;
Pouring out a rush of birds;
A flow of clear liquid
On a cloudless day.
Not like the black oil stains we live in,
Not like the factory air engulfing us;
Not this plastic death in a can.[41]

The entombed water, birds and measureless blue sky of an originary natural experience seep back into the intoxicated body. His sensuous portals swinging wide in the breeze of a narcotic rush, the young Rodriguez revisits the land of his ancestors, which is cast into relief as the negative of the existent, 'not like' the suffocating and poisonous air of *el barrio*. It is not, of course, the adolescent Rodriguez who feels this, but the mature poet looking back on that experience in the 'profane illumination' of distance, who produces it as such. Walter Benjamin invented this phrase to account for the revolutionary impact of Surrealist writing;[42] not that there is anything too 'surreal' about the liberated sensorium of Rodriguez here, but the narcotic emancipation of urban space from its imprisoning everyday forms is an analogous one.

The whole episode takes place in an indeterminate zone, a place that Michel Foucault would have called a 'heterotopia'.

> There are . . . probably in every culture, in every civilization, real places – places that do exist and that are formed in the very founding of a society – which are something like counter-sites, a kind of effectively enacted utopia in which the real sites, all the other real sites that can be found within the culture, are simultaneously represented, contested, and inverted. Places of this kind are outside of all places, even though it may be possible to indicate their location in reality. Because these places are absolutely different from all the sites that they reflect and speak about, I shall call them, by way of contrast to utopias, heterotopias.[43]

The LA river is surely such a place, at once between the *barrio* and Anglo Los Angeles, between culture and nature, and yet at the same time possessing its own secretive and volatile topography. The great concrete slabs entombing a once meandering river also lay the ground for that river's free use in ethnic reverie and poetic redemption.

Memory is the privileged phenomenological category of Rodriguez's verse. It straddles not only the distance between Chicago and Los Angeles, but that between Mexico and America itself. In another poem, 'Jesus Saves', the poetic persona willfully misreads a poster bearing those words as a man's name. 'He' thereby becomes an object of class and ethnic envy.

> I wish I were that guy . . .
> then I wouldn't be
> this chocked-faced pirate on city
> seas, this starved acrobat of the alcoves
> loitering against splintered doors.
> Then I wouldn't be this aberration
> who once had a home, made of stone even,
> and a woman to call wife.
> In the old country,
> I worked since I was seven!
> I knew the meaning
> of the sun's behest
> for pores to weep.
> But now such toil is allowed
> to rot like too many berries on a bush.
> . . .
> But here I am a grieving poet,
> a scavenger of useless literature;
> they mean nothing in this place . . .
> my metaphoric manner,
> the spectacle of my viscous verse
> nothing!
> I am but a shadow on the sidewalk,
> a spot of soot on a block wall;
> a roll of dice tossed across
> a collapsing hallway in a downtown
> SRO hotel.[44]

The lived antithesis between a traditional Latin American economy south of the border, its peasant agriculture and oral culture, and the vacuum of late capitalism's economy and culture for the dispossessed, is aesthetically realized in this verse as a formal asymmetry. 'Here' in Los Angeles, the ethnic worker has his uselessness and parasitism branded upon his body: 'chocked-faced pirate' 'starved acrobat' 'aberration' 'scavenger' 'shadow' 'spot of soot'. Much like late-Coleman's atomized subject, Rodriguez figures his immigrant peasant persona as an effacement within the urban grid.

The greatest lack felt by the Mexican immigrant, a lack which afflicts his body and reduces it to insect-like leanness, is that of work. 'In the old country', work is a behest of nature itself, a right as inalienable as heat from the sun; while in post-industrial America, the 'natural' fruits of toil rot on the branches of overconsumption, racism, an insuperable class structure, and the production of poverty. Similarly, the cultural labour of the poet is meaningless in post-industrial LA, where metaphor has no soil and verse no root structure. Memory alone can retain the knowledge of another culture, another economy which, no matter how unequal and divided, at least respects the meaning and dignity of both agricultural and cultural work. The poem is the space of this encounter between the memory of work, home and wife, and the presence of nothingness, between two irreconcilable chronotopes whose contradiction is lived by the Mexican immigrant.

Memory also defamiliarizes the hopeless present of post-industrial urban space by memorializing the advanced industry it displaces. The poet can speak as the unofficial mourner over the grave of this industry and the ethnic working-class communities it once supported:

> Bethlehem Steel's
> shift-turn whistles
> do not blast out
> in Maywood anymore.
>
> Mill workers no longer congregate
> at Slauson Avenue bars
> on pay day.
>
> Bethlehem's soaking pits
> are frigid now . . .   ('Bethlehem No More'[45])

Each sentence constructs a pivot between industrial past and post-industrial present, in a consistent movement of denial and negation. The name Bethlehem (previously one of the great employers in the region) itself acquires a quasi-mythical stature through repetition in the poem, drawing on its Biblical heritage to cast irony on its present incarnation as a tomb of dead labour. Issuing from this carefully measured syntax is the controlled force of elegy, which turns everything it touches into an occasion for affective recovery of the thing lost. Inevitably we will ourselves back to a moment untouched by contemporary blight. Yet with calm insistence, the verse confirms the worst:

> But Bethlehem you are no more.
> We have made you rich;
> rich enough to take our toil
> and invest it elsewhere.

Rich enough
to make us poor again.

In this *finalé*, the proper noun 'Bethlehem' is dialogized and reattrib-
uted, not to the particular mill over which it stood, but to the
multinational corporation it denotes. The second person address
accuses this now eerily insubstantial entity of the deepest and
commonest of 'postmodern' economic betrayals: to have fed on a
given labour pool only so long as another, cheaper pool could not be
safely exploited, and then to have ditched the former without
ceremony. This briefest of poetic notes to the whole, vast process of
deindustrialization in the First World achieves, through its brevity,
the shock of a cognitive jolt. The cognitive map of Los Angeles'
'internationalization' of space begins here, with this elegy for lost
industry, lost jobs, and lost hope.

Nor has Rodriguez flinched from exploring the worst aspects of
the social space produced by deindustrialization. Homelessness has
rarely known the kind of poetic attention given it by Rodriguez in
his poem, 'A Harvest of Eyes'. Seeking neither to justify the unjustifi-
able, nor ennoble the human beings degraded by it, Rodriguez
instead finds a way of constructing a chronotope of homelessness:

A street finds its song in the murmur
of a woman's heart as she lies on the sidewalk.
Conversations in concrete promise nothing.
The rustling of vines along an unkept lawn
is a man finding a place to sleep.[46]

We will note that this homeless space assumes an aural rather than
visual character. The absence of work and of shelter results in a
withering away of the principal organ of postmodern culture, the
eye, and a recuperation of the sensuous ear. The street no longer has
a prospect, but a song, whose vocal organs are the coronary muscles
of a destitute woman. Similarly, the man searching for a resting place
manifests himself synecdochally through a rustle of vines, and not
the demeaning spectacle of a shambling lumpenproletarian. Strangely, this lateral shift of the poem's sensual organ alters the quality of
time in this space; time assumes the dignity of a human duration, an
abiding and a dwelling, rather than the flashy and instantaneous
temporality of postmodern vision.

Rodriguez, like Coleman before him, follows a predictable path
from the discovery and articulation of ethnic representational spaces
(in his case, Mexico, Catholicism, the sun and sky, rivers, work
songs), through the distorting and confining structures of spatial

practice in the *barrio* (listless waiting, unemployment, violence, ramshackle housing, homelessness, drugs), to a critique of late capitalism itself, its determinate production of 'underdevelopment' within and around the spaces of inordinate wealth. Yet unlike Coleman, he has at his disposal a much more centred and confident sense of self, which is a product of his gender and distinct ethnicity. Thus, the oft-repeated 'I' of these poems, while from time to time it walks amongst the living dead, retains an autonomous and incontestable identity, buttressed by tattoos, the Church, cars, the desire of women, and an assumed homosociality. It is the strong residue of Hispanic modernism in Rodriguez's verse, a residue with a history. For it was not until the 1960s that Chicano literature emerged as such, having until that time lived a fugitive and anonymous existence in other forms. Under the influence of Américo Paredes in that decade, the existing traditional folk form of the *corrido*, or Mexican ballad, was fused with Anglo-American modernism in an openly political literary hybrid that fueled the broader social movement.[47] José Montoya, Rodolfo 'Corky' Gonzalez, Juan Gomez-Quiñonez, Tomás Rivera and Ricardo Sánchez all followed the example set by Paredes, by producing quasi-heroic poetic narratives of masculine heroes struggling gamely against the obdurate racism of the *gringo*. This androcentric aesthetic has yet to be entirely dissipated, despite the best efforts of many Chicana poets to redress the gender imbalance of this cultural code.[48] Rodriguez himself could scarcely escape the strong influence of this existing code, and it would be petty to condemn his use of a strong male subjectivity as such: it is an admirable source of dissident identity. Indeed, when we position this robust, masculine, Hispanic self alongside the existential void of Bret Ellis's characters, the obsessive malevolence of Cooper's wolves, the frenzied hysteria of James Ellroy's detectives, or indeed the quintuply alienated persona of Wanda Coleman's verse, we begin to appreciate the legacy of Chicano tradition in Los Angeles as an available representational space for the production of hard-won individual identities.

Meanwhile, one body of work in Los Angeles has attempted to circumvent the inevitable complaints raised against both the solid subjectivity of a Rodriguez, and the desperately victimized personae of a Wanda Coleman. Sesshu Foster, one of the co-editors of the ground-breaking *Invocation LA* in 1989, has refused any endorsement of stable poetic 'selves', presumably seeing these as the imperative of a dominant culture, while working towards a genuinely plural speaking voice. Foster's polyphonic ghetto vignettes bring into focus the actual diversity, the hybridity and multiculturalism of communities on the ground, as well as the undiminished degree of everyday violence visited upon working-class 'others' in minoritized Los Angeles.

It is Foster's poetic technique that most clearly distinguishes him from his contemporaries. He has developed a form which, uniquely, sidesteps all appearance of lyricism. Lyricism is an affectation of both Rodriguez and Coleman: a relatively short verse form dominated by short lines, stanzas, one more or less contained 'thought' per poem, and a basic expressivity. Foster retains only the brevity of form, and substitutes for the rest a new assortment of technical features. To get an idea of this form, and its aesthetic effects, here is a typical untitled piece from his volume, *City Terrace: Field Manual* (1996), that has the virtue of representing precisely the multicultural Los Angeles we have been seeking:

> In Mediterranean LA there's a fresh sea breeze, the
> Spanish oaks don't hide the young woman's corpse,
> raped and strangled, you'll never see those eyes which
> in life would have bruised your heart, sands of the
> Sahara blow down Vermont, take a left on Pico through
> Little San Salvador, shifts in timeless winds reveal the
> fifteen-year-old boy shot twice through the back by
> sheriff's deputies as he ran from the stolen vehicle, you
> fucked up, in Siberian LA taiga obscures the horizon,
> who knows where you may end up, dark clouds blow
> sleet and sheets of rain down Alameda, the train station
> disappears in the blizzard, Olvera Street with icicles, five
> below zero at Siquieros' *América Tropical*, the crucified
> Indian is pecked by the gringo eagle, burnt out on
> Turkish LA, you cough where homeless children play
> along immense adobe walls in sandals and huaraches . . .
> the sirens . . . Thai LA . . . the victims . . . the seamstresses
> and garment workers returning . . . the sun like a cracked
> egg . . . Scottish LA . . . bones, twine, tufts of hair . . .[49]

The most notable absence from all of this is of course any sustained subjectivity, whose closest approximation is the infrequent second person address; but this pronoun 'you' hardly designates a stable person or identity. Rather, it is scrambled over the crazy-quilt of ethnic Los Angeles like a tattered thread through a labyrinth. The poem's ambition would seem to be the representation of an 'objective' space uncompromised by any specific subjectivity. Yet what could be more resolutely impressionistic than this disjointed and increasingly uncertain catalogue of violent urban domains? Although the verse begins on a high point of 'objective', indicative certainty, its final lines degenerate into fragments of phrases, gutteral growls of woe. What intervenes, the polyphonic variety of cultures that have claimed LA, destabilizes the discourse's grasp on its own material. For this material, this radical spatial and cultural hetero- geneity, and the crude murderousness of its way of life, defies all hitherto existing modes of figuration. Even the recourse to the representational space of the wind and weather, which loosely links the first thirteen lines or so, fails hopelessly to contain the immanent dynamic of what it has been called upon to mediate.

We will note, however, how the ruined space of the body emerges here as a wretchedly persistent figure. From the raped and strangled girl, to the boy shot in the back by deputies, to the crucified Indian, and finally to the gruesome bones and tufts of hair, Foster's poem seeks to ground his affective intensity in the broken bodies of those who have gone under. No one race or ethnicity seems to suffer more than the others in this brutal Los Angeles. Class, inflected by ethnicity, is the principal determinant of this universal suffering: the Thai garment workers and seams- tresses, the unemployed Salvadoran car thief, the homeless Turkish children, as well as the anonymous rape victim, all bear upon their bodies the double stigmata of being ethnically 'other' and working class.

Foster's form is determined by his content: an urban space so riven by difference, injustice and inequality is not only inadequate to lyricism, but baffles all existing representational strategies. His disjointed vignettes and lengthy, impacted lines, shot through with surreal moments of metaphoric play, constitute a working solution to the problems posed by this unrepresentable space. Occasionally, Foster's impersonal impressionism is interrupted by a genuine narrative drive, which has the virtue, in the context of his collection, of allowing for periods of readerly relaxation and direct pedagogy:

> . . . Far
> from rent control and the beach, LAPD censors a life.
> Someone said they saw Gilberto trying to climb the
> fence. He'd gone down to watch. Someone else said
> Gilberto was trying to run away. One cop said they
> shouted a warning. Another cop said one kid had a
> gun. They shot Gilberto in the back, one time, that's
> all. It was enough: 15 years old. Old folks' fingertips

dusty from venetian blinds, wooden slats from the '50s,
watching turrets move through the ruined mini-mall.
Nicotine stains on fingertips. When the cop is scared,
yelling at you, he'll point his automatic pistol and
order you to lie on the pavement. 'Don't look at me!
Put your nose on the fuckin' street!' Your belly is
cold, water rushing down the asphalt in front of gutted
buildings. Are your eyes beautiful in the dark?[50]

Only one fragment of a longer poem, already these lines contain three distinct sections and moods, which are unmarked by any transitions or breaks. The first, narrative section concerns another police shooting of an unarmed child; its method is direct statement and the quasi-legal presentation of evidence. The second, appearing as though from another dimension, is an oblique reference to the spectacle of the 1992 riots themselves, here condensed into the synecdoche of 'turrets' in a 'ruined mini-mall'. Finally, the concluding portion turns didactically to the second person and represents the very experience of racist police harrassment. The tone of casual distance makes for a rather Brechtian intensification of cognitive labour somehow to accept this as an instruction booklet (a 'field manual', as the collection is entitled) for ghetto survival.

The absence of transitions and the discordance of person, mood and point-of-view, foment a characteristic elasticity and subtlety of poetic texture. Foster's complex chronotope of Los Angeles is an elegant collage of different representations, all of which circle around and refer back to the difficulties of identity in a minoritized space dominated by police power and coercion. Yet even the Carceral City is challenged by the proliferating otherness it pretends to control.

Show me some ID. Centerline of every boulevard in
town, a border where you cannot reveal all identities;
cannot peel light Chinese bones to their stares, cannot
cry Mexican oil for their car parts, cannot fart Indian
air for their Anglo fetishes.[51]

The sheer multiplicity of ethnic LAs has muddled the representational order of things. While the authorities demand stable and readily recognizable badges of identity, the urban reality has obviated any such possibility. The clichés of Anglo stereotype (those convenient representations of ethnic space) are mercilessly ridiculed in this verse, which refuses them in the face of that abrupt opening command to 'show some ID'. The command is taken up again later in the poem.

> . . . On the corner of City Terrace and Eastern, they
> shine the spotlight in your eyes and any ID you show
> them will be self-reflexive. Thin, logically thin plastic
> will show them a picture of a past without visible scars,
> breath, heat, labor. When they pat down your pockets,
> kick your ankles apart, nudge your elbows higher –
> empty the paper bag you carry onto the sidewalk –
> call your picture ID in to the computer downtown –
> when they look at your face, they will not see anyone
> they recognise

Between 'you' and 'them', this drama of reification and misrecognition is played out under the glare of a police spotlight. On 'their' side: the light, the 'logically thin' ID card, the physical power to command, and the 'computer downtown'; on 'your' side: a personal history of 'scars, breath, heat, labor', and a paper bag. Yet the final lines insist that for all this manifest inequality of equipment, the official 'ID' is undone by its own hypostasis, its incapacity to register the 'scars, breath, heat, labor' of individual being. The hegemony of white vision is internally flawed precisely due to its rationalization of seeing: no matter how much data is collected about a 'face', the inability to recognize 'anyone' is built into the programme.

This mini-drama suggests that the larger story of Foster's poetry is the perennial violence inflicted by the Los Angeles authorities on the various minorities of 'multicultural LA', a record of systematic injustice against a non-white majority. In 1992, the Coalition Against Police Abuse issued a Report on the LAPD's record of racist violation of rights between the years 1965–91.[52] Its findings confirmed the worst. The frequency of incidents of police killing unarmed citizens rose dramatically in the mid-late 1970s, tapered off slightly in the early 1980s, and then reached unparalleled heights in the mid-1980s, with no less (and certainly more, according to the *Los Angeles Times*) than thirty-seven killed between 1984 and 1987 alone. The victims of this bloody campaign have almost all been young black and Chicano men. The campaign has had one clear object: to produce the urban 'hyper-segregation'[53] that the first Foster poem we considered tried but consciously failed to thread into a whole. By systematically killing young 'ethnic' men, the LAPD has enforced a rigid apartheid between the ghettos and white LA, as the resentment caused by their treatment has led to escalating popular hostility and resistance, which calls for greater and greater levels of armed 'containment' of gangs and their wider communities. Marc Cooper comments:

In a city increasingly cleaved between rich and poor, white and non-white, between sparkling new Mercedes-Benzes and 74 Chevies, between $30-million mini-mansions and $600-a-month roach-infested apartments, the white minority that continues to exercise a monopoly over political power . . . asks few questions of the 8,300 cops charged with upholding civilization. The faceless, non-white, increasingly foreign-born, ever-more-desperate underclass, in the wake of Reaganomics and the white-led taxpayers' revolt of Proposition 13, has been virtually abandoned by every arm of the state, be it local, regional or national.[54]

Foster has endeavoured to retrieve the everyday stories of oppression told by the 'faceless, non-white, increasingly foreign-born, ever-more-desperate underclass', and adapt them for poetic use.

The 'you' of the following poem is forcibly driven into its space, as a challenge simply to survive, let alone 'map' it:

When the 3 year old cries, who was beaten to death, you
will hear that weeping in your throat like gravel. The
7 year old, raped and strangled, her body set on fire in
the public park, she will be your suffocation. Your eyes
will be stung by those fields of ash, your lungs filigreed
with that pitch smoke. You will dream sometimes that
you sleep in blue rooms of a feverish, unconscious
people. You will not even know that you yearn to walk
in the quiet forest away from everything they call this
'civilization'. Instead, you will smell inside of your
longing that urine taint of penitentiary concrete, gray
waste of steel time, and in the nearest shop window
plate glass, you will see in the corner of your eye, me:
a man with your face and life imprisonment so far from
his sweet wife. Faster than a riptide: the city will carry
you out on a sea of fear, hatred, poverty, ignorance.
You will walk in the dust of the avenue, stupefied by
slaughter. Women murdered by men having a bad
day will echo in your footsteps. An overfed shit-faced
apologist will whine across the TV sets of the nation
that this world is a universe of injustice, but it will be
you who breathes it in and tastes it, once, twice, three
times to its bitterest depths.

– *Sobre todo, séan siempre capáz de sentir en lo más hondo cualquier*
injusticia cometida contra cualquiera en cualquier parte
del mundo.   Che (last letter to his children)[55]

The city as an open grave, within which the second person self wanders bruised and forlorn: such would be one way to crystallize Sesshu Foster's oppressive urban chronotope. To expand upon its constitution, one would necessarily have to account for the persistent figure of the dead child's body, which here receives its most vivid incarnation in those two opening images of inexplicable violence. My feeling is that these corpses function as something like the insistence of the real in a shifting and spectral urban media-space – 'the TV sets of the nation' – much as Watts once functioned for the earlier Naturalism of Wanda Coleman. In this sense, there is a clear line of continuity, albeit with serious differences, between the carnal aesthetics of Dennis Cooper, and Foster's more polemical poetics. The body, dead, dismembered and defunct, is as Baudrillard memorably put it, the unredeemable gift that cuts directly against the grain of the exchange principle.[56] It is the incontestable evidence of an act which the system cannot answer without undoing itself.

The well-nigh sublime space of the dead body is then articulated with a representational space – the 'fields of ash', 'pitch smoke', and 'blue rooms' – which clearly seeks to establish itself as 'visionary', a Dantean tour of Hell. And this in turn is constructed against the utopian space of the 'quiet forest', again invoking Dante, and promoting a non-urban strand of imagery, the most appalling thing about which being that 'you will never even know that you yearn to walk' there. So infinitessimal and indistinct has the utopian imagination become in 'ethnic' Los Angeles, that the subject addressed by the poem is programmed in advance not to register its poetic traces.

'Instead', as a rare transitional marker insists, the shade-like subject will introject this blasted, vicious space as an *incarceration of time*. Here, our search for the definition of Foster's chronotope may have ended. Note how the olfactory sense is introduced to mediate 'external' and 'internal' space, a nodding of the head at phenomenology and Proust's *petite madeleine*; but in Foster's chronotope, the only memory dislodged from lost time by this sensory incident is one of imprisonment and the 'gray / waste of steel time' which describes precisely the temporal qualities of the present itself. And in this confirmation of entrapment, we suddenly are delivered Foster himself, or his poetic image, caught and stranded in the plate-glass shop window : 'a man with your face and life imprisonment so far from / his sweet wife'. This is the closest we come to subjectivity itself, this realization that the 'you' of the whole poem is a first person objectified through the displacement and dispossession of commercial display.

Scarcely has this moment of realization occurred, than 'the city' bears 'you' away from 'me' again, and back to the flattened space of reified abstractions: fear, hatred, poverty, ignorance. Then, more

death and deadening stupefaction, before the advent of TV, to figure
the representation of national space in Los Angeles; the 'overfed'
face of a Rush Limbaugh-clone broadcasting its 'whine' into every
living room in the nation. The 'universal' concept of injustice being
bandied across the screen fits poorly with 'your' daily diet of the
same. 'Your' limp progress through the devastated cityscape of this
poem has defined injustice in a concrete aesthetic sense, arising from
the body and it senses. It is no accident that sight, sound, taste, smell
and touch have all been used to flesh out this chronotope; Foster's
point would seem to be that it is only by realizing injustice as a
remorseless assault on the sensorium that the body will want again
to shuffle it off – politics beginning in the intimate spaces of 'you', as
they did in Cooper.

Meanwhile the concluding transcript of Che Guevara's last letter
to his children confirms the pathos of the 'child' as a symbol in this
chronotope, and strives to make a representational fold connecting
the daily violence of late capitalist LA and the distant jungles of
Bolivia where *guerilla* armies take on state power. As a total performance, the poem is exemplary of Foster's ability to cross borders and
encourage a political intelligence without insisting on any 'untouch-
able' representational space of ethnic identity. Indeed, it is only after
a moment of reflection that the realization comes powerfully home:
ethnicity has not even figured in this poem, which has preferred to
address 'injustice' as an issue affecting the totality of ethnic and
working-class communities, and not any particular one of them.

It is in this sense that the structural politics of class, rather than the
identity politics of a given race or ethnicity, are figured by Foster as
the basis of a new urban consciousness of the oppressed. The trick in
much of his verse is to bear witness to the production of an urban
space that is then treated as a reified self-sufficient entity, a second
nature that devours lives as fuel.

> . . . How
> does this city stay alive? They feed it, women whose
> hands are folded into bread, into clothes, wards of
> hospital beds, smoothing out wrinkled faces of children.
> Men who truck loads of food, heavy equipment, 8-foot
> diameter concrete pipes into the inner city. Through
> triumphal arches of light and smoke coming from
> their own homes. Men who hang fences, walk the
> streets, women who stack money in the vaults. Cry
> into telephones. Paperhangers, check chasers, men with
> evil devices, women with ideas to match. The young

and their empty sacrifice, looking for parties, fucked on
film where identity's erased. Chicken shacks, lube joints,
neo-Hawaiian apartments, burglar-barred and run-down,
the swimming pool filled with gravel and palm trees
planted in it. Even children make it work like this,
running across avenues, hit by cars going nowhere.[57]

The now familiar figure of the sacrificed child concludes an encyclo-
pedic list of the labour by which Los Angeles is daily produced. If
this is a new proletarian poetry, however, it is one devoid of any
trace of romanticism or heroism, and derives its cognitive excitement
from a tactical refusal of the whole 'post-industrial' hypothesis.
Industry is everywhere in Los Angeles; indeed, the poem insists that
industry *is* Los Angeles. The men, women and children who
produce the city, whose bodies are so demonized and hounded by
state power, who have had their being and identity 'erased' by the
city's most powerful industry – this silent minor-majority has found
a respectful and disabused voice in Sesshu Foster.

I have not wanted to suggest that Foster is somehow 'against' race
or ethnicity as a representational space. On the contrary, his several
poems dedicated to Japanese victimization in the city, and his
constant exploration of Chicano identity and history, would instantly
defeat any such claim. What I do want to argue is that, for Foster,
race is not in itself an answer or a ground; rather, it is the outline of a
problem, a problem of form as much as content. In a city of so many
intertwining ethnic identities, the choice to essentialize any one of
them in a literary form is an act of regrettable false consciousness.
Foster's poetic form turns relentlessly on the question of white
domination, but never opts for a particular ethnic representational
space as a viable locus of 'authenticity' from which to contest its
effects. The poetry's radical sincerity consists in this rejection of
precisely the enclosures of ethnicity we have seen burdening (and
animating) Rodriguez and Coleman. Nor would I want to ascribe
this too easily to Foster's own hybrid ethnic identity, both Chicano
and Japanese. Instead, the most valuable point seems to me to be the
closeness of Foster's attention to an everyday life that is fragmented
into so many racial and ethnic constituencies, but which retains the
same basic form across all of them. The belligerence of power, the
destruction of infrastructures, the sickening pathos of raped and
murdered children, and the deeper, unrecognized truth of alienated
labour: black, brown, yellow or red, 'you' live this conspiracy of
forces day to day in 'your' very body. And how remarkable this

recourse to the second person is in Foster's chronotope. In place of an 'I' or 'we' that is automatically exclusive, the open second person pronoun takes every non-white reader (and perhaps a few white ones) in hand, as the poetry's syntax, like some latter-day Vergil, guides them to the edges of the urban map and beyond. Transcending the politics of identity and of difference alike, Foster's indeterminate 'you' may turn out to be the aesthetic prefiguration of a new and militant political rhetoric. If so, this rhetoric's first ambition would surely be nothing less than the transformation of the everyday life it so patiently traces.

5

Realism and beyond

Again, and finally, the question returns: is a realism desirable which
would cut the beast of LA along the joints, surgically remove the
layers of simulation superadded to the city, and yield us the 'thing
itself'?[1] Or is our earliest point still valid, that aesthetics are fundamental to the city's production, not superadded but *a priori*, and that
as a result culture and space here refer to each other in an excess of
representation, whose only real aesthetic consequence is the resort to
'artificiality'? Quite apart from this dialectical knot, the fact that the
concept of totality, to which that of realism has long been attached,
has been deposed by the logic of minoritarianism (indeed, in Los
Angeles, had never really come into being), frustrates any possibility
of a realist aesthetic in this city. It is in this sense that Los Angeles is
the preeminent habitat of 'minor' literature in Deleuze and Guattari's sense; albeit in a mode more often closer to Naturalism than
Kafka's allegories.[2] Lefebvre's 'abstract space' is so much more fully
developed and administered here, that the hysterical contradictions
of Prague at the fall of the Habsburg empire look Byzantine by
comparison. The political mistake, however, as Bret Easton Ellis's
characters repeatedly make it, would surely be to imagine that
abstract space therefore holds incontestable sway over everyday life.
It is a mistake symptomatic of its age precisely in its forgetfulness
about history.

As Lefebvre was at pains to demonstrate, the very oppositions
that abstract space mystifies (homogeneity/fragmentation; quan-
tity/quality; centre/margin) are restless and dynamic. Inevitably,
Lefebvre thought, they must themselves begin to dictate a shift in the
reified patterns of late capitalist urban life – an homogenized multi-
tude of fragments being, surely, as unsustainable as a restless

margin, without a constantly maintained political pressure on social space. So that, in his theory, abstract space gives way on occasion to the appearance of what he calls 'contradictory to differential space', a space of upsurge and struggle.[3] In this way, history can provide occasions for the reappearance of the totality, otherwise kept at arm's length by spatial seriality and the intensities of group territoriality; and which also in turn, as we shall see, allows for the redoubling of state power over the totality through panoptical and military strategies. It is in the dialectical oscillations between abstract and differential space that the totality reemerges from the political unconscious, for with the return of political confrontation to everyday life it is not so much the immanent groups and spaces themselves, as their ultimate relatedness and inequalities, that is at issue. And recent Los Angeles history, for all its reluctance on this score, has issued a violent reminder that the retreat into various 'cultural identities' can never altogether repress the social contradictions between these and other groups in the production of space itself.

On 29 April 1992, these rumbling social energies exploded in Los Angeles, as thousands of Latino, black, Korean and white citizens abandoned their everyday spatial practices and for three days and nights held hostage the official myths of multiculturalism which justified segregation, exclusion and oppression. This dramatic reawakening of the totality in Los Angeles brought home the possibility of some fuller cognitive cartography of the postmodern metropolis than had hitherto been imagined. For in the political ferment of those riots, modes of territorial being that had until yesterday existed in disregard of each other, suddenly discovered themselves side by side in spontaneous praxis, negotiating their frustrated interests in destructive as well as cooperative forms.

The comfortable vision of an integrated 'mosaic' of cultures with which the city authorities had been dissembling the mounting tensions of a restructured urban economy,[4] dissolved into massmediated scenes of looting, larceny, fire-bombing, beating and death. Over 16,291 people were arrested during the unrest. 'The Fire Department received 5,537 structure fire calls and responded to an estimated 500 fires. An estimated 4,000 businesses were destroyed. Fifty-two people died and 2,383 people were injured . . . Property damage and loss have been estimated at between $785 million and $1 billion'.[5] Such figures make this incident the costliest social revolt in twentieth-century American domestic history; but rather than dwell on this media carnival of apocalypse and the facile anti-urban polemics it provoked, it seems of much greater moment to concentrate upon the opportunity afforded by this 'return of totality' to the streets of Los Angeles for the advent of a renewed holistic representation, or a *return of realism itself*, at the level of its aesthetic mediation. If ever any event were to cancel the psychic claims of territoriality and abstraction, and pave the way for a new realism of urban relations, this was undoubtedly it. Our guiding question in this chapter will be, not whether such a realism was possible (it was, as we shall see), but whether its actual achievements managed to surmount the problems of representational immanence treated in this book; and whether the very mediation of such public violence by corporate spectacle did not actually undermine the realist possibility from within, and so entail its immediate surcease.

The work which commands our attention as an ostensible 'answer' to the call for realism immediately after May 1992 is Anna Deavere Smith's authoritative one-woman performance work, *Twilight: Los Angeles 1992*. Indeed, in preparing for this work, Smith was repeatedly provoked by a popular desire for an all-embracing voice or vision – a Realism – able to pull the dissociated urban shards together in an act of aesthetic unification: 'one of the questions I was most frequently asked when I was interviewed about *Twilight* was "Did you find any one voice that could speak for the entire city?" I think there is an expectation that in this diverse city, and in this diverse nation, a unifying voice would bring increased understanding and put us on the road to solutions'.[6] Yet, despite the temptations of seeing herself in that vatic and omniscient role, Smith was at pains to distance herself from this anachronistic wish. 'There is little in culture or education that encourages the development of a unifying voice', she rightly insisted.[7] So, while the desire called Realism is everywhere to be found in the conditions of possibility of this work, what we shall be interested in determining is how, in its articulation, the simplistic recourse to nineteenth-century representational certainties is resisted; and what strategies are invoked instead to answer that desire. What should be confessed well in advance, however, is that Smith's work is not 'literary' as such, but 'dramatic' in a rather original way, and merely sets the example of what a reconfigured literary anti-Realist realism might resemble.[8]

Our principal difficulty in analyzing Smith's performance work will thus be literary-critical, since the object of attention is no longer merely a printed text (though it is that), but also a body in motion upon a stage, a production design, and an audience. This obviates the possibility of 'close reading' as such, especially as Smith's method is anti-authorial and involves no original writing. Clearly, then, our usual strategy of chronotopic investigation through stylistic and formal analysis will not be applicable here, and we will have to rely more upon an interpretation of histrionic technique than on any other critical method.

In May 1992, not a month after the riots had broken out, Smith was commissioned by Gordon Davidson at the Mark Taper Forum in LA, 'to write a one-woman performance piece about the civil disturbances in that city in April 1992'.[9] As a solo woman writer and performer already established as a dramatist of civil unrest with *Fires in the Mirror* (about black vs. Hasidic Jewish violence in Crown Heights, Brooklyn), Smith's various productions over the previous fifteen years had been assembled together under the general title of 'On the Road: A Search for American Character'.[10] This larger entity, which she conceives of loosely as a series, acquires its formal unity from its consistent dramatic methodology. This evolved from a conviction that 'if I listened carefully to people's words, and particularly to their rhythms, . . . I could use language to learn about my own time. If I could find a way to really inhabit the words of those around me, . . . I could learn about the spirit, the imagination, and the challenges of my time, firsthand'.[11] Smith's implicit belief in the speech rhythms of real others, as an allegorical mode of access to larger sociological and historical processes, has remained the mainstay of her performance method.

> If we were to inhabit the speech patterns of another, and walk in the speech of another, we could find the individuality of the other and experience that individuality viscerally. I became increasingly convinced that the activity of reenactment could tell us as much, if not more, about another individual than the process of learning about the other by using the self as a frame of reference. The frame of reference for the other would *be* the other.[12]

This commitment has required a corresponding development of her acting skills to the highest imaginable level. Her quest for technical perfection colours the entirety of her art, and is the leading formal edge of what might be mistaken for a 'content-based' aesthetic. Her critics and commentators concur that Smith's performance is 'a feat of technical virtuosity'.[13] 'Technically, she has such a high command of various voices that her change of tone may lead audiences to believe she has changed a face'.[14]

Apart from the refinement of her acting skills in catching and reproducing the precise mix of quirks and mannerisms that makes up each of her 'subjects', Smith's method is deceptively straightforward. She conducts an interview with a given individual, tapes the interview, and after spending hours with the recorded material, selects the section of the subject's responses which she feels most precisely captures that individual's character: 'I try to find a section that I don't have to interrupt'.[15] What is at stake here, despite the aversion from writing and attraction to voice, is not some cult of 'presence', but precisely the deconstruction of the traditional sense of identity, which is to say, *self-presence*, or the Cartesian *cogito*. Smith's tactic of appropriating the other effectively expels her own psychological being from her body, and accepts the other as an animating spirit.

As a value, this 'identity' of the other denotes not his or her public mask as such, but all that has not yet been subsumed into the machines of abstraction which govern late-capitalist space. It consists in the ungrammatical slips of spoken discourse, the ceasurae of unplanned utterances, the unconscious gestural economy of hand, body and face, the sudden flash of insight on the hoof, and so on.[16] Iterable discourse, then, is less important for the manifestation of 'character' than some obscure, subterranean energy that flickers through the interstices of words, a subliminal poetics of body rhythm and unsubsumed somatic nature. Smith's own task is to track this inscrutable energy by working homeopathically from the linguistic surface down into the marrow of identity: 'The point is simply to repeat it [the other's utterance] until I begin to feel it and what I begin to feel is his song and that helps me remember more about his body . . . My body begins to do the things that he probably must do inside while he's speaking'.[17]

To account for this remarkable artistic practice, I want to suggest that it functions precisely as a negation of media stereotyping and 'myth', and thus as an exemplary realism. Roland Barthes' impassioned critique of contemporary myth as elaborated by the media explicitly uses the terms of evacuation and voiding: 'The function of myth is to empty reality: it is literally a ceaseless flowing out, a haemorrhage, or perhaps an evaporation, in short a perceptible absence.'[18] The media performs this evacuation of the real in the very act of representing it: taking hold of the body, with all its perverse originality, it transforms it into an absence, a *crypt* as we said in our engagement with Dennis Cooper. Any art, such as Cooper's, which would restitute the body's peculiar reality from under the pall of such mythic absence is then charged with a 'realism' hitherto unknown in cultural history. Instructively enough, at his death, Henri Lefebvre – whose theory of the 'metaphorization' of the body under media society as a voiding chimes aptly with Barthes'[19] – had begun work on a lengthy philosophical treatise on what he called 'rhythm analysis', a term presumably borrowed from the phenomenologist Gaston Bachelard.[20] In it, he intended to clarify the essential features of just this unmapped domain of human activity, as yet not fully colonized by the techniques of domination. It was to complete his copious work on the social production of space, a last turn to the intimate spatial practices of bodies, and the instinctual production of body rhythms even within the abstractions of capitalist social space. He wrote:

> The body's inventiveness needs no demonstration, for the body itself reveals it, and deploys it in space. Rhythms in all their multiplicity interpenetrate one another . . .
> It is possible to envision a sort of 'rhythm analysis' which would address itself to the concrete reality of rhythms, and perhaps even to their use (or appropriation). Such an approach would seek to discover those rhythms whose existence is signalled only through mediations, through indirect effects or manifestations. Rhythm analysis might eventually even displace psychoanalysis, as being more concrete, more effective, and closer to a pedagogy of appropriation (the appropriation of the body, as of spatial practice).[21]

I want to suggest that Anna Deavere Smith is an artist of these very rhythms, and an exemplary pedagogue of what is at stake in 'the appropriation of the body' *vis-à-vis* the media abstractions it negates. Through her appropriations of the rhythms of others, she makes them the objects of aesthetic attention, and liberates their elemental structures for cognition; which is the very inverse of mythic 'absence'. For, as she suggests, these rhythms are loaded with meaning, allegorical of their 'times' in ways which only the applied concentration of a theatrical audience, before a carefully structured artwork, can fully appreciate. In everyday life, these rhythms slip unnoticed through the cracks of 'spatial practice', and fail to disclose their truth content. In the media, they are converted into a death-mask of social being. In art, they are formally redeemed.

The first critical point about Smith's mimesis and estrangement of body rhythms is that these molecular structures of everyday life are smaller than the larger performative structures of ethnicity and gender. By tracking identity home to the peculiar play of gesture, habit, tone and voice of specific individuals, she circumvents the very group identities or minorities we observed earlier to be claiming provenance over much artistic and literary production today. Such a tactic radicalizes the notion of identity itself. If postmodern America is erected on the banal image of a 'melting pot', then Smith is determined to work against all that is passive in that representation of space. 'I've been wondering how to find the tools for thinking about difference as a very active negotiation rather than an image of us all holding hands. There are too many contradictions, problems, and lies in American society about the melting pot'. In place of this image, she proposes a careful attention to the ways in which bodies negotiate and navigate impersonal abstraction. 'Motion is what I'm interested in right now. People who talk about motion, who use the word move. In my show I've become interested in which characters can move in the space and which ones can't'.[22] At issue here is the differences bodies make to their surrounding spaces: do they inscribe themselves within it, or are they written by it into passive roles? Movement alters the space, invests it with an energy and a trajectory, appropriates it for a specific agency.

Yet it is of course her body we see on stage, and not those of her subjects. The distance between the two, between appearance and reference, remains constantly in view. No matter how virtuosic her ability to perform the other, her own being openly denotes itself as well, in its invariant skin colour, sex, and basic physical proportions. 'On stage, that is, Smith is a single figure. Her body persists as one thing, an iconic presence'.[23] The fact that she is a black woman is never concealed beneath make-up or too much costume; instead, this mute facticity glares back at the audience through the technically accomplished performance as a kind of extra-diegetic character in its own right. In an address on theatre in higher education, Smith explicitly acknowledged this. 'Yes, my entry into theatre is political. Largely because of my race and gender. I am political without opening my mouth. My presence is political. The way I negotiate my presence becomes political'.[24] The various real-life characters she painstakingly recreates are mediated by a bodily presence whose very nature in contemporary America proclaims a political identity. This identity, the 'black woman', only infrequently agrees with the identity she is conjugating on stage; and where that identity is white and male, the politics of the disjunction are particularly acute.

And yet, Smith was at pains throughout the process of preparing *Twilight* to resist as much as possible the implicit politics of her flesh: 'My predominant concern about the creation of *Twilight* was that my own history, which is a history of race as a black and white struggle, would make the work narrower than it should be.'[25] To correct this 'natural' bias, Smith went so far as to hire several multicultural intellectuals as dramaturges, including Latinos, Asian-Americans, and another African-American.[26] So while the 'black woman' is ever present, it is never stressed. It is then left to the audience to think through the many levels of irony when, for instance, Smith plays white LAPD Sergeant Charles Duke, explaining why Rodney King was beaten so severely:

> Prior to this
> we lost upper-body-control holds,
> in 1982.
> If we had upper-body-control holds
> involved in this,
> this tape woulda never been on,
> this incident woulda lasted about
> fifteen seconds.
> The reason that we lost upper-body-control holds . . .
> because we had something like
> seventeen to twenty deaths in a period of about 1975–76 to
>   1982, and
> they said it was associated with its being used on Blacks
> and Blacks were dying.
> Now,
> the so-called community leaders
> came forward and complained
> *(He drinks water)*
> and they started a hysteria . . .[27]

As she recreates Duke's conviction that upper-body-control holds were an excellent preventive measure, despite all the deaths, and swings a police baton to demonstrate the problems with the way it was used in the Rodney King beating, Smith never inserts any overt irony, or steps outside of her role in conventional Brechtian style. The resultant *Verfremdungseffecte* springs rather from the incongruity of her body in that role to begin with. This has a far greater impact than mere caricature. For it is a dynamic tension which nevertheless allows Duke to reach his own 'poetic moment', slightly after the quoted extract, in which he theorizes that the excessive use of force in the King case was part of an unofficial policy by Chief Daryl Gates and the Command Staff to protest the banning of upper-body-control holds. By beating people into submission and breaking bones, he suggests, the LAPD hoped to create enough public outcry to force the reinstatement of their preferred method of control. It is at this moment that the performing body and her role shift into some strange sort of alignment, and the distance reduces to a minimum: the moment of cognitive revelation, or truth. By admitting Duke's being into her body, Smith has angled for a rush of enlightenment to clarify certain issues about the civil unrest. Yet, for all the rationality of these discursive interests, we have seen that Smith's performance method remains steadfastly 'primitive', an instance of what Richard Schechner calls *shamanism*.[28] Her deep mimesis of the other is acutely complicated by these possibly irreconcilable tendencies: the intersubjective search for truth, and the homeopathic magic of imitation.

In their *Dialectic of Enlightenment*, Theodor Adorno and Max Horkheimer teased endlessly at the knot of contradictions between enlightenment and magic. On the one hand, enlightenment works by the abstract principles of quantity and identity, but ruthlessly abolishes distinct qualities and differences; on the other, magic respects these last, but the shaman retains disproportionate charismatic power by virtue of his ability to represent nature. Enmeshed in a dialectical history, enlightenment and magic tirelessly chase each others' tails: the sheer quantification of an exchange economy veers irrevocably into the contemporary magic of commodity fetishism. Yet they remain distinctly opposed as concepts. Adorno's *Aesthetic Theory* theorized this tension between magic and enlightenment as the constitutive aporia of all art. 'The aporia of art, pulled between regression to literal magic or surrender of the mimetic impulse to thinglike rationality, dictates its law of motion; the aporia cannot be eliminated. The depth of the process, which every artwork is, is excavated by the unreconcilability of these elements; it must be imported into the idea of art as an image of reconciliation.'[29] The aesthetics of Anna Deavere Smith occupies just this aporetic yet reconciliatory ground, between identity and difference, truth and magic, self and other. She entertains a magical apprehension of the other, whose specific qualities require specific representation; yet her overall artistic interest is in enlightening the public about the social truths of events.[30]

It is at this juncture of contradictory forces that we can begin to determine how the 'private space' of Smith's body is suited to serve as a metaphorical stage for the missing public space of Los Angeles. For it is not simply that Smith undertakes the specific representation of *another* in the interest of truth; it is rather that Smith's shamanistic ritual of enlightenment passes through a genuine multiplicity of others. Depending on where she performed *Twilight*, Smith incarnated anything between thirty and forty individuals on stage, from many different parts of the city and a full gamut of ethnicities. The published text of the performance includes no fewer than fifty distinct voices. Each real-life character, be it a Korean merchant disabled by the riots, a former president of the LA Police Commission, intellectuals like Mike Davis and Homi Bhabha, Congresswoman Maxine Waters, or any number of others, Smith fairly applies the same commitment to specific representation and rhythm-analytic mimesis we have already explored. Yet the overall effect of dialogic polyphony exceeds any expectation we might have had of a 'realistic' cross-section of the city, and makes unique demands on our very ability to read this performance or its text, projecting us into an apprehension of the social as a swarm of differences united by crisis.

So it is that Smith's larger works (*Fires in the Mirror* and *Twilight*) come to stand, in their very complexity, for something outside them that is lacking, clearing some aesthetic space for the advent of a public space to come. Cornel West has suggested that '*Fires in the Mirror* is a grand example of how art can constitute a public space that is perceived by people as empowering rather than disempowering.'[31] Because she refuses to endorse any of what West calls the 'tribal mentalities' of America in her art, Smith liberates the notion of speaking from the bad protectionism of identity politics. Nothing could be greater anathema to Smith's aesthetics of difference than the familiar essentialisms of ethnicity which restrict both art and public space to one-way monologism:

> In theatre we have not fully realized what the drama of race is. This is because we have been creating it as a series of monologues. One race speaks, the other listens. In mainstream theatre, it often happens that artists of color go onto the stage and perform for largely white audiences. They talk, white people watch . . .
> . . . What I am proposing is creating theatre that juxtaposes worlds that are far apart in order to create an aesthetic contrast out of politically explosive interactions. We could then capture a raw natural genuine modern drama which could ultimately

influence how societies negotiate difference.

... If we could dance the steps of ethnicity, across the boundaries of ethnicity, we could give American culture something it needs: a beautiful revelation of what lives inside ethnic houses. Now we are living in a society that daily moves farther and farther behind its fortresses. We cannot afford to be fortressed . . .

Theatre in the last twenty years has been ethnocentric . . . Now, I think, is the time to create ways of moving between the fortresses, and in so doing to encourage a generation of artists who live in work, and for lack of a better image, in *boats*.[32]

This manifesto would look utopian indeed, were it not for the fact that Smith appears to have succeeded in realizing some of her desired goals. Diane Wood Middlebrook opines that 'There is no dominant point of view in these works – what she offers us does not incite us to judgment, although it does try to bring something to closure. Hers is a complex and subtle art, a sort of postmodern urban *Rashomon*.'[33] Carol Martin remarks that 'The authority of one group over another, of one individual over others, is undermined by the presence of Smith as the one person through whom so many voices travel. Smith gives these people the chance to speak as if to each other – in much the same way a "spirit doctor" brings ancestors or other spirits in contact with the living – in the presence of the community of the audience.'[34] This observation seems almost right. The identity of Smith's body, animating the inexhaustible diversity of others' rhythms and utterances, undermines not the *authority* (for she is deeply interested in personal authorship), but the *ability to dominate* of everyone represented, as much as herself. Through this tactical refusal of the traditional function of identity, Smith has initiated a very postmodern kind of aesthetics, where difference and identity mutate into each other ceaselessly, without any pretence to a final word. What distinguishes her from many of the other writers examined in this thesis, apart from form and technique, is this spontaneous deconstruction of her own identity and space-time as a privileged platform, in the name of a genuine minoritization.

Which is not to say that there are not precedents of a sort for Smith's performance art in the American theatre; certainly, the 1930s saw a proliferation of types of 'documentary theatre', as well as the oral history projects of Studs Terkels and others.[35] Smith's accent on verité and authenticity is properly to be thought of in conjunction with such state-funded projects and collectivist enterprises of a more 'Modernist' political era. Where her work differs markedly from these archetypes, however, is in three specific respects: the limitation to her own body as a mimetic and allegorical vehicle; the aesthetic investment in homeopathy or 'magic'; and the refusal of any final perspective or frame in which the various contents could ultimately be judged. In this 'theatre that juxtaposes worlds that are far apart in order to create an aesthetic contrast out of politically explosive interactions', there can be no final arbiter, no Party or group whose claim on reality surpasses that of any other. Smith's postmodernism consists primarily in this: that between the molecular level of body rhythms and radical individualism, and the molar level of the civil event itself, in all its contradictory vastness, the moment of a properly collective consciousness never arises. Smith's emphasis is on the construction of individual lines of flight between group chronotopes. Encouraged to attend to the rhythmic differentials between the diverse human particulars recreated by Smith, the audience is left to draw together what remains latent in that hetero-clite evidence: the truth of the city as a contingent universal, a momentary constellation conjured into being by Smith's aesthetic homeopathy. Her succession of becomings pursues this truth with formidable formal integrity; yet it precludes that requisite property of all political art hitherto conceived: a privileged social agency in which the possibility of effecting political change is identified.

Politics here is, I think, aesthetically conceived. The 'explosive political interactions' Smith sets in train are a formal conceit rather than a traditionally staged dramatic confrontation. It is in the montage-like arrangement of her monologues that the interactions become 'explosive'. For the formal law of solo performance art is that the various characters can never meet in anything other than an adjacent or sequential sense. Constrained by her commitment to solo artistry and to the deep integrity of each 'other', Smith has no means at her disposal to build the very bridges for which her aesthetic cries out; unless it is the invariant being of her own body, which is surely less a bridge than another molecular structure in its own right. There is of course an implicit form to the way Smith has arranged her sequence of characters.[36] Within this structure, the many voices in each section enter into dialogical relationships of dissonance and resonance, and the forward momentum of it all compensates some-what for the lack of a middle ground between radical particularism and universal intelligibility. Yet this lack is felt, and may be called a flaw for the very reason that *Twilight* is a work of art. As Adorno wrote, 'only because no artwork can succeed emphatically are its forces set free; only as a result of this does art catch a glimpse of reconciliation.'[37] Above all, what is missing, precisely in accordance with her reconciliatory credo, is the political sense that domination and abstraction do after all structure the postmodern metropolis, no matter how 'minoritized' and fractured it is; aesthetic 'explosiveness' rings rather hollow in the absence of this fundamental truth.

Thus Smith's work, while touching so profoundly upon many of the more salient contemporary artistic and political issues – issues of identity and difference, self and other, minority and domination, public and private – is best described as a kind of 'postmodern realism'. In undertaking to represent, in the manner of realism, a faithful image of the city's diverse constituency, Smith paradoxically shifts to the leftward limit of postmodernist aesthetic practice itself, towards straightforward nominalism. Thus the work unexpectedly satisfies both the more sophisticated aesthetic intelligence of the age, and the popular desire for wisdom about the most destructive civil unrest of the epoch. In walking the uneasy line between popular and élite 'taste', *Twilight* achieves that most unlikely result of artistic success in the best sense of the phrase. And yet, for a political work of art, it is strangely lacking in political insight.

Perhaps, however, the surest political and aesthetic values of Smith's art inhere in its formal climax: the ultimate, eponymous figure of 'Twilight' himself, gang member and architect of the historic gang truce that has lasted these many years. Twilight is Smith's own personal favourite from the fifty or so characters performed in her play, and it is him she once recommended the curious District Attorney of Los Angeles to meet.[38] Twilight is presented to us seated in a restaurant in a shopping-centre. He is 'short, graceful, very dark-skinned. He is soft-spoken and even in his delivery. He is very confident.'[39] It is this magnetic sense of calm certainty, fostered outside the official educational and familial institutions, out on the streets so feared by the majority of LA citizens, that arrests us, as this young black man, the reviled, stereotyped scapegoat for all the city's crime and violence, proceeds to deconstruct the social imago imposed on his body (even as Smith does her own).

> Twilight Bey,
> that's my name.
> When I was
> twelve and thirteen,
> I stayed out until, they say,

until the sun come up.
Every night, you know,
and that was my thing.
I was a
watchdog.
You know, I stayed up in the neighborhood,
make sure we wasn't being rolled on and everything
and when people
came into light
a what I knew,
a lot a people said,
'Well, Twilight, you know,
you a lot smarter and you have a lot more wisdom than those
twice your age'.
And what I did, you know,
I was
at home writing one night
and I was writing my name
and I just looked at it and it came ta me:
'twi',
abbreviation
of the word 'twice'.
You take away the 'ce'.
You have the last word,
'light'.
'Light' is a word that symbolizes knowledge, knowing,
wisdom
within the Koran and the Holy Bible.
Twilight.
I have twice the knowledge of those my age,
twice the understanding of those my age.
So twilight
is
that time
between day and night.
Limbo,
I call it limbo.
So a lot of times when I've brought up my ideas to my
    homeboys,
they say,
'Twilight,
that's before your time,
that's something you can't do now'.
When I talked about the truce back in 1988,
that was something they considered before its time,
yet
in 1992
we made it
realistic.

So to me it's like I'm stuck in limbo,
like the sun is stuck between night and day
in the twilight hours.
I'm in an area not many people exist.[40]

Here is what Lefebvre calls a 'representational space' that revives belief in the very mediatory ground we have felt lacking in the work itself. Twilight's 'limbo', where his precocious intelligence and self-less social responsibility moves restlessly like the missing next tick of the clock, is perhaps the most exciting of all the chronotopes explored in this thesis. It is an 'active negotiation', in Smith's words, of the many geographies of a city that has preferred to forget about Twilight and his people. Patrolling his neighbourhood all night from age thirteen, playing prophet with the syllables of his name, augur of all the good that is 'before his time', Twilight and his creative limbo will either triumph over that malignant 'production of space' or be crushed to fodder by it. His anticipatory, transitional 'space-time' is proof that the system works only by harbouring, in the unlikely depths of its own machinery, sparks of a future it can neither control nor imagine.

Yet how persuasive after all is Smith's postmodern realism in the face of all we have learned since the rebellion about the capacity of this social space to recontain and administer anew the contradictions there unchained? In Kim Stanley Robinson's 'Orange County' trilogy, there is a moment of prophecy which galvanizes for us the overriding issue at stake in the fragmentation and minoritization of space in the Greater Los Angeles region: namely, its pitiless abstraction. Jim McPherson lectures his friends on the 'great gridwork of light' that is the region's freeway system, circa the mid-twenty-first century:

> We're at the centre of the world . . . Orange County is the end of history, its purest product. Civilization kept moving west for thousands of years, in a sunset tropism, until they came to the edge here on the Pacific and they couldn't go any farther. And so they stopped here and *did* it. And by that time they were in the great late surge of corporate capitalism, so that everything here is purely organized, to buy and sell, buy and sell, every little piece of us.[41]

What Jim's little group is gathered together to do at the 'center of the world' is perform an archaeological (and illegal) act of historical rescue from this purified abstraction of space. Directly beneath what is now the 'Fluffy Donuts Video Palace' is the site of an old wood-frame elementary school, now buried under several cubic feet of concrete. In the dark of night, the group's saws and needlejacks pry open the concrete tomb of history, and finally the alien *thunk* of a shovel on wood greets their ears; it is a solid hardwood beam, from which they slice a small souvenir. 'Jim regards it dubiously. So this is the past . . .'[42]

Science fiction has the virtue of extrapolating tendencies of the present into a possible future, in which we glimpse our own social processes from the outside, estranged, rendered properly incomprehensible. How is it that we could have participated and collaborated in this social entombment of our own history, our nature, our spirit? Is it possible that, some few years hence, we will have obliterated all aspects of what has put us at a distance from the market, that 'every little piece of us' will soon have been assimilated to the parcelliza-tions of exchange value? Will future acts of recovery of our represen-tational spaces necessarily be terroristic, furtive, illegal; will they be perpetrated at all? And so what of today: do these precious spaces still exist for us as they did for our grandparents, or have they already entered the simulacrum? Pick up a piece of the past and we already 'regard it dubiously'. The same goes for every shred of apparently representational space. Ethnicity, community, theatre, home, bedroom, sexuality, subjectivity: real or simulated? Authentic or pastiche?

A hermeneutics of suspicion quarantines every molecule of meaning left to us, and this because reflection is barred from any significant articulation with activity as such, or social change and those groups or classes by which it is effected. What withers in abstract space is *use*. Abstraction guarantees reproduction: 'buying and selling', land rent, property speculation, accumulation, deindus-trialization, out-marketing, carceralization. These are not 'uses' of space, so much as they are strategies designed to dominate and profit from it. Such strategies are no doubt quite 'flexible', and it is not inconceivable that the meaning of the various forms of particu-larism considered in this book is ultimately to drape the withering-away of spatial use-value with the manifestations of difference.

All celebrations of the diversity and range of cultures in Los Angeles the Heteropolis today are therefore false to the degree that they occlude the fundamental homogeneity of its space; the restric-tion of its limitless possible uses to serial and routine practices of reproduction. Charles Jencks writes of 'a city which quite naturally tolerates difference, inconsistency and contradiction';[43] yet one wants to know more about this 'tolerance', its 'naturalness', and what exactly the grammatical subject of the 'city' in this sentence actually refers to – all its citizens, its police force, its administrators and politicians, its artists? No; the 'city' in Jencks' sentence is surely nothing other than abstraction itself, for it is abstraction which reads inconsistency as 'natural' and which is quite happy to tolerate it under the liberal banner of 'difference'. And even if Anna Deavere Smith's *Twilight* resisted the comfortable banality of 'natural toler- ance', we still noted there a deficiency in thinking about domination and abstraction which rendered her subject to the charge of nomin- alism. The riots of 1992 had a consequence not often remarked upon, which confirms the ultimate domination of difference by the abstract: namely, the fact that they were quelled by tanks and marines, a full-scale imposition of military power which rendered the 'heteropolis' utterly subservient to state power and surveillance. Add to this the obvious fact that the whole episode was completely mediatized by corporate television, from the Rodney King beating to the helicopter aerials of the mass violence itself, and you are left with the inescapable conclusion that what might have appeared as the reclamation of social space for social agents through popular and violent protest, can equally well be construed as the ideal oppor- tunity for state and corporate strategy to reimpose and upscale its powers of violent abstraction.

From the perspective of political power, the grid of the city is resolved into a pattern of spatial nodes: nodes of accumulation, centralizations of capital and power within the urban fabric and linked to national governmentality and transnational corporations, around which are then arranged the multifarious economic margin- alia of space – blighted zones of deprivation, underdevelopment, migrant populations, homelessness, and so forth. Here the classic economic question of property reasserts itself with a vengeance: no longer the property of things in space (factories, goods, wealth), but of space itself, 'real' estate as such. With this emergent conception of the city as a dialectic of space,[44] a contradiction between centres of accumulation, decision-making, knowledge and culture, and margins of poverty and dead or living labour, the function of abstraction is made apparent. It is to contain and defuse these contradictions, render them neutral or void by virtue of its exorbitant metaphors.

What we have been proposing in this book is that certain cultural acts are themselves 'uses', of a highly limited, imaginary or symbolic sort to be sure, of the social space of the city. In other words, the symbolic or allegorical or figurative representation of space is a use, or better, an appropriation of it: a *detournement* of abstraction through the residual filters of phenomenology, nature, ethnicity, community, libido, ego, sexuality, and so on, which have not altogether been neutralized by exchange value. This is a process of 'rescue' or reclamation that dates back to the Romantic period, continues in altered conditions during Modernism, and today persists in embattled and minor gestures: a fractured history of resistance to imperious abstraction which seizes on representational spaces as uncolonized *loci* of felt qualities. Perhaps literary history has not sufficiently highlighted the necessary spatial aspects of this resistance. Romanticism exploited the representational spaces of Nature and the Ego; Modernism of Consciousness, the Unconscious and Memory (as well as the more traditionally cited Time and Tradition); while postmodernism looks predisposed to exploiting ethnicity and the body, not as extrinsic representations, but as felt and lived intensities. One can see quite clearly how inaccessible these 'lived' spaces are to the visual media; and I have endeavoured again and again to argue for literary style as their surest indelible repository. Because literature works with language, it inevitably burrows into the preserves of individual lived experience which film, video and television simply cannot penetrate (it may of course find them empty, as with Bret Ellis, but precisely that absence is felt as a critical discovery); and such lived experience is generally mediated by larger group identities which even Anna Smith, in her virtual taboo upon them, did not quite manage to dispel.

Nor is it entirely certain that these minoritized representational spaces are not themselves capable of wider kinds of allegorical application throughout the global marketplace. Unguessed-at affinities between, say, illegal Chicano immigrants in LA and the ex-Communist poor of Eastern Europe are suggested by T. Coraghessan Boyle in *The Tortilla Curtain* (1995), not only in its title, but in reflections such as this:

> She was a fool to have left, a fool to have listened to the stories, watched the movies, read the *novelas*, and more of a fool to ever for a second have envied the married girls in Tepoztlán whose husbands gave them so much when they came home from the North. Clothes, jewelry, a new TV – that wasn't what you got. You got this. You got streets and bums and burning pee.[45]

It's a lesson not a few post-Communist countries are now busy and painfully learning: the promises of abstract space and consumerism are universal by nature; and so, increasingly, are their consequences, 'streets and bums and burning pee'. Such lessons are applicable across neo-capitalist space, and the final turn to the body here is an index of the appeal of what remains of representational space for politics in general today. If it hurts, then it must be history, we might say; and history is not altogether unalterable, except after the fact. We may have been fools to listen to the stories and watch the movies, but literature can still carry out some covert action against them, remind us of the latent contradictions, illustrate them by articulating the divorced spheres of abstract Knowledge and lived experience.

If so, then how best to do so? The excitement generated by Anna Deavere Smith's admirable work looks rather evanescent now, as televisual talking heads have yet again neutered the theatrical rhythmanalysis of her expressive bodies. If her 'realism' of the body and *civitas* functioned as an inversion of media myth, those stereotypes and clichés of identity in America endure in spectacular undeath across the nation, in stark indifference to her labours. Indeed, it seems ultimately futile to resist or deny the domination of space by image and spectacle: the way in which *déja-vu* is part of the logic of space itself – our already having seen and known everything. In fact, if there is to be an effective literary engagement with the contemporary, it will have to pass, as several of the writers discussed in this book have attempted to pass, through the abstraction of space itself, rather than cling stubbornly to the concrete fragments of everyday life as though that abstraction were somehow avoidable. Yet, unlike Ellroy and Mosley, whose deliberate passage through the crime genre signalled their shared consciousness of 'mediation' by mass-reproducible forms, a proper encounter with the present will have perforce to represent the present, and not a convenient period of the past; and unlike Ellis and Cooper, it will also have to articulate a wide and complex web of relations between the ethnic and racial 'fortresses' of the city, and not treat abstraction simply as a white man's burden.

I want very briefly here to suggest that the lineaments of this new possibility for fiction of and about Los Angeles (and so, of and about postmodern society at large) do exist, and can be observed functioning in highly charged manner in Gary Indiana's novel, *Resentment* (1997). Now, while Indiana is a gay writer and his central protagonists are sexualized in a similar way, this does not simply consign the novel to a minority status, or if it does so it is in the understanding that this status is in any event ineluctable and the starting point of any Los Angeles fiction. What is of much greater importance is how this 'position' is not identified with any special-ized chronotope that is not the chronotope of the heterogeneous majority itself: namely, the chronotope of the media, of saturated broadcasting, of image society itself, as a universal spectacle into which the cultural-identity fragment is absorbed. 'Los Angeles' in this novel is not, in this sense, a particular stretch of suburbia, or network of roads, or interior domestic intensity; it is that incessant flow of visual and discursive messages in which 'Los Angeles' is spectacularized and reified as myth.

Taking as its point of departure not the riots, but the celebrity trials of the Menendez brothers and O.J. Simpson, *Resentment* refuses all temptations of immediacy, and prefers instead to demonstrate the degree to which the abstract spectacle of those trials structured everyday life itself – in the movement of its characters, their dialo-gues, working lives, relations, and fates. In this work, not the city but its abstract projection into a theatre of sensations is the basis of narrative form:

> I have, in fact, inserted into the action of this book many structural details, and even stray chunks of *ipsissima verba*, related to those cases [*California v. Menendez, California v. Simpson*], as shorthand references to generic public spectacles which millions have witnessed in one or another mediated form, and which, from the perspectives of absurdity and pathos . . . provided their own satirical embellishments.
> . . . [It is] a kind of reverse *roman a clef* in which what has already occurred in 'life' as collective spectacle functions as honorary ballast for an entirely speculative fictional narrative.[46]

For these reasons, events as narrated do not appear unmediated, as if dropped from an authorially immaculate conception, but emerge with all the embarrassed difficulty of having always already been represented. Unlike Bret Easton Ellis's deadpan and affectless prose, then, Indiana's comes laced with all the accumulated irony and venom of years of literary *resentment* against spectacle and stereotype. Consider in the following early extract how the well-nigh Dickensian base-line satire of corrupt and impure language-use is radicalized by the absence of an authorial absolute, a 'style' which would stand as a corrective to the debased clichés. The device of importing quoted extracts from the media 'analysis' of the trials to ridicule them is double-edged to the degree that the media language generates a necessary momentum of its own within the narrative voice.

> [I]t was assumed that the deaths of Fidel and Peggy Martinez were *gangland killings*, or, as was sometimes reported, *gangland-style* killings, since Fidel Martinez, a video distribution company executive, was reputed to have had so-called *gangland connections* or *gangland associates*, though it was often noted that a double murder involving fifteen shotgun blasts could not be accurately described as gangland-*style* killings, even if they had in fact been *gangland* killings, since the established *style* of gangland killings is a single bullet fired from a pistol or revolver into the base of the skull, rather than five to ten rounds of birdshot and buckshot fired wildly from a shotgun. The Beverly Hills Police Department, which only handles an average of two homicides per year, in the wake of these violent deaths, surmised that the murders were indeed some type of *gang-related* or *mob-connected* killings, despite their lack of so-called gangland *style*, and pursued this avenue of thinking in its investigations . . .[47]

The satire here is complex and multi-layered, but also fresh and accessible. First, at the level of content, this murder of a child-abusing 'video distribution company executive' by his two spoilt sons proves comically insoluble by the BHPD without the fantasized construct of presumably ethnic criminal gangs and mobs, located outside Beverly Hills and originating ultimately in the image-banks of Hollywood itself. Next, at the level of style, the italicized phrases retain all their media banality within the more open and flexible, yet non-judgemental discursive space of the narrator; the stupidity of the police is associated directly with the stupidity and stereotypicality of the language in which the crime is mediated. And finally, at a rather higher and philosophical level, surely what is at stake in this passage is nothing other than the demise of the real itself, whose substitution by a self-sufficient structure of signifiers within a tightly organized code is carried through with po-faced thoroughness by the narratorial voice: the emergence of one element of the code, 'gangland', generates all of the other semes which go with it (gangland-style, gangland-associates, gang-related, mob-connected, the single bullet, etc.), in a system which then demands a disciplined set of actions and responses, entirely detached from the 'double murder involving fifteen shotgun blasts' it would seem to want to address.

As a result of this complex intertwining of distinct satiric layers, the sentences in Indiana's prose – unlike so much of contemporary Los Angeles fiction – surmount the syntactical unidimensionality of parataxis. Encouraged as it were by the conceptual freedom of allowing the debased content of image society and abstract space to satirize itself, the style luxuriates in relative spaciousness, since all it is effectively required to do in order to achieve this end is, precisely, *subordinate* certain clauses to others:

> Carlos never understood why Felix went sobbing to the quack when he had his so-called attack of conscience, since neither of them trusted Pot, as Carlos called him, in the first place, Pot short for toilet where you dropped your shit, Carlos says, even when Fidel and Peggy were around the brothers had been circumspect, because Pot and Fidel had some deal where Pot told Fidel whatever Carlos and Felix told him, not everything but anything important, anything clinically significant, which is one reason Felix never told Pot about these feelings he gets about other boys, or the BJs he and Poppy gave each other, or stuff him and Carlos did a few times years ago, Fidel would have hit the ceiling even though Fidel had those feelings himself obviously and furthermore acted on them with his own children, and just forget telling Pot about Fidel . . .[48]

This 'sentence' continues for a further page, and what distinguishes it above all from the long sentence we examined in Ellis's *Informers* is the arrangement of the clauses themselves within a clearly hypotactic schema, designed purely to display the 'satirical embellishments' of the spectacle to best effect. The deft use of conjunctions, sentence adverbs, elaborations and asides is the predominant means whereby Indiana secures his effects; his hypotaxis is a virtual three-dimensional inflation of one-dimensional materials, and thereby a satiric deformation of stereotype achieved principally through style.

So if Indiana's novel is ultimately to be thought of as a development of the great first satire of Los Angeles' image-worship, Nathanael West's *Day of the Locust* (1939), it is nonetheless postmodern to the degree that its grotesquerie is intensely understated and confined to the movements of a prose-style rather than enacted in excessive modernist gestures á la West. Which is not to say that there are not many rather conventional and tired rehearsals of themes here, as in the following familiar laments about abstract space itself:

> . . . because everything here is disconnected. There is no connection, Seth says, between this room and this hotel and the city around it, this room and this hotel have nothing to do with anything. Everyone in this city is in transit from one place to someplace else, crossing vast dead space to get from one dead thing to another, one moment of life to another, and in between, nothing . . .[49]

> He says he cannot figure out the reverse route back to Hollywood via freeway, there are too many changes, he keeps getting lost on surface roads, winding up in Glendale or the forbidding tracts of emptiness behind Griffith Park, roads bare of traffic that look like crime scenes, derelict freight-yards and cul-de-sacs, seedy nowhere villages and blank passages of useless landscape.[50]

But the more typical stylistic successes of the novel point elsewhere, to a fine-tuned postmodern satire of the postmodern, which in contradistinction to all of the works treated hitherto in this book, seizes onto the progressive side of abstraction itself. It is this, indeed, which I want to offer as the ultimate word on this whole dilemma of representation in the contemporary city.

There is something of value, as Indiana sees it, in the peculiar dynamic of abstraction in Los Angeles, which, contrary to some other forms of abstraction in ideology and commodification across the globe, cannot but celebrate and mythologize its own mechanics, its own manifest artifice. It is for this reason that Los Angeles has most often been conceived of as un-American in the context of the nation's democratic charter with its citizens. No representation of LA has seemed more attractive to middle-class, middle-brow America in recent years than this 'fallen' one. It is as though the dystopian Los Angeles social imaginary, first constructed by writers like West, Chandler and Horace McCoy, then appropriated ironically by the local tourist and real-estate industries, has been exported to the nation at large, which can feed off this potent reminder of all that is wrong with uncontrolled urban capitalism and congratulate itself that not everything is that bad. The packaging of Los Angeles as the great 'wrong place'[51] has been particularly useful, of course, over the last twenty years, since the Reagan administration began its remorseless budgetary campaign against the nation's cities, and needed a justificatory scapegoat, as we shall see.

Steve Erickson's visionary novel *Amnesiascope* (1996) imagines an American near-future in which a new-Right moralism has gained incontestable national ascendancy and effectively sequestered LA (the vice, the crime, the spectacle, the falsity) from the body of the nation. As a consequence, as Erickson astutely points out, the very idea of America has been split down the middle:

> LA is all that's left of America the Delirious. Long ago, in the movie theaters of the land, LA collectivized the American dark; it cleaned up the depraved whispers and messier impulses of America's deeper recesses and reduced them to archetypes or,

even better, commodities. LA insisted that the subconscious didn't own us but we owned it; a more American aspiration is hard to imagine. Now east of LA rolls America the Mean. The thin membrane between the delirious and the mean, between LA and the rest of the country, is an America of the mind that will explode any moment, if it has any life left in it at all, or will expire with a hush . . . Now in LA, street by street, block by block, step by step, door by door, all that's left of the old America is under siege. I catch sight of it from time to time: a fleeting glimpse at the top of the stairs, or outside rustling in the bushes. This is the old America of legend and distant memory, that invested no faith in the wisdom of history and no hope in the sham of the future, the old America that invented itself all over from the ground up every single day. It's the brazen America, the reckless one, the one with the lit fuse, the America that ejaculates not by habit but for the intoxicating pleasure of it . . .[52]

This bifurcated national identity, both puritanical and decadent at once, authentic and simulated, repressive and libidinous, is in many senses as old as the Republic itself; yet what Erickson is rightly indicating is the degree to which 'LA' has recently figured in the New Right's demonization of precisely the liberationist and democratic moments of America's constitution. Erickson's affirmation of the 'authenticity' of LA's inauthenticity is of a piece with Jean Baudrillard's spirited assays on the city: one must learn to accept LA's playful simulacrum as America's greatest legacy to the world.[53] This is a tactic of reading the city which makes best sense when it is seen as a dialogical rejoinder to what the rest of America – 'America the Mean' – is saying about it.

It is this larger and pernicious social text, to be found refracted across innumerable political, journalistic, literary and critical modes, which has made Los Angeles 'probably the most mediated town in America, nearly unviewable save through the fictive scrim of its mythologizers.'[54] Less a real city than a tissue of discourses through which it might be discussed and explained by outsiders, 'Los Angeles' exists principally, for most Americans, as 'a series of tropes. The list of these topics outlines the range of strategies for argumentation as well as the parameters of a sufficient description of "Los Angelesness" . . . All this tends to produce inconclusive ways of speaking rather than ways of knowing. Los Angeles has a rhetoric but no epistemology.'[55] Of course, this book has been an attempt to redress this absence of an epistemology of LA, based on readings of literary efforts to appropriate its space; meanwhile, however, the balance of power rests with the experts and soothsayers ensconced in comfortable suburban havens, who are free to direct urban policy in California with manifest disregard for the poorer people who live in its cities.

As Lewis Lapham reminds us, the fulsome anti-urban bias of much of this 'expert' commentary comes with a long and inglorious history:

> The American ruling and explaining classes tend to live in the suburbs, or in cities as indistinguishable from suburbs as West Los Angeles and the government preserves of Washington, D.C., and their fear and suspicion of the urban landscape (as well as the urban turn of mind) would have been well understood by the gentlemen who founded the Republic in Philadelphia in 1787. The idea of a great city has never occupied a comfortable place in the American imagination. Much of the country's political and literary history suggests that the city stands as a metaphor for depravity – the port of entry for things foreign and obnoxious, likely to pollute the pure streams of American innocence. Virtue proverbially resides in villages and small towns, and for at least two hundred years the rhetoric of urban reform has taken its images from the Bible and the visionary poets.[56]

To have imagined America as a village of free-floating individuals is the root of the crime here, as so few of the country's great intellectuals have been concerned to affirm the full nature of modern democracy as an *urban* project. But that this pervasive anti-urbanism in America's representational history should recently have settled on Los Angeles as its favourite whipping-boy will surprise no one who has attended to the persistent representation of this city as the end of the line of America itself, the site of its vulgar Culture Industry, and of its most heterogeneous and explosive immigration. To the degree that LA is taken by the nation's opinion-makers to be broadly representative of the urban future in America, so it has come to be repudiated as what must at all costs be avoided, the living laboratory of future shock, where the very essence of America is dissipated and lost.

What have the results of this revulsion from the urban been in recent years? When the Reagan administration began its federal war on American cities, the spirit of corporate capitalism ushered in by the Right was expected to shift the burden of financial 'responsibility' for the nation's cities from the state to the private sector.[57] Disinvestment quickly abandoned the urban cores to Social Darwinism, as the overall federal contribution to the budgets of big cities fell by 64% after 1980: a $26 billion shortfall which cities had to make up for by gutting community funding, job training, subsidized housing and everything else but more police to fight the resultant increase in crime. Privatization programmes put thousands in the public sector out of work. The federal War on Drugs meanwhile converted down-town streets into literal warzones, with high-tech machinery and weaponry trained on the cities' children to terrify them into apparent submission. Behind the scenes, the real process was being further consolidated: the subsidized retreat of white money to suburban edge cities, now bloated with greater tax revenues than all the inner cities put together.[58] Thus was created for the first time a 'suburban majority' whose surplus of votes, taxes and lobbyists over the residual inner-city constituencies has meant that government no longer has to concern itself with the urban question at all.

In Los Angeles, this spatial redistribution of the structure of political power became manifest culturally in a host of films which, since Ridley Scott's epochal *Blade Runner* of 1982, represented the city as a doomed, apocalyptic space, a strategy clearly meant to wipe the city itself off the national imaginary. *Terminator* I and II, *Predator* 2, *Strange Days*, *Colors*, *Falling Down*, *Speed*, *Escape From LA*, *Independence Day*, and *Volcano*, all variously project Los Angeles on the verge of a pure disaster, either natural or social, which would forever put to rest the unaskable question of its 'renewal'. The regressive, non-democratic, suburban imaginary of Spielberg's *E.T.: The Extraterrestrial* supplanted the risky, dangerous urban imagin-ary of, say, Altman's *The Long Goodbye*. Middle America began to protect itself from the risk-taking essential to any genuine democ-racy, and this amnesia about its vital urban heritage, this retreat into small-town mentality and security, has also been increasingly dominating the nation's literary scene. Richard Ford, David Gu-terson, and the assorted fall-out of Raymond Carver's 'dirty realism': what could better reflect the reinvention of an American literary tradition after 'white flight' and Reaganism than literary tendencies such as these?

Torn between wanting to be rid once and for all of Los Angeles, and the puerile optimism that, with enough 'workfare' and effective policing, it and other cities will one day be clean and decent again, Middle America has politely declined to expend any extensive thought, dialogue or funding on the urgent regeneration of urban areas. The casualty of this neglect is democracy itself, which simply cannot be practised in the gated, affluent suburbs or on the Shopping

Network. Kevin R. McNamara insists courageously on what is at stake in recuperating America's urban imagination:

> If the virtue of urban culture is its ability to shock us out of ourselves, our cities will never be risk free, smooth-functioning organisms or machines. If cities are geographic pockets of concentrated difference, it is incumbent upon all citizens not to withdraw from life in common by practicing a limiting identity politics or becoming preoccupied with inner space, but to find common ground on which to rebuild cities as physical, political, and ethical spaces shared by different communities whose overlappings weave the social fabric. Cities will remain 'dangerous' because tolerance is a quality more often demanded than supplied.[59]

It is an urgency shared, albeit more brilliantly, by Lewis Lapham himself:

> The hatred of cities is the fear of freedom. Freedom implies change, which implies friction, which implies unhappiness, which disturbs the nervous complacency of the admissions committee at the country club. Because the city promises so many changes and transformations (a good many of them probably dangerous or unhealthy), the act of decision presents itself as a burden instead of an opportunity . . . Until we learn to value the idea of the city, we can expect to see the streets paved with anger instead of gold.[60]

The problem, however, is that in the long abeyance of clear policy decisions and federal commitments to urban programmes since the 1970s, what we have been calling the full-throttle 'production of space' in urban America has facilitated a virtually incontestable political dominion by capital over *the practice of everyday life itself*. Michel de Certeau's optimism about the spontaneous acts of pedestrians in American cities once held out the belief in freedom's imminence, given a simple shift in the interpretive framework:

> [O]ne can try another path: one can analyse the microbe-like, singular and plural practices which an urbanistic system was supposed to administer or suppress, but which have outlived its decay; one can follow the swarming activity of these procedures that, far from being regulated or eliminated by panoptic administration, have reinforced themselves in a proliferating illegitimacy, developed and insinuated themselves into the network's surveillance, and combined in accord with unreadable but stable tactics to the point of constituting everyday regulations and surreptitious creativities that are merely concealed by the frantic mechanisms and discourses of the observational organization.[61]

Yet this advocacy of a millipedal democracy failed to recognize the *creative* domination of space by power, and its inexhaustible capacity to curtail the appropriative tactics of 'users': for instance, in Los Angeles, the eradication of pedestrian space itself. Edward Soja's clear-eyed and vigilant analysis of Los Angeles' six geographies cuts like a surgeon's scalpel through any misty-eyed nostalgia for the 'good old days' of the city.[62] Not only did such days never exist, but their appearance today would entail the miraculous reversal of decades of calamitous failure on the part of elected officials to halt or even curb the wholesale abstraction and fragmentation of urban life by the power of capital. Our investigations of some of the city's writing has shown the limitations to urban consciousness in a city overwhelmingly controlled by a spectral class which does not even reside there. Life-long locals and self-conscious authors have found it impossible or impracticable to overcome the contradictions of postmodern urban space, let alone forge some ideal 'common ground on which to rebuild'.

What I think it is permissible to say in conclusion, however, is that perhaps the 'common ground' is there in the very baleful monstrosity of abstraction itself, which in Los Angeles is delirious and positively volatile. As Erickson, Baudrillard and Indiana remind us, that monstrous spectacle which the city makes of itself is exactly the novelty it has contributed to the world; a vast, garish and hysterical self-display that ecstatically deterritorializes itself, in a highly unstable metastasis of global dimensions. We began this book by quoting Bertolt Brecht on Los Angeles, troubled by this vulgar 'atlantis' of signs and spectacles, unable to see anything but the despicable political economy subtending it. Yet it was Brecht himself who insisted so bravely on the evident contradiction that history progresses by its bad side: 'Don't start from the good old things but the bad new ones'.[63] The 'good old' representational spaces we have seen explored and used in literary appropriations of Los Angeles' social space are of course not as dispensable as this maxim would have us think. No doubt they will go on radiating their obscured values for a long time to come. Race, ethnicity, memory, the body and all the other 'spaces' analyzed in this book as critical weapons against abstraction have, precisely, a kernel of lived truth which the latter so obviously lacks. Yet it is the latter which continues to dominate and control everyday life itself. Perhaps if there were some way of joining it on its own ground and catching it in the act, its manifest untruth might be transposed into an effective and critical knowledge. This is ultimately what Jameson means by cognitive mapping: 'the new political art . . . will have to hold to the truth of postmodernism, that is to say, to its fundamental object – the world space of multinational capital – at the same time at which it achieves a breakthrough to some as yet unimaginable new mode of representing this last, in which we may again begin to grasp our positioning as individual and collective subjects and regain a capacity to act and struggle which is at present neutralized by our spatial as well as our social confusion.'[64] In the meantime, and as a preparation for the rigours of such a 'breakthrough', Los Angeles' 'fundamental object', its abstract and delirious representationality, might be a reasonable place to start. Rather than drawing back from it into treasured representational spaces, or moralizing about it impotently, it is just conceivable that, once accepted as a legitimate object for representational capture, LA's provocatively abstract space may prove the best ground currently available for clearing up some of our spatial and social confusion. Here it is, 'the old America that invented itself all over from the ground up every single day. It's the brazen America, the reckless one, the one with the lit fuse, the America that ejaculates not by habit but for the intoxicating pleasure of it . . .' The bad new thing is old enough after all, if you present it the right way; it only remains to devise an aesthetic and a literature adequate to it.

Notes

Epigraph

1 Antonin Artaud, From 'To Have Done with the Judgment of God', translated by Clayton Eshleman, in Jerome Rothenberg and Pierre Joris (eds.), *Poems for the Millennium; The University of California Book of Modern and Postmodern Poetry: Volume Two: From Postwar to Millennium* (Berkeley and Los Angeles, 1998), p. 34.

Introduction

1 Charles Jencks, *Heteropolis: Los Angeles, the Riots and the Strange Beauty of Hetero-Architecture* (London, 1993), pp. 24–5.
2 Edward W. Soja, 'Los Angeles, 1965–1992: From Crisis-Generated Restructuring to Restructuring-Generated Crisis', in Allen Scott and Edward W. Soja (eds.), *The City: Los Angeles and Urban Theory at the End of the Twentieth Century* (Berkeley and Los Angeles, 1996), pp. 445–6.
3 Steve Erickson, *Amnesiascope* (New York, 1996), p. 47.
4 Wanda Coleman, *Native in a Strange Land: Trials and Tremors* (Santa Rosa, CA, 1996), p. 197.
5 Mike Davis, *City of Quartz: Excavating the Future in Los Angeles* (London, 1990), p. 40.
6 Kathleen Tynan, 'Literary Letter from Los Angeles: Why They Live Here', *New York Times Book Review* (November 18, 1979), p. 11.
7 Quoted in Matthew Tyrnauer, 'Who's Afraid of Bret Easton Ellis?' *Vanity Fair* (August, 1994), p. 125.
8 Friedrich Nietzsche, *On the Genealogy of Morals*, translated by Walter Kaufmann and R. J. Hollingdale (New York, 1969), p. 36.
9 Paul Beatty, *The White Boy Shuffle* (Boston, 1996), p. 76.
10 Gilles Deleuze and Félix Guattari, *Kafka: Towards a Minor Literature*, translated by Dana Polan (London, 1986), p. 17.

1 **The representation of Los Angeles**

1 Bertolt Brecht, 19 January, 1942, *Journals: 1934–1955*, translated by Hugh Rorrison, edited by John Willett (London, 1993), p. 193.
2 'Although LA and Miami are real cities, they are built on the power of dreamscape, collective fantasy, and façade. This landscape is explicitly produced for visual consumption'. Sharon Zukin, *Landscapes of Power: From Detroit to Disneyworld* (Oxford, 1991), p. 219.
3 See Lewis Lapham, 'City Lights', in *Hotel America: Scenes in the Lobby of the Fin-de-Siècle* (London, 1995), pp. 197–202.
4 See Norman M. Klein, *The History of Forgetting: Los Angeles and the Erasure of Memory* (London, 1997), p. 55.
5 James Joyce, *Ulysses* (London, 1992), p. 45.
6 Jean Baudrillard, *Simulations*, translated by Paul Foss, Paul Patton and Philip Beitchman (New York, 1983), pp. 1–79.
7 Edward W. Soja, *Thirdspace: Journeys to Los Angeles and Other Real-and-Imagined Places* (Oxford, 1996), pp. 64–5.
8 Henry James, 'The American Scene' in *Collected Travel Writings: Great Britain and America* (New York, 1993), p. 425.
9 Klein, *History of Forgetting*, p. 27.
10 Misapprehensions which Mike Davis sees as having got the human settlement of the region off on entirely the wrong foot. See Davis, 'Los Angeles After the Storm: The Dialectics of Ordinary Disasters', *Antipode*, vol. 27, no. 2, (1995), pp. 221–41. Expanded version in his *Ecology of Fear: Los Angeles and the Imagination of Disaster* (London, 1999), pp. 5–55.
11 For instance, see Carey McWilliams, *California: The Great Exception* (New York, 1949).
12 The first of these was in Edward W. Soja's book *Postmodern Geographies: The Reassertion of Space in Critical Theory* (London, 1989), pp. 190–248.
13 Quoted in Carey McWilliams, *Louis Adamic and Shadow America* (Los Angeles, 1935), pp. 79 and 81.
14 Carey McWilliams, *Southern California Country: An Island on the Land* (New York, 1946), p. 359.
15 Michael J. Dear, H. Eric Schockman and Greg Hise (eds.), *Rethinking Los Angeles* (London, 1996), pp. 6–8.
16 The classic account of LA as a self-divided urban agglomeration remains Robert Fogelson's *The Fragmented Metropolis: Los Angeles, 1850–1930* (Cambridge, MA, 1967).
17 Martin Wachs, 'The Evolution of Transportation Policy in Los Angeles: Images of Past Policies and Future Prospects', in Allen J. Scott and Edward W. Soja (eds.), *The City: Los Angeles and Urban Theory at the End of the Twentieth Century* (London, 1996), pp. 106–59.
18 Michael Dear, 'In the City, Time Becomes Visible: Intentionality and Urbanism in Los Angeles, 1781–1991', in Scott and Soja (eds.), *The City*, p. 92.

19 An emergence being charted (and denounced) on the spot by Theodor W. Adorno and Max Horkheimer, *Dialectic of Enlightenment*, translated by John Cumming (London, 1986), pp. 120–67.

20 'In the social production of their life, men enter into definite relations that are indispensable and independent of their will, relations of production which correspond to a definite stage of development of their material productive forces. The sum total of these relations of production constitutes the economic structure of society, the real foundation, on which rises a legal and political superstructure and to which correspond definite forms of social consciousness. The mode of production of material life conditions the social, political and intellectual life process in general. It is not the consciousness of men that determines their being, but, on the contrary, their social being that determines their consciousness'. Karl Marx, 'Preface to *A Contribution to the Critique of Political Economy*', in Marx and Engels, *Selected Works*, vol. 1 (Moscow, 1973), p. 503.

21 Mike Davis, *City of Quartz: Excavating the Future in Los Angeles* (London, 1990), p. 23.

22 Quoted in David Reid, 'Introduction', to Reid (ed.), *Sex, Death and God in LA* (London, 1994), p. xxxiv.

23 McWilliams, *Southern California Country*, p. 13.

24 Klein, *History of Forgetting*, p. 9.

25 McWilliams, *Southern California Country*, pp. 183–201.

26 Brecht, *Journals 1934–1955*, p. 366.

27 Alex Abella, *The Killing of the Saints* (London, 1992).

28 Bebe Moore Campbell, *Brothers and Sisters* (New York, 1994).

29 David Fine, *Los Angeles in Fiction* (Alberquerque, 1984), p. 2.

30 Lionel Rolfe, *In Search of . . . Literary LA* (Los Angeles, 1991), p. 90.

31 Fredric Jameson, *The Cultural Turn: Selected Writings on the Postmodern, 1983–1998* (London, 1998), p. 111.

32 Henri Lefebvre, *The Production of Space*, translated by Donald Nicholson-Smith (Oxford, 1991).

33 Perry Anderson, *The Origins of Postmodernity* (London, 1998), p. 56.

34 Raymond Williams, *The Country and the City* (London, 1993), esp. pp. 215–47.

35 Williams, 'The Metropolis and the Emergence of Modernism', in Timms and Kelley (eds.), *Unreal City: Urban Experience in Modern European Literature and Art* (Manchester, 1985), pp. 14–15.

36 Perry Anderson, 'Modernism and Revolution', *New Left Review* 144 (March-April 1984), pp. 95–113.

37 Walter Benjamin, *Charles Baudelaire: A Lyric Poet in the Era of High Capitalism*, translated by Harry Zohn (London, 1989).

38 Fredric Jameson, *Postmodernsim, or, the Cultural Logic of Late Capitalism* (London, 1991), pp. 309–10.

39 See for instance Neil Smith, *Uneven Development: Nature, Capital and the Reproduction of Space* (Oxford, 1990).

40 Kristin Ross, *The Emergence of Social Space: Rimbaud and the Paris Commune* (Houndmills, 1988), p. 56.

41 Lefebvre, *Production of Space*, pp. 30 ff.

42 Cf. Jameson's spirited reading of Giovanni Arrighi's *The Long Twenti-eth Century*, entitled 'Culture and Finance Capital', which charts the leapfrogging expansionism of Capital from Renaissance Italy to the saturated volumes of contemporary globalization, in Fredric Jameson, *The Cultural Turn*, pp. 136–61.

43 Henri Lefebvre, *The Survival of Capitalism: Reproduction of the Relations of Production*, translated by Frank Bryant (London, 1976), p. 83.

44 Lefebvre, *Production of Space*, pp. 316–17.

45 Geoff King, *Mapping Reality: An Exploration of Cultural Cartographies* (Houndmills, 1996), p. 10.

46 Henri Lefebvre, *Writings on Cities*, translated and edited by Eleonore Kofman and Elizabeth Lebas (Oxford, 1996), p. 77.

47 Edward W. Soja and Allen J. Scott, 'Los Angeles: Capital of the Late Twentieth Century', *Environment and Planning D: Society and Space* 4 (1986), p. 249.

48 Fredric Jameson, 'On Raymond Chandler', *The Southern Review*, vol. 6, no. 3 (1970), p. 629.

49 To which work Jameson explicitly owes many of his own insights into the spatial order of postmodernism; see especially his 'Spatial Historiographies', subsection in *Postmodernism*, pp. 364–76. The un-initiated will enjoy learning that Jameson was responsible for in-viting Lefebvre to participate in the History of Consciousness program at the University of California in Santa Cruz in 1983–4; and that in 1984, Jameson, Lefebvre and Edward Soja were to be found 'wandering through the Bonaventure' hotel, scene of Jameson's most memorable evocation of postmodern hyperspace. See Soja, *Third-space*, p. 196.

50 To see an earlier attempt at doing so, see my 'Grounding Theory: Literary Theory and the New Geography', in Martin McQuillan *et al.* (eds.), *Post-Theory: New Directions in Criticism* (Edinburgh, 1999), pp. 200–8.

51 Lefebvre, *Production of Space*, pp. 38–9.

52 Ibid., p. 44.

53 Ibid., pp. 41–2.

54 Rubén Martínez, 'La Placita', in Reid (ed.), *Sex, Death and God in LA*, p. 233.

55 Zukin, *Landscapes of Power*, pp. 221–41.

56 Davis, *City of Quartz*, pp. 223–60.

57 Rubén Martínez, *The Other Side: Fault Lines, Guerilla Saints, and the True Heart of Rock 'n' Roll* (London, 1992).

58 Dolores Hayden, *The Power of Place: Urban Landscapes as Public History* (London, 1995), esp. pp. 82–97.

59 For this concept of 'becoming-animal' see Gilles Deleuze and Félix Guattari, *A Thousand Plateaus: Capitalism and Schizophrenia*, translated by Brian Massumi (London, 1988), pp. 232–309.

60 Scott L. Bottles, *Los Angeles and the Automobile: The Making of the Modern City* (London, 1987).

61 Michel de Certeau, *The Practice of Everyday Life*, translated by Steven Rendall, (London, 1988), pp. 91–110.

62 David Rieff, *Los Angeles: Capital of the Third World* (London, 1992), p. 137.
63 A tradition inaugurated by Claude Lévi-Strauss, in 'The Structural Study of Myth', in *Structural Anthropology*, translated by C. Jacobson and B. G. Schoepf (New York, 1963), pp. 206–31. This would later be worked up into a substantial literary theory in its own right by Fredric Jameson in *The Political Unconscious: Narrative as a Socially Symbolic Act* (Ithaca, NY, 1981), esp. pp. 77–80.
64 See Marc Augé, *Non-Places: Introduction to an Anthropology of Supermodernity*, translated by John Howe (London, 1995).
65 Fredric Jameson, 'Cognitive Mapping', in *Marxism and the Interpretation of Culture*, Lawrence Grossberg and Cary Nelson (eds.) (London, 1988), p. 351.
66 Jameson, *The Cultural Turn*, p. 111.
67 Jameson, *Postmodernism*, p. 47.
68 Ibid., pp. 417–18. See also Georg Lukács, *History and Class Consciousness: Studies in Marxist Dialectics*, translated by Rodney Livingstone (London, 1971), esp. pp. 46–81, 149–209.
69 In a sliding scale of spatial orders in the contemporary world, Neil Smith enumerates the following: 'body, home, community, urban, region, nation, global'. See Smith, 'Homeless/Global: Scaling Places', in Jon Bird *et al.* (eds.) *Mapping the Futures: Local Cultures, Global Changes* (London, 1993), p. 101.
70 Mikhail Bakhtin, 'Forms of Time and of the Chronotope in the Novel', *The Dialogical Imagination: Four Essays*, edited by Michael Holquist, translated by Caryl Emerson and Michael Holquist (Austin, 1981), p. 84.
71 Ibid.
72 Michael Sorkin, 'Explaining Los Angeles', in *Exquisite Corpse: Writing on Buildings* (London, 1991), pp. 48–60. For more on apocalypse, see also Mike Davis' remarkable chapter, 'The Literary Destruction of Los Angeles', in his *Ecology of Fear: Los Angeles and the Imagination of Disaster* (London, 1999), pp. 273–356.
73 Slavoj Žižek, 'Multiculturalism, or, the Cultural Logic of Multinational Capitalism', *New Left Review* 225 (September–October, 1997), pp. 44–6.
74 For an excellent introduction to these issues, see Mike Davis, 'Chinatown, Revisited?: The "Internationalization" of Downtown Los Angeles', in Reid (ed.), *Sex, Death and God in LA*, pp. 19–53.

2 Neo-noir and the archaeology of urban space

1 Mike Davis, *City of Quartz: Excavating the Future in Los Angeles* (London, 1990), p. 23.
2 J. U. Peters, 'The Los Angeles Anti-Myth', in Charles L. Crow (ed.), *Itinerary Seven: Essays on California Writers* (Bowling Green, 1978), pp. 21–34.
3 David Fine, 'Introduction', *Los Angeles in Fiction* (Alberquerque, 1984), p. 7.

4 Davis, *City of Quartz*, p. 38.
5 For an instance of that respect, see Edmund Wilson, 'The Boys in the Back Room', in *Classics and Commercials: A Literary Chronicle of the Forties* (New York, 1958).
6 The concept is defined by Norman M. Klein as a host of more or less unconscious, popular assumptions about society and the built environment. Klein, *The History of Forgetting: Los Angeles and the Erasure of Memory* (London, 1997), pp. 9–13.
7 Ibid., p. 55.
8 Thomas Pynchon, *Vineland* (London, 1991), pp. 325–6.
9 See my 'Noir and the Racial Unconscious', *Screen* vol. 39, no. 1 (Spring, 1998), 22–35.
10 Franco Moretti, *Signs Taken for Wonders* (London, 1983), p. 138.
11 David Schmid, 'Imagining Safe Urban Space: The Contribution of Detective Fiction to Radical Geography', *Antipode*, vol. 27, no. 3 (1995), 242–69.
12 Barry Long, 'Dark Passages', *The Weekend Review* (*Australian*) (March 4–5, 1995), 7.
13 John G. Cawelti, *Adventure, Mystery, and Romance* (London, 1976), p. 141.
14 Raymond Chandler, *The Simple Art of Murder* (London, 1950), p. 333.
15 Dennis Porter, *The Pursuit of Crime: Art and Ideology in Detective Fiction* (London, 1981), p. 169.
16 Raymond Chandler, *Selected Letters of Raymond Chandler*, edited by Frank MacShane (London, 1981), p. 48.
17 Chandler, *Raymond Chandler Speaking*, edited by Dorothy Gardiner and Katherine Sorley Walker (London, 1962), p. 75.
18 Chandler, *Selected Letters*, p. 87.
19 Fredric Jameson, 'On Raymond Chandler', *Southern Review*, vol. 6, no. 3 (1970).
20 Ibid., p. 131.
21 T. J Binyon, *'Murder Will Out': The Detective in Fiction* (Oxford, 1989), pp. 108–18.
22 Edward W. Soja uses this term to account for the extreme levels of surveillance and discipline in Los Angeles. See his 'Los Angeles, 1965–1992: From Crisis-Generated Restructuring to Restructuring-Generated Crisis', in Allen J. Scott and Edward Soja (eds.), *The City: Los Angeles and Urban Theory at the End of the Twentieth Century* (London, 1996), pp. 448–50.
23 Jean Baudrillard, *America* (London, 1988), p. 107.
24 James Ellroy, *My Dark Places* (London, 1996), p. 101.
25 Ibid., p. 103.
26 Quoted in Paul Scanlon, '"Demon Dog" Has His Day', *GQ* (US), (October, 1992), 206.
27 Davis, *City of Quartz*, p. 251.
28 See for instance the scenes in *LA Confidential* (London, 1990), pp. 61–4; 144–6.
29 Ibid., p. 295.

30 Edward W. Soja, *Postmodern Geographies: The Reassertion of Space in Critical Social Theory* (London, 1989), p. 236.
31 James Ellroy, *The Black Dahlia* (London, 1993), pp. 53–4.
32 Ellroy, *LA Confidential* (London, 1990), pp. 95–6.
33 Davis, *City of Quartz*, p. 233.
34 Ellroy, *Black Dahlia*, p. 235.
35 Ibid., pp. 299–300.
36 Ellroy, *The Big Nowhere* (London, 1994), p. 44.
37 Theodor W. Adorno, *Notes to Literature*, volume two, edited by Rolf Tiedemann, translated by Shierry Weber Nicholsen (New York, 1992), p. 136.
38 Ellroy, *LA Confidential*, p. 63.
39 Ellroy, *Black Dahlia*, p. 206.
40 Ellroy, *LA Confidential*, p. 71.
41 Ibid., p. 400.
42 Ibid., p. 146, passim.
43 Ellroy, *White Jazz* (London, 1992), p. 124.
44 Quoted in Scanlon, 'Demon Dog', pp. 204–6.
45 Ellroy, *Black Dahlia*, p. 77.
46 Josh Cohen, 'James Ellroy, Los Angeles and the Spectacular Crisis of Masculinity', *Women: a cultural review*, vol. 7, no.1 (Spring, 1996), 5.
47 See Joan Copjec, 'The Phenomenal Nonphenomenal: Private Space in *Film Noir*', in Joan Copjec (ed.), *Shades of Noir* (London, 1993), pp. 167–98.
48 Ellroy, *Big Nowhere*, p. 166.
49 See Laura Mulvey, 'Visual Pleasure and Narrative Cinema', *Screen*, vol. 16, no. 3 (1975); reprinted in Gerald Mast and Marshall Cohen (eds.), *Film Theory and Criticism: Introductory Readings*, 3rd ed. (Oxford, 1985), pp. 803–16. See also Sigmund Freud, 'On Narcissism', in *On Metapsychology*, vol. 11, Penguin Freud Library (London, 1991), esp. pp. 80–5.
50 Franco Moretti, *Signs Taken for Wonders*, p. 135.
51 Ellroy, *Big Nowhere*, pp. 130–2.
52 Ibid., p. 153.
53 John Gregory Dunne's *True Confessions* (London, 1978) took the same point of departure. See also T. Hamm, 'Fragments of Postwar Los Angeles: The Black Dahlia in Fact and Fiction', *Antipode*, vol. 28, no.1 (1996), 24–41.
54 Ellroy, *Black Dahlia*, p. 87.
55 Copjec, *Shades of Noir*, pp. 182–3.
56 Ellroy, *Big Nowhere*, pp. 436–9, 461.
57 Ellroy, *White Jazz*, p. 49.
58 Jim Shelley, 'A Genre's Demon Dog', *The Guardian Weekend* (January 7, 1995), 19.
59 Murphet, 'Noir and the Racial Unconscious'.
60 Toni Morrison, *Playing in the Dark: Whiteness and the Literary Imagination* (London, 1992), pp. 14–15.
61 Lawrence B. de Graaf, 'The City of Black Angeles: Emergence of the

Los Angeles Ghetto, 1890–1930', in Theodore Kornweibel, Jr. (ed.), *In Search of the Promised Land: Essays in Black Urban History* (London, 1981), pp. 161–81.

62 B. Ruby Rich, 'Dumb Lugs and Femmes Fatales', *Sight and Sound*, vol. 5, no. 11 (1995), 12.

63 In much the same way, Judith Butler has argued that the non-conviction of the LAPD officers in the Rodney King case rested on the jury's apparently counterintuitive sense that King, not the policemen, was in charge of the situation, was the violent, threatening one – a conviction based on a racist 'white paranoia which projects the intention to injure that it itself enacts'. So too, *film noir*, in appropriating and rewiring the 'authentic' black paranoia on the streets, projects its own white violence 'on increasingly larger scales' to encompass the universe itself. Butler, 'Endangered/Endangering: Schematic Racism and White Paranoia', in Robert Gooding-Williams (ed.), *Reading Rodney King/Reading Urban Uprising* (London, 1993), pp. 15–22.

64 Chandler, *Selected Letters*, pp. 43, 87; my emphasis.

65 Jameson, 'Allegorizing Hitchcock', in *Signatures of the Visible* (London, 1992), p. 105.

66 Henry Louis Gates, Jr., *The Signifying Monkey: A Theory of Afro-American Literary Criticism* (Oxford, 1988), p. xxiv.

67 Walter Mosley, *White Butterfly* (London, 1993), p. 7.

68 Lynell George, *No Crystal Stair: African-Americans in the City of Angels* (London, 1992), p. 194.

69 Walter Mosley, *Devil in a Blue Dress* (London, 1991), pp. 48–50.

70 Mosley, *Black Betty* (London, 1994), p. 163.

71 Mosley, *Devil in a Blue Dress*, p. 11.

72 Theodore O. Mason, Jr., 'Walter Mosley's Easy Rawlins: The Detective and Afro-American Fiction', *Kenyon Review*, vol. 14, no.4 (1992), 178.

73 Mosley, *A Red Death* (London, 1992), p. 221.

74 Gaston Bachelard, *The Poetics of Space*, translated by Maria Jolas (Boston, 1994).

75 Mosley, *Black Betty*, p. 4.

76 Mosley, *White Butterfly*, pp. 45–6.

77 Mosley, *A Little Yellow Dog* (London, 1996), p. 234.

78 Mosley, *White Butterfly*, pp. 96–7.

79 Mosley, *Little Yellow Dog*, p. 60.

80 Mosley, *Red Death*, p. 4.

81 Mosley, *Black Betty*, p. 26.

82 Charles Scruggs, *Sweet Home: Invisible Cities in the Afro-American Novel* (London, 1993).

83 Mosley, *White Butterfly*, pp. 61–2.

84 Fredric Jameson, 'The Synoptic Chandler', in Copjec (ed.), *Shades of Noir*, pp. 35–6.

85 Mosley, *Little Yellow Dog*, p. 20.

86 Gilles Deleuze and Félix Guattari, *Kafka: Towards a Minor Literature*, translated by Dana Polan (London, 1986), p. 17.

3   Postcards from sim-city

1   Henri Lefebvre, *The Production of Space*, translated by Donald Nicholson-Smith (Oxford, 1991), pp. 75–6.
2   Ibid., p. 98.
3   Norman M. Klein, *The History of Forgetting: Los Angeles and the Erasure of Memory* (London, 1997), p. 253.
4   David Thomson, 'Uneasy Street', in David Reid (ed.), *Sex, Death and God in LA* (London, 1994), pp. 325–7.
5   Edward W. Soja, 'Los Angeles, 1965–1992: From Crisis-Generated Restructuring to Restructuring-Generated Crisis', in Allen J. Scott and Edward Soja (eds.), *The City: Los Angeles and Urban Theory at the End of the Twentieth Century* (London, 1996), pp. 451 and 452.
6   Stanley Aronowitz, 'The Critic as Star', *Dead Artists, Live Theories* (London, 1994), p. 54.
7   Fredric Jameson, *Postmodernism, or, the Cultural Logic of Late Capitalism* (London, 1991), pp. 10–12.
8   Carey McWilliams, *Southern California Country: An Island on the Land* (New York, 1946), p. 362.
9   Elizabeth Young, 'Vacant Possession: *Less Than Zero* – A Hollywood Hell', in Elizabeth Young and Graham Caveney (eds.), *Shopping in Space: Essays on 'Blank Generation' Fiction* (London, 1993), p. 23.
10 Bret Easton Ellis, *Less Than Zero* (London, 1986), p. 61.
11 Joan Didion, *Slouching Towards Bethlehem* (Harmondsworth, 1981), p. 83.
12 Didion, *Play It As It Lays* (New York, 1979), pp. 15–16.
13 Ellis, *Less Than Zero*, p. 100.
14 Bret Easton Ellis, *The Informers* (London, 1994), pp. 96–7.
15 Nikki Sahlin, '"But This Road Doesn't Go Anywhere": The Existential Dilemma in *Less Than Zero*', *Critique*, vol. 33, no. 1, (1991), 23–42.
16 Graham Caveney, 'Notes Degree Zero: Ellis Goes West', in Young and Caveney (eds.), *Shopping in Space*, pp. 123–9; Peter Freese, 'Bret Easton Ellis, Less Than Zero: Entropy in the MTV Novel?', in Reingard M. Nischik and Barbara Korte (eds.), *Modes of Narration: Approaches to American, Canadian and British Fiction* (Würzburg, 1990), pp. 68–87.
17 Elizabeth Young, 'Vacant Possession'.
18 Pamela Thurschwell, 'Elvis Costello as Cultural Icon and Cultural Critic', in Kevin Dettmar and Willliam Richey (eds.), *Reading Rock and Roll* (New York, 1999).
19 Freese, 'Bret Easton Ellis', p. 71.
20 Young, 'Vacant Possession', p. 19.
21 *Time* (June 10, 1985), p. 80.
22 Jean Baudrillard, Interview, translated by Nancy Blake, in Giancarlo Politi and Helena Kontova (eds.), *Flash Art: Two Decades of History XXI Years* (Cambridge, MA, 1990), p. 157.
23 Ellis, *Less Than Zero*, pp. 139–40.
24 Ernst Bloch, *The Utopian Function of Art and Literature: Selected Essays*,

translated by Jack Zipes and Frank Mecklenburg (London, 1988), p. 208.

25 Ibid., p. 215.

26 Roland Barthes, *Writing Degree Zero and Elements of Semiology*, translated by Annette Lavers and Colin Smith (London, 1984), p. 64.

27 Marc Augé, *Non-Places: Introduction to an Anthropology of Supermodernity*, translated by John Howe (London, 1995).

28 Didion, *Play It As It Lays*, pp. 169–70.

29 Matthew Tyrnauer, 'Who's Afraid of Bret Easton Ellis?' *Vanity Fair* (August, 1994), 96.

30 Ellis, *Less Than Zero*, p. 125.

31 Ibid., p. 136.

32 Joan Didion, *Play It As It Lays*, p. 212.

33 Ellis, *Informers*, pp. 18–19.

34 Ibid., p. 32.

35 Ibid., pp. 19–20; 168.

36 Ibid., pp. 53; 56; 60.

37 Ibid., p. 138.

38 Ellis, *Less Than Zero*, p. 168.

39 Fredric Jameson, *Postmodernism*, pp. 43–4.

40 Ellis, *Informers*, p. 134.

41 George Bataille, *Literature and Evil*, translated by Alastair Hamilton (London, 1997).

42 Jean Baudrillard, *Symbolic Exchange and Death*, translated by Iain Hamilton Grant (London, 1993), pp. 101–12.

43 'There is no such thing as the social production of reality on the one hand, and a desiring-production that is mere fantasy on the other', declare Deleuze and Guattari, thereby extinguishing the role of the unconscious as the dark intermediary of precisely these two realities in Freudian theory. Gilles Deleuze and Félix Guattari, *Anti-Oedipus: Capitalism and Schizophrenia*, translated by Robert Hurley, Mark Seem and Helen R. Lane (Minneapolis, 1983), p. 28. It was Jameson, however, who popularized the notion of the death of the unconscious in postmodernism: 'the prodigious new expansion of multinational capital ends up penetrating and colonizing those very precapitalist enclaves (Nature and the Unconscious) which offered extraterritorial and Archimedean footholds for critical effectivity'. Jameson, *Postmodernism*, p. 49.

44 Jean Baudrillard, *Symbolic Exchange*, p. 97.

45 Fredric Jameson, *The Geopolitical Aesthetic* (London, 1993), pp. 200–1.

46 Herbert Marcuse, *Eros and Civilization* (London, 1969), pp. 59–74.

47 In what follows, I have decided to move more or less freely between Cooper's texts, since they seem (like Ellroy's) to emerge each time from unchanging obsessions and formal devices, as though social and historical change, not to mention biographical development, did not affect this writing practice. This leads to some interesting comparisons with one of his literary mentors in the French erotic tradition, Jean Genet. 'All the basic themes of his thought and life are to be found in each of his works; one

recognises the same motifs from book to book: would anyone dream of reproaching him for this? If so, one would have to condemn Dostoievsky for having written the same novel over and over and Kafka for having written the same story a hundred times'. Jean-Paul Sartre, *Saint Genet: Actor and Martyr* (London, 1988), p. 484.

48 Dennis Cooper, *Try* (London, 1994), p. 45.

49 This insistence on the negativity of gay sexuality with regard to the dominant sexual representation has not endeared Cooper to the gay movement at large, which has been more interested in constructing homosexuality as a positive and affirmative identity. Gay activists even went so far as to send Cooper death threats on a reading tour of his most disturbing novel, *Frisk*. See Charlotte Innes, 'Emerging from the Scary Shadows of Human Behaviour', *Los Angeles Times* (Oct 9, 1994), E 13.

50 George Bataille, writing on the aesthetic of the Marquis de Sade, reduces its logic to the following phrases: 'The object as such (a human being) would still be indifferent – it must be modified so that the necessary suffering should be obtained from it. To modify it means to destroy it', Bataille, *Literature and Evil*, p. 115.

51 'In Cooper's system, the subject of desire is never the object of desire; the unidirectionality of desire is modeled on the relation of the spectator to the screen, which also figures both the subject's melancholia and his fetishistic awe of the object', Earl Jackson, Jr., *Strategies of Deviance: Studies in Gay Male Representation* (Bloomington, 1995), p. 193.

52 Dennis Cooper, *The Tenderness of the Wolves* (New York, 1982), p. 56.

53 Ibid., pp. 57, 58.

54 Ibid., p. 59.

55 Baudrillard, *Symbolic Exchange*, p. 126.

56 The principle of shit is articulated most coherently by Philippe in *Closer*, whose paedophilic and necrophilic comrades collectively discover its essence: 'It was their major find. It formed a kind of stumbling block, in one's words, between them and their wish. It was, in another's terms, death's mace'. Cooper, *Closer* (London, 1992), p. 108.

57 Ibid., p. 61.

58 Cooper, *Tenderness*, p. 38.

59 Cooper, *Try*, p. 100.

60 Earl Jackson, Jr., *Strategies of Deviance*, p. 184.

61 Cooper, *Closer*, pp. 100; 117.

62 Ibid., p. 127.

63 Ibid., p. 36.

64 Lawrence A. Rickels, *The Case of California* (London, 1991), p. 2, passim.

65 Cooper, *Wrong* (London, 1994), p. 42.

66 Cooper, *Tenderness*, p. 55.

67 Matias Viegener, 'Men Who Kill and the Boys Who Love Them', *Critical Quarterly*, vol. 36, no. 1 (1994), 108.

68 Quoted in Kasia Boddy, 'Conversation with Dennis Cooper', *Critical Quarterly,* vol. 37, no. 3 (1995), 104.
69 William Carlos Williams, 'Prologue to Kora in Hell', *Selected Essays* (New York, 1969), p. 16.
70 Cooper, *Frisk* (London, 1992), p. 124.

4   Cities within the city: Third World in the First

1 David E. James, 'Poetry/Punk/Production: Some Recent Writing in LA', in E. Ann Kaplan (ed.), *Postmodernism and Its Discontents* (London, 1988), pp. 163–84.
2 See *Poetry/LA 1–21: A Celebration* (Los Angeles, 1993) and separate issues 17–21; J. Woetzel, M. McLaughlin, and C. Westphal (eds.), *The Southern California Anthology 1984,* introduction by John Rechy, (Santa Barbara, 1984); and M. McLaughlin and C. Westphal (eds.), *The Southern California Anthology 1985* (Los Angeles, 1985).
3 Michelle T. Clinton, Sesshu Foster and Naomi Quiñonez (eds.), *Invocation LA: Urban Multicultural Poetry* (Los Angeles, 1989), p. ix.
4 Zena Pearlstone, *Ethnic LA* (Beverly Hills, 1990), p. 25.
5 *LA 2000: a City for the Future,* Final Report, Los Angeles 2000 Committee (Los Angeles, 1988), p. 52.
6 Mike Davis, *City of Quartz: Excavating the Future in Los Angeles* (London, 1990), p. 86.
7 Laurence B. de Graaf, 'The City of Black Angels: Emergence of the Los Angeles Ghetto, 1890–1930', in Theodore Kornweibel, Jr. (ed.), *In Search of the Promised Land: Essays in Black Urban History* (London, 1981), pp. 161–81.
8 Paul Bullock, 'Watts: Before the Riot', in Paul Bullock (ed.), *Watts: The Aftermath – An Inside View of the Ghetto by the People of Watts* (New York, 1969), pp. 11–19.
9 Noel Cohen (ed.), *The Los Angeles Riots: A Socio-Psychological Study* (London, 1970).
10 David O. Sears, 'Urban Rioting in Los Angeles: A Comparison of 1965 with 1992', in M. Baldassare (ed.), *The Los Angeles Riots: Lessons for the Urban Future* (Oxford, 1994), p. 238.
11 Thomas Pynchon, 'A Journey Into the Mind of Watts', *New York Times Magazine* (June 12, 1966), 35 and 78.
12 Ibid., p. 78.
13 Manuel Castells, *The City and the Grassroots: A Cross-Cultural Theory of Urban Social Movements* (London, 1983), p. 53.
14 Mike Davis, *City of Quartz,* pp. 67–8.
15 This observation is based on an extensive personal interview held with Coleman at her home in December 1996.
16 Wanda Coleman, *Native in a Strange Land: Trials and Tremors* (Santa Rosa, 1996), p. 201.
17 Tony Magistrale, 'Doing Battle with the Wolf: A Critical Introduction to Wanda Coleman's Poetry', *Black American Literature Forum,* vol. 23, no. 3 (1989), 540.

18 Wanda Coleman, 'Clocking Dollars', in *African Sleeping Sickness: Stories and Poems* (Santa Rosa, 1990), p. 218.
19 Coleman, *Imagoes* (Santa Rosa, 1983), p. 31.
20 Coleman, *Heavy Daughter Blues: Poems and Stories 1968–1986* (Santa Rosa, 1987), p. 14.
21 Ibid., p. 47.
22 Ibid., p. 107.
23 Coleman, *Imagoes*, p. 149.
24 Coleman, *Mad Dog Black Lady* (Santa Rosa, 1979), p. 3.
25 Coleman, *Imagoes*, p. 162.
26 Coleman, *Heavy Daughter Blues*, p. 107.
27 Coleman, *Imagoes*, p. 95.
28 Coleman, *African Sleeping Sickness*, p. 291.
29 Julian Stallabrass, *Gargantua: Manufactured Mass Culture* (London, 1996), p. 179.
30 Ibid., p. 178.
31 Coleman, *African Sleeping Sickness*, p. 291.
32 David Rieff, *Los Angeles: Capital of the Third World* (London, 1992). Fredric Jameson writes with some passion about the 'Third World side of American life today – the production of poverty and misery, people not only out of work but without a place to live, bag people, waste and industrial pollution, squalor, garbage, and obsolete machinery' Jameson, *Postmodernism, or, the Cultural Logic of Late Capitalism* (London, 1991), p. 128.
33 Coleman, *African Sleeping Sickness*, p. 295.
34 Pearlstone, *Ethnic LA*, pp. 53–60.
35 Ibid., p. 53.
36 P. A. Morrison and I. S. Lowry, 'A Riot of Color: The Demographic Setting', in Mark Baldassare (ed.), *The Los Angeles Riots*, p. 23.
37 Luis J. Rodriguez, *The Concrete River* (Willimantic, 1991), p. 12.
38 Rodriguez, *Poems Across the Pavement* (Chicago, 1989), p. 41.
39 Rodriguez, *Always Running, La Vida Loca: Gang Days in LA* (New York, 1994).
40 Rodriguez, *Concrete River*, p. 35.
41 Ibid., p. 39.
42 Walter Benjamin, *One Way Street and Other Writings*, translated by Edmund Jephcott and Kingsley Shorter (London, 1985), pp. 225–39.
43 Michel Foucault, 'Of Other Spaces', translated by Jay Miskowiec, *Diacritics* (Spring, 1986), 24.
44 Rodriguez, *Concrete River*, pp. 86–7.
45 Ibid., p. 101.
46 Ibid., p. 104.
47 José E. Limón, *Mexican Ballads, Chicano Poems: History and Influence in Mexican-American Social Poetry* (Oxford, 1992), pp. 81–4.
48 M. E. Sánchez, *Contemporary Chicana Poetry: A Critical Approach to an Emerging Literature*, (London, 1985).
49 Sesshu Foster, *City Terrace: Field Manual* (New York, 1996), p. 4.
50 Ibid., p. 19.

51 Ibid., p. 96.
52 Brian Cross, *It's Not About a Salary..*, pp. 319–30.
53 Los Angeles was classified as 'hyper-segregated' by a University of Chicago study analysing 252 American cities. Marc Cooper, 'LA's State of Siege: City of Angels, Cops from Hell', in Don Hazen, (ed.), *Inside the LA Riots: What Really Happened – and Why it Will Happen Again, Essays by More Than 60 of America's Leading Independent Writers and Journalists* (n.p., 1992), pp. 12–19.
54 Ibid., p. 14.
55 Foster, *City Terrace*, p. 126.
56 Jean Baudrillard, *Symbolic Exchange and Death*, translated by Iain Hamilton Grant (London, 1993), pp. 36–8.
57 Foster, *City Terrace*, p. 144.

5   Realism and beyond

1 This presumes the possibility that if such a gesture could be made today, it would in that case be identifiable as 'realism'. It is equally conceivable, however, that 'realism' is an historically and socially contingent phenomenon, whose larger philosophical project was Enlightenment itself; in which case the nineteenth-century Realists' vocation was nothing less than 'the production of a whole new world – on the level of the symbolic and imaginary – which will henceforth constitute the objective lived appearance of that equally objective production of the infrastructure of the emergent market system of industrial capitalism. What is at stake in their cultural production is therefore the retraining, the collective re-education, of a whole population whose mentalities and habits were formed in the previous mode of production, feudalism or the *ancien régime*.' Fredric Jameson, 'The Realist Floorplan', in *On Signs*, edited by Blonsky (Baltimore, 1985), pp. 373–4. I prefer, with Brecht, to keep alive the possibility of realist aesthetic practice outside of this obviously foundational moment.
2 Gilles Deleuze and Félix Guattari, *Kafka: Towards a Minor Literature*, translated by Dana Polan (London, 1986).
3 'Hence a quite specific dialectical process is set in train: on the one hand, the state's reinforcement is followed by a weakening, even a breaking-up or withering-away; on the other hand local powers assert themselves vigorously, then lose their nerve and fall back. And so on – in accordance with a cycle and with contradictions which must, sooner or later, achieve resolution.' Henri Lefebvre, *The Production of Space*, translated by Donald Nicholson-Smith (Oxford, 1991), p. 382.
4 *LA 2000: a City for the Future*, Final Report, Los Angeles 2000 Committee (1988).
5 Melvin L. Oliver, James H. Johnson, Jr., and Walter C. Farrell, Jr., 'Anatomy of a Rebellion: A Political-Economic Analysis', in *Reading Rodney King/Reading Urban Uprising*, edited by Robert Gooding-Williams (London, 1993), p.118.

6 Anna Deavere Smith, *Twilight: Los Angeles, 1992* (New York, 1994), pp. xxiv-v.
7 Ibid., p. xxv.
8 Christopher Nash addresses the tradition of 'anti-Realist' literature in his *World Postmodern Fiction: A Guide* (Burnt Mill, 1993).
9 Smith, *Twilight*, p. xvii.
10 See the full chronological survey of some eighteen pieces in Carol Martin, 'Anna Deavere Smith: The Word Becomes You; An Interview by Carol Martin', *The Drama Review*, vol. 37, no. 4 (1993), 47.
11 Smith, *Fires in the Mirror: Crown Heights, Brooklyn and Other Identities* (London, 1993), p. xxv.
12 Ibid., p. xxvii.
13 Carol Martin, 'Anna Deavere Smith', p. 45.
14 W. H. Sun and F. C. Fei, 'Masks or Faces Re-Visited: A Study of Four Theatrical Works Concerning Cultural Identity', *The Drama Review*, vol. 38, no. 4 (1994), 131.
15 Martin, 'Anna Deavere Smith', p. 57.
16 See Smith, *Fires in the Mirror*, p. xxxi.
17 Martin, 'Anna Deavere Smith', p. 57.
18 Roland Barthes, 'Myth Today', in *Mythologies* (London, 1973), p. 143.
19 Henri Lefebvre, *Production of Space*, p. 98.
20 '. . . I once said that by examining the rhythms of life in detail, by descending from the great rhythms forced upon us by the universe to the finer rhythms that play upon man's most exquisite sensibilities, it would be possible to work out a rhythmanalysis that would tend to reconcile and lighten the ambivalences that psychoanalysts find in the disturbed psyche,' Gaston Bachelard, *The Poetics of Space*, translated by Maria Jolas (Boston, 1994), p. 65.
21 Henri Lefebvre, *Production of Space*, p. 205. For Lefebvre's late efforts in this vein, see Lefebvre and Catherine Régulier, 'Le projet rhythmanalytique', *Communications*, 41 (1985), and Lefebvre and Régulier, 'Rhythmanalysis of Mediterranean Cities', in *Writings on Cities*, translated and edited by Eleonore Kofman and Elizabeth Lebas (Oxford, 1996), pp. 228–40.
22 Martin, 'Anna Deavere Smith', pp. 53–4.
23 Alice Rayner, 'Improper Conjunctions: Metaphor, Performance, and Text', *Essays in Theater/Études Théâtrales*, vol. 14, no. 1 (1995), 10.
24 Anna Deavere Smith, 'Not So Special Vehicles', *Performing Arts Journal* 50/51 (1995), 80.
25 Smith, *Twilight*, p. xxii.
26 Smith, 'Not So Special Vehicles', p. 86.
27 Smith, *Twilight*, p. 62.
28 Richard Schechner, 'Acting as Incorporation', *The Drama Review*, vol. 37, no. 4 (1993), 63–4.
29 Theodor W. Adorno, *Aesthetic Theory*, edited by Gretel Adorno and Rolf Tiedemann, translated by Robert Hullot-Kentor (London, 1997), p. 54.
30 See also my 'Identity and Difference in the Performance Art of Anna Deavere Smith', in *Wasafiri*, 27 (Spring 1998), 29–33.

31 Cornel West, 'Foreword', in Smith, *Fires in the Mirror*, p. xix.
32 Smith, 'Not So Special Vehicles', pp. 80, 84, 85–6.
33 Diane Wood Middlebrook, 'The Artful Voyeur', *Transition* 67 (1995), 186.
34 Martin, 'Anna Deavere Smith', p. 45.
35 See Alfred Kazin, *On Native Grounds* (London, 1943); William Stott, *Documentary Expression and Thirties America* (New York, 1973); Mordecai Gorelik, *New Theatres for Old* (New York, 1940). A new critical treatment of this period and its documentary tendencies is available in Michael Denning's wonderful *The Cultural Front* (London, 1997).
36 The performance begins with a Chicano prologue about ethnic chauvinism in general, moves to a first 'act' on 'The Territory' of multi-ethnic LA without specific references to the rebellion, then a second act devoted to Rodney King and the trial entitled 'Here's a Nobody', followed by a long third section about the riots themselves called 'War Zone', a penultimate act called 'Twilight' dealing with the immediate aftermath, and last a short act entitled 'Justice', being a final call for peace and reconciliation.
37 Adorno, *Aesthetic Theory*, pp. 54–5.
38 Smith, 'Not So Special Vehicles', p. 79.
39 Smith, *Twilight*, p. 253.
40 Ibid., pp. 253–5.
41 Kim Stanley Robinson, *The Gold Coast* (London, 1990), p. 3.
42 Ibid., p. 7.
43 Charles Jencks, *Heteropolis: Los Angeles, the Riots and the Strange Beauty of Hetero-Architecture* (London, 1993), p. 34.
44 It is a conception we owe above all to the pathbreaking work of Edward W. Soja, in his *Postmodern Geographies: The Reassertion of Space in Critical Theory* (London, 1989), esp. pp. 190–248.
45 T. Coraghessan Boyle, *The Tortilla Curtain* (New York, 1996), p. 233.
46 Gary Indiana, 'Author's Note', *Resentment* (London, 1998), p. iii.
47 Indiana, *Resentment*, p. 6.
48 Ibid., pp. 152–3.
49 Ibid., p. 9.
50 Ibid., p. 28.
51 See Graham Clarke, 'The Great Wrong Place: Los Angeles as Urban Milieu', in Graham Clarke (ed.), *The American City: Literary and Cultural Perspectives* (London, 1988).
52 Steve Erickson, *Amnesiascope* (New York, 1996), pp. 126–7.
53 Jean Baudrillard, *America*, translated by Chris Turner (London, 1988), esp. pp. 51–63.
54 Michael Sorkin, *Exquisite Corpse: Writing on Buildings* (London, 1991), pp. 48–9.
55 Ibid., p. 53.
56 Lewis Lapham, 'City Lights' in *Hotel America: Scenes in the Lobby of the Fin-de-Siècle*, (London, 1995), p. 199.
57 Dilys M. Hill, 'Domestic Policy in an Era of "Negative" Government' in *The Reagan Presidency: An Incomplete Revolution?*, edited by Dilys

M. Hill, Raymond A. Moore and Phil Williams (Houndmills, 1990), pp. 173–4.
58 Mike Davis, 'Who Killed LA? A Political Autopsy', *New Left Review* 197 (1993), p. 20.
59 Kevin R. McNamara, *Urban Verbs: Arts and Discourses of American Cities* (Stanford, 1996), p. 247.
60 Lapham, 'City Lights', p. 202.
61 Michel de Certeau, *The Practice of Everyday Life*, translated by Steven Rendall (London, 1988), p. 96.
62 Edward W. Soja, 'Los Angeles, 1965–1992: From Crisis-Generated Restructuring to Restructuring-Generated Crisis', in *The City*, edited by Allen Scott and Edward W. Soja (Berkeley, 1996), pp. 426–62.
63 Quoted in Walter Benjamin, 'Conversations with Brecht', in *Understanding Brecht*, translated by Anna Bostock (London, 1998), p. 121.
64 Fredric Jameson, *Postmodernism, or the Cultural Logic of Late Capitalism* (London, 1991), p. 54.

Bibliography

Abella, Alex. *The Killing of the Saints* (London, 1992).

Acosta, Oscar Zeta. *The Revolt of the Cockroach People* (San Francisco, 1973).

Adamic, Louis. 'Los Angeles! There She Blows!', *The Outlook* (13 August, 1930), 563–5 and 594–7.

    Laughing in the Jungle: The Autobiography of an Immigrant in America (New York, 1932).

Adorno, Theodor W. *The Culture Industry: Selected Essays on Mass Culture*, edited by J. M. Bernstein (London, 1991).

    Notes to Literature, Volume Two, edited by Rolf Tiedemann, translated by Shierry Weber Nicholsen (New York, 1992).

    Aesthetic Theory, edited by Gretel Adorno and Rolf Tiedemann, translated by Robert Hullot-Kentor (London, 1997).

Adorno, Theodor W. and Max Horkheimer. *Dialectic of Enlightenment*, translated by John Cumming (London, 1986).

Ain, J. et al., (eds.). *Poetry Los Angeles* (London, 1958).

Anderson, Perry. 'Modernism and Revolution', *New Left Review* 144 (March-April 1984), 95–113.

    The Origins of Postmodernity (London, 1998).

Aronowitz, Stanley. *Dead Artists, Live Theories* (London, 1994).

Attali, Jacques. *Noise: The Political Economy of Music*, translated by Brian Massumi, Theory and History of Literature, vol. 16 (Manchester, 1985).

Augé, Marc. *Non-Places: Introduction to an Anthropology of Supermodernity*, translated by John Howe (London, 1995).

Babitz, Eve. *Black Swans – Stories* (New York, 1993).

Bachelard, Gaston. *The Poetics of Space*, translated by Maria Jolas (Boston, 1994).

Bahr, Eugene, and Carolyn See. *Literary Exiles in Los Angeles* (Los Angeles, 1988).

Baker, Jr., Houston A. *Blues, Ideology, and Afro-American Literature: A Vernacular Theory* (London, 1984).

Bakhtin, Mikhail. *The Dialogical Imagination: Four Essays*, edited by

Bibliography

Michael Holquist, translated by Caryl Emerson and Michael Holquist (Austin, 1981).

Baldassare, Mark (ed.). *The Los Angeles Riots: Lessons for the Urban Future* (Oxford, 1994).

Balibar, Etienne and Immanuel Wallerstein. *Race, Nation, Class: Ambiguous Identities*, translated by Chris Turner (London, 1991).

Banham, Rayner. *Los Angeles: The Architecture of Four Ecologies* (London, 1971).

Barthes, Roland. *Image Music Text*, edited and translated by Stephen Heath (London, 1977).

Mythologies (London, 1973).

Writing Degree Zero and Elements of Semiology, translated by Annette Lavers and Colin Smith (London, 1984).

S/Z, translated by Richard Miller (Oxford, 1993).

Bataille, George. *Literature and Evil*, translated by Alastair Hamilton (London, 1997).

Baudrillard, Jean. *America*, translated by Chris Turner (London, 1988).

Interview, translated by Nancy Blake, in Giancarlo Politi and Helena Kontova (eds.), *Flash Art: Two Decades of History XXI Years* (Cambridge, MA, 1990).

Simulations, translated by Paul Foss, Paul Patton and Philip Beitchman (New York, 1983).

Symbolic Exchange and Death, translated by Iain Hamilton Grant (London, 1993).

Beatty, Paul. *Joker, Joker, Deuce* (New York, 1994).

The White Boy Shuffle (Boston, 1996).

Benjamin, Walter. *One Way Street and Other Writings*, translated by Edmund Jephcott and Kingsley Shorter (London, 1985).

Charles Baudelaire: A Lyric Poet in the Era of High Capitalism, translated by Harry Zohn (London, 1989).

Understanding Brecht, translated by Anna Bostock (London, 1998).

Berman, Marshall. *All That Is Solid Melts Into Air: The Experience of Modernity* (New York, 1982).

Binyon, T. J. *'Murder Will Out': The Detective in Fiction* (Oxford, 1989).

Bloch, Ernst. *The Utopian Function of Art and Literature: Selected Essays*, translated by Jack Zipes and Frank Mecklenburg (London, 1988).

Bloch, Ernst, *et al. Aesthetics and Politics*, edited by Ronald Taylor (London, 1980).

Boddy, Kasia. 'Conversation with Dennis Cooper', *Critical Quarterly*, vol. 37, no. 3 (1995).

Bottles, Scott L. *Los Angeles and the Automobile: The Making of the Modern City* (London, 1987).

Boyle, T. Coraghessan. *The Tortilla Curtain* (New York, 1996).

Brecht, Bertolt. *Journals 1934–1955*, edited by John Willett, translated by Hugh Rorrison (London, 1993).

Brennan, Tim. 'Off the Gangsta Tip: A Rap Appreciation, or Forgetting about Los Angeles', *Critical Inquiry*, vol. 20, no. 4, (1994), 663–93.

Bukowski, Charles. *Hollywood* (Santa Rosa, 1994).

Bullock, Paul. 'Watts: Before the Riot', in *Watts: The Aftermath—An Inside View of the Ghetto by the People of Watts*, edited by Paul Bullock (New York, 1969).

Butler, Judith. 'Endangered/Endangering: Schematic Racism and White Paranoia', in Robert Gooding-Williams (ed.), *Reading Rodney King/ Reading Urban Uprising* (London, 1993), pp. 15–22.

Cain, James M. *The Postman Always Rings Twice* (New York, 1934).
Mildred Pierce (New York, 1941).

Cameron, Ian (ed.). *The Movie Book of Film Noir* (London, 1992).

Campbell, Bebe Moore. *Brothers and Sisters* (New York, 1994).

Cappetti, Carla. *Writing Chicago: Modernism, Ethnography, and the Novel* (New York, 1993).

Castells, Manuel. *City, Class and Power*, translated by Elizabeth Lebas (London, 1978).
The City and the Grassroots: A Cross-Cultural Theory of Urban Social Movements (London, 1983).
The Informational City: Information Technology, Economic Restructuring, and the Urban Regional Process (Oxford, 1989).

Cawelti, John G. *Adventure, Mystery, and Romance* (London, 1976).

Caws, Mary Ann (ed.). *City Images: Perspectives from Literature, Philosophy and Film* (London, 1991).

Chandler, Raymond. *The Simple Art of Murder* (London, 1950).
Raymond Chandler Speaking, edited by Dorothy Gardiner and Katherine Sorley Walker (London, 1962).
Selected Letters of Raymond Chandler, edited by Frank MacShane (London, 1981).
Three Novels: The Big Sleep; Farewell, My Lovely; The Long Goodbye (Harmondsworth, 1993).

Christopherson, S. and M. Storper. 'The City as Studio; the World as Back Lot: The Impact of Vertical Disintegration on the Location of the Motion Picture Industry', *Environment and Planning D: Society and Space*, 4 (1986), 305–20.

Clarke, Graham. 'The Great Wrong Place: Los Angeles as Urban Milieu', in Graham Clarke (ed.), *The American City: Literary and Cultural Perspectives* (London, 1988).

Clinton, Michelle T. *High Blood/Pressure* (Los Angeles, 1986).

Clinton, Michelle T., Sesshu Foster, and Naomi Quiñonez (eds.). *Invocation LA: Urban Multicultural Poetry* (Los Angeles, 1989).

Cohen, Josh. 'James Ellroy, Los Angeles and the Spectacular Crisis of Masculinity', *Women: a cultural review*, vol. 7, no. 1 (Spring, 1996), 1–15.

Cohen, Noel (ed.). *The Los Angeles Riots: A Socio-Psychological Study* (London, 1970).

Coleman, Wanda. *Mad Dog Black Lady* (Santa Rosa, 1979).
Imagoes (Santa Rosa, 1983).
Heavy Daughter Blues: Poems and Stories 1968–1986 (Santa Rosa, 1987).
A War of Eyes and Other Stories (Santa Rosa, 1988).
African Sleeping Sickness: Stories and Poems (Santa Rosa, 1990).
Hand Dance (Santa Rosa, 1993).

Bibliography

Native in a Strange Land: Trials and Tremors (Santa Rosa, 1996).

Colomina, Beatriz (ed.). *Sexuality and Space* (New York, 1992).

Cooper, Dennis. *The Tenderness of the Wolves* (New York, 1982).

He Cried: For Chris Lemmerhirt (San Fransisco, 1984).

Frisk (London, 1992).

Closer (London, 1994).

Try (London, 1994).

Wrong (London, 1994).

The Dream Police: Selected Poems, 1969–1993 (New York, 1995).

Guide (London, 1998).

Cooper, Marc. 'LA's State of Siege: City of Angels, Cops from Hell', in Don Hazen (ed.), *Inside the LA Riots: What Really Happened – and Why it Will Happen Again, Essays by More Than 60 of America's Leading Independent Writers and Journalists* (Institute for Alternative Journalism, 1992), pp. 12–19.

Copjec, Joan (ed.). *Shades of Noir: A Reader* (London, 1993).

Craven, Bruce. *Fast Sofa* (New York, 1993).

Cross, Brian. *It's Not About a Salary . . . Rap, Race and Resistance in Los Angeles* (London, 1993).

Cuadros, Gil. *City of God* (San Francisco, 1994).

Davis, Mike. 'Chinatown Part Two? The "Internationalization" of Downtown Los Angeles', *New Left Review* 164 (1987), 65–86.

'Urban Renaissance and the Spirit of Postmodernism', in E. Ann Kaplan (ed.), *Postmodernism and Its Discontents* (London, 1988), pp. 79–87.

City of Quartz: Excavating the Future in Los Angeles (London, 1990).

'Who Killed LA? A Political Autopsy', *New Left Review* 197 (1993), 3–28.

'Who Killed Los Angeles? Part Two: The Verdict is Given', *New Left Review* 199 (1993), 29–54.

'The Empty Quarter', in David Reid (ed.), *Sex, Death and God in LA* (London, 1994), pp. 54–71.

'Los Angeles After the Storm: The Dialectics of Ordinary Disasters', *Antipode* vol. 27, no. 2, (1995), 221–41.

Ecology of Fear: Los Angeles and the Imagination of Disaster (London, 1999).

De Certeau, Michel. *The Practice of Everyday Life*, translated by Steven Rendall (London, 1988).

De Graaf, Laurence B. 'The City of Black Angels: Emergence of the Los Angeles Ghetto, 1890–1930', in *In Search of the Promised Land: Essays in Black Urban History*, edited by Theodore Kornweibel, Jr. (London, 1981), pp. 161–81.

Dear, Michael J. 'Postmodernism and Planning', *Environment and Planning D: Society and Space* 4 (1986), 367–84.

Deleuze, Gilles and Félix Guattari. *Anti-Oedipus: Capitalism and Schizophrenia*, translated by Robert Hurley, Mark Seem and Helen R. Lane (Minneapolis, 1983).

A Thousand Plateaux: Capitalism and Schizophrenia, translated by Brian Massumi (London, 1988).

Kafka: Towards a Minor Literature, translated by Dana Polan (London, 1986).

Didion, Joan. *Play it as it Lays* (New York, 1979).

Slouching Towards Bethlehem (Harmondsworth, 1985).

Dunne, John Gregory. *True Confessions: a Novel* (London, 1978).

Playland (London, 1994).

Ellis, Bret Easton. *Less Than Zero* (London, 1986).

American Psycho (London, 1991).

The Informers (London, 1994).

Ellroy, James. *The Black Dahlia* (London, 1993).

White Jazz (London, 1993).

The Big Nowhere (London, 1994).

Dick Contino's Blues and Other Stories (London, 1994).

LA Confidential (London, 1994).

American Tabloid (London, 1995).

My Dark Places (London, 1996).

Erickson, Steve. *Arc d'X* (London, 1994).

Amnesiascope (New York, 1996).

Faulkner, William. 'Golden Days', in *The Penguin Collected Stories of William Faulkner* (Harmondsworth, 1985), pp. 701–26.

Fenton, Frank. *A Place in the Sun* (London, 1943).

Fine, David (ed.). *Los Angeles in Fiction* (Alberquerque, 1984).

Fitzgerald, F. Scott. *The Love of the Last Tycoon: A Western*, edited by Matthew J. Bruccoli (London, 1995).

Fogelson, Robert M. *The Fragmented Metropolis: Los Angeles, 1850–1930* (Cambridge, MA, 1967).

Ford, Richard. *Independence Day* (London, 1996).

Foster, Sesshu. *City Terrace: Field Manual* (New York, 1996).

Foucault, Michel. 'Of Other Spaces', translated by Jay Miskowiec, *Diacritics* (Spring, 1986), 22–7.

Frampton, Kenneth. *Modern Architecture: A Critical History*, 3rd edition (London, 1992).

Freese, Peter. 'Bret Easton Ellis, Less Than Zero: Entropy in the MTV Novel?', in *Modes of Narration: Approaches to American, Canadian and British Fiction*, edited by Reingard M. Nischik and Barbara Korte (Würzburg, 1990), pp. 68–87.

Freud, Sigmund. *On Metapsychology*, vol. 11, Penguin Freud Library (London, 1991).

Gates, Jr., Henry Louis. *The Signifying Monkey: A Theory of Afro-American Literary Criticism* (Oxford, 1988).

'Two Nations, Both Black', in *Reading Rodney King/Reading Urban Urpising*, edited by Robert Gooding-Williams (London, 1993), pp. 249–54.

Gayle, Jr., Addison (ed.). *The Black Aesthetic* (Garden City, NY, 1971).

Gelfent, Blanche. *The American City Novel*, 2nd edition (Norman, 1970).

Gelley, Alexander. 'City Texts: Representation, Semiology and Urbanism', in *Politics, Theory, and Contemporary Culture*, edited by Mark Poster (New York, 1993), pp. 237–60.

Bibliography

George, Lynell. *No Crystal Stair: African-Americans in the City of Angels* (London, 1992).

Gómez-Peña, Guillermo. *Warrior for Gringostroika* (Saint Paul, 1993).

Gooding-Williams, Robert (ed.). *Reading Rodney King/Reading Urban Uprising* (London, 1993).

Gottdiener, M. and A. P. Lagopoulos (eds.). *The City and the Sign: An Introduction to Urban Semiotics* (New York, 1986).

Grapes, Jack (ed.). *The New Los Angeles Poets* (Los Angeles, 1990).

Gregory, Derek. *Geographical Imaginations* (Oxford, 1994).

Greimas, A. J. *On Meaning: Selected Writings in Semiotic Theory*, translated by Paul J. Perron and Frank Collins (London, 1987).

Gudis, C. (ed.). *Helter Skelter: LA Art in the 1990s* (Los Angeles, 1992).

Hamm, Theodor. 'Fragments of Postwar Los Angeles: The Black Dahlia in Fact and Fiction', *Antipode*, vol. 28, no. 1 (1996), 24–41.

Harvey, David. *The Condition of Postmodernity: An Inquiry into the Origins of Cultural Change* (Oxford, 1990).

'Militant Particularism and Global Ambition: The Conceptual Politics of Place, Space, and Environment in the Work of Raymond Williams', *Social Text* 42 (1995), 69–98.

Haut, Woody. *Pulp Culture: Hardboiled Fiction and the Cold War* (London, 1995).

Hayden, Dolores. *The Power of Place: Urban Landscapes as Public History* (London, 1995).

Hazen, Don (ed.). *Inside the LA Riots: What Really Happened – and Why it Will Happen Again, Essays by More Than 60 of America's Leading Independent Writers and Journalists* (Institute for Alternative Journalism, 1992).

Hill, D. M. 'Domestic Policy in an Era of "Negative" Government' in *The Reagan Presidency: An Incomplete Revolution?*, edited by Dilys M. Hill, Raymond A. Moore and Phil Williams (Houndmills, 1990), pp. 161–78.

Himes, Chester. *Lonely Crusade* (London, 1950).

If He Hollers Let Him Go (New York, 1986).

hooks, bell. *Yearning* (Boston, 1990).

Hurm, Gerd. *Fragmented Urban Images: The American City in Modern Fiction from Stephen Crane to Thomas Pynchon* (Frankfurt am Main, 1991).

Innes, Charlotte. 'Emerging from the Scary Shadows of Human Behaviour', *Los Angeles Times* (Oct 9, 1994), E 13.

Jackson, Jr., Earl. *Strategies of Deviance: Studies in Gay Male Representation* (Bloomington, 1995).

Jackson, Helen Hunt. *Ramona. A Story* (Boston, 1886).

James, David. E. 'Poetry/Punk/Production: Some Recent Writing in LA', in E. Ann Kaplan (ed.), *Postmodernism and Its Discontents* (London, 1988), pp. 163–84.

James, Henry. *The American Scene*, in *Collected Travel Writings: Great Britain and America* (New York, 1993).

Jameson, Fredric. 'On Raymond Chandler', *The Southern Review*, vol. 6, no. 3 (1970), 624–50.

Marxism and Form: Twentieth-Century Dialectical Theories of Literature (Princeton, 1974).

The Political Unconscious: Narrative as a Socially Symbolic Act (Ithaca, 1981).

'The Realist Floor-Plan', in *On Signs*, edited by Blonsky (Baltimore, 1985), pp. 373–83.

'Cognitive Mapping', in *Marxism and the Interpretation of Culture*, edited by Lawrence Grossberg and Cary Nelson (London, 1988), pp. 347–57.

Postmodernsim, or, the Cultural Logic of Late Capitalism (London, 1991).

Signatures of the Visible (London, 1992).

The Geopolitical Aesthetic: Cinema and Space in the World System (London, 1993).

The Seeds of Time (Chichester, 1994).

'Is Space Political?', in *Anyplace*, edited by Cynthia C. Davidson (London, 1995), pp. 192–205.

'Actually Existing Marxism', in *Marxism Beyond Marxism*, edited by Saree Makdisi, Cesare Casarino, and Rebecca E. Karl (London, 1996), pp. 14–54.

The Cultural Turn: Selected Writings on the Postmodern, 1983–1998 (London, 1998).

Jencks, Charles. *Heteropolis: Los Angeles, the Riots and the Strange Beauty of Hetero-Architecture* (London, 1993).

Joyce, James. *Ulysses* (London, 1992).

Kaplan, E. Ann (ed.). *Postmodernism and its Discontents* (London, 1988).

Katz, C. 'Reflections while Reading *City of Quartz* by Mike Davis', *Antipode*, vol. 25, no. 2 (1993), 159–63.

Keil, R. 'The Urban Future Revisited: Politics and Restructuring in Los Angeles after Fordism', *Strategies* 3 (1990), pp. 105–29.

Kelley, Robert D. G. *Race Rebels: Culture, Politics, and the Black Working Class* (New York, 1994).

Kerr, Philip. *Gridiron* (London, 1995).

Kestner, J. A. *The Spatiality of the Novel* (Detroit, 1978).

King, Geoff. *Mapping Reality: An Exploration of Cultural Cartographies* (Houndmills, 1996).

Klein, Norman M. 'Open Season: A Report on the Los Angeles Uprising', *Social Text* 34 (1993), 115–20.

The History of Forgetting: Los Angeles and the Erasure of Memory (London, 1997).

Kling, R., S. Olin, and M. Poster (eds.). *Postsuburban California: The Transformation of Orange County since World War II* (Oxford, 1991).

Knight, Stephen. *Form and Ideology in Crime Fiction* (Bloomington, 1980).

Kornweibel, Jr., T. (ed.). *In Search of the Promised Land: Essays in Black Urban History* (London, 1981).

Krieger, M. H. 'Ethnicity and the Frontier in Los Angeles', *Environment and Planning D: Society and Space* 4 (1986), 385–90.

Krutnik, Frank. *In a Lonely Street: Film Noir, Genre, Masculinity* (London, 1991).

Bibliography

LA 2000: a City for the Future. Final Report, Los Angeles 2000 Committee (1988).

Lapham, Lewis H. *Hotel America: Scenes in the Lobby of the Fin-de-Siècle*, (London, 1995).

Lefebvre, Henri. *The Survival of Capitalism: Reproduction of the Relations of Production*, translated by Frank Bryant (London, 1976).

Critique of Everyday Life, Volume One, translated by John Moore (London 1991).

The Production of Space, translated by Donald Nicholson-Smith (Oxford, 1991).

Writings on Cities, translated and edited by Eleonore Kofman and Elizabeth Lebas (Oxford, 1996).

Lévi-Strauss, Claude. 'The Structural Study of Myth', in *Structural Anthropology*, translated by C. Jacobson and B. G. Schoepf (New York, 1963), pp. 206–31.

Levick, M. and S. Young. *The Big Picture: Murals of Los Angeles* (London, 1988).

Limón, José E. *Mexican Ballads, Chicano Poems: History and Influence in Mexican-American Social Poetry* (Oxford, 1992).

Lipsitz, George. *Dangerous Crossroads: Popular Music, Postmodernism and the Poetics of Place* (London, 1995).

'Cruising Around the Hegemonic Bloc', *Cultural Critique* (1986/87), 157–77.

Long, Barry. 'Dark Passages', *The Weekend Review* (*Australian*) (March 4–5, 1995), 7.

Lukács, Georg. *History and Class Consciousness: Studies in Marxist Dialectics*, translated by Rodney Livingstone (London, 1971).

Studies in European Realism, translated by Edith Bone (London, 1972).

Lurie, Alison. *The Nowhere City* (London, 1986).

Lynch, Kevin. *The Image of the City* (London, 1968).

What Time is This Place? (London, 1972).

Magistrale, Tony. 'Doing Battle with the Wolf: A Critical Introduction to Wanda Coleman's Poetry', *Black American Literature Forum*, vol. 23, no. 3 (1989), 539–54.

Marchand, B. *The Emergence of Los Angeles: Population and Housing in the City of Dreams 1940–1970* (London, 1986).

Marcus, Greil. *Lipstick Traces: A Secret History of the Twentieth Century* (London, 1989).

In the Fascist Bathroom: Writings on Punk 1977–1992 (London, 1993).

Marcuse, Herbert. *Eros and Civilization* (London, 1969).

Martin, Carol. 'Anna Deavere Smith: The Word Becomes You; An Interview by Carol Martin', *The Drama Review*, vol. 37, no. 4 (1993), 45–62.

Martínez, Ruben. *The Other Side: Fault Lines, Guerilla Saints, and the True Heart of Rock 'n' Roll* (London, 1992).

Marx, Karl. 'Preface to *A Contribution to the Critique of Political Economy*', In Marx and Engels, *Selected Works*, vol. 1 (Moscow, 1973).

Mason, Jr., T. O. 'Walter Mosley's Easy Rawlins: The Detective and Afro-American Fiction', *Kenyon Review*, vol. 14, no. 4 (1992), 173–83.

Massey, Doreen. 'Politics and Space/Time', *New Left Review* 196 (1992), 65–84.

Mazón, M. *The Zoot Suit Riots: The Psychology of Symbolic Annihilation* (Austin, 1984).

McCoy, Horace. *They Shoot Horses Don't They?* (New York, 1935).

McLaughlin, M. and C. Westphal (eds.). *The Southern California Anthology 1985* (Los Angeles, 1985).

McNamara, Kevin R. *Urban Verbs: Arts and Discourses of American Cities* (Stanford, 1996).

McWilliams, Carey. *Louis Adamic and Shadow America* (Los Angeles, 1935).

Southern California Country: An Island on the Land (New York, 1946).

California: The Great Exception (New York, 1949).

Michaels, L. David Reid, and R. Sherr (eds.). *West of the West: Imagining California* (London, 1989).

Middlebrook, Diane W. 'The Artful Voyeur', *Transition* 67 (1995), 186–95.

Mitchell, J. P. *Race Riots in Black and White* (Englewood Cliffs, NJ, 1970).

Mohr, W. (ed.). *The Streets Inside: Ten Los Angeles Poets* (Santa Monica, 1978).

Moretti, Franco. *Signs Taken for Wonders*, translated by Susan Fischer, David Forgacs and David Miller, 2nd edition (London, 1988).

Morrison, P. A. and I. S. Lowry. 'A Riot of Color: The Demographic Setting', in Mark Baldassare (ed.), *The Los Angeles Riots: Lessons for the Urban Future* (Oxford, 1994), pp. 19–46.

Morrison, Toni. 'City Limits, Village Values: Concepts of the Neighborhood in Black Fiction', in *Literature and the Urban Experience*, edited by Michael C. Jaye and Ann Chalmers Watts (New Brunswick, NJ, 1981).

Playing in the Dark: Whiteness and the Literary Imagination (London, 1992).

Mosley, Walter. *Devil in a Blue Dress* (New York, 1991).

A Red Death (New York, 1992).

White Butterfly (New York, 1993).

Black Betty (London, 1995).

A Little Yellow Dog (London, 1996).

Mulvey, Laura. 'Visual Pleasure and Narrative Cinema', *Screen*, vol. 16, no. 3 (1975).

Murphet, Julian. 'Grounding Theory: Literary Theory and the New Geography', in *Post-Theory: New Directions in Criticism*, edited by Martin McQuillan, *et al.* (Edinburgh, 1999), pp. 200–8.

'Identity and Difference in the Performance Art of Anna Deavere Smith', in *Wasafiri* 27 (1998), 29–33.

'Noir and the Racial Unconscious', *Screen* vol. 39, no. 1 (1998), 22–35.

Oliver, Melvin L., James H. Johnson, Jr., and Walter C. Farrell, Jr. 'Anatomy of a Rebellion: A Political-Economic Analysis', in *Reading Rodney King/Reading Urban Uprising*, edited by Robert Gooding-Williams (London, 1993), pp. 117–41.

Pearlstone, Zena. *Ethnic LA* (Beverly Hills, 1990).

Bibliography

Peters, J. U. 'The Los Angeles Anti-Myth', in *Itinerary Seven: Essays on California Writers*, edited by Charles L. Crow (Bowling Green, OH, 1978), pp. 21–34.

Pfeil, Fred. *White Guys: Studies in Postmodern Domination and Difference* (London, 1995).

Pike, Burton. *The Image of the City in Modern Literature* (Princeton, 1981).

Pile, Steve. *The Body and the City: Psychoanalysis, Space and Subjectivity* (London, 1996).

Poetry/LA 1–21: A Celebration (Los Angeles, 1993).

Porter, Dennis. *The Pursuit of Crime: Art and Ideology in Detective Fiction* (London, 1981).

Prendergast, Christopher. *Paris and the Nineteenth Century* (Oxford, 1992).

Priestman, M. *Detective Fiction and Literature: The Figure in the Carpet* (Houndmills, 1990).

Pynchon, Thomas. 'A Journey Into the Mind of Watts', *New York Times Magazine* (June 12, 1966), 34–35+.

   The Crying of Lot 49 (London, 1979).

   Vineland (London, 1990).

Rand, Chris. *Los Angeles: The Ultimate City* (Oxford, 1967).

Rayner, A. 'Improper Conjunctions: Metaphor, Performance, and Text', *Essays in Theater/Études Théâtrales*, vol. 14, no. 1 (1995), 3–13.

Rayner, Richard. *Los Angeles Without a Map* (London, 1989).

Reid, David (ed.). *Sex, Death and God in LA* (London, 1994).

Rich, B. Ruby. 'Dumb Lugs and Femmes Fatales', *Sight and Sound* (November, 1995), 6–10.

Rickels, Lawrence A. *The Case of California* (Baltimore, 1991).

Rieff, David. *Los Angeles: Capital of the Third World* (London, 1992).

Robinson, Kim Stanley. *The Gold Goast* (London, 1990).

Robinson, W. W. *Los Angeles: A Profile* (Norman, 1968).

Rodriguez, Louis J. *Poems Across the Pavement* (Chicago, 1989).

   The Concrete River (Willimantic, 1991).

   Always Running, La Vida Loca: Gang Days in LA (New York, 1994).

Rolfe, Lionel. *In Search of . . . Literary LA* (Los Angeles, 1991).

Ross, Kristen. *The Emergence of Social Space: Rimbaud and the Paris Commune* (Houndmills, 1988).

   'Watching the Detectives', in *Postmodernism and the Re-Reading of Modernity*, edited by Francis Barker, Peter Hulme and Margaret Iversen (Manchester, 1992), pp. 46–65.

Sahlin, Nikki. '"But This Road Doesn't Go Anywhere": The Existential Dilemma in *Less Than Zero*', *Critique*, vol. 33, no. 1 (1991), 23–42.

Sánchez, M. E. *Contemporary Chicana Poetry: A Critical Approach to an Emerging Literature* (London, 1985).

Sanchez, Thomas. *Zoot-Suit Murders* (New York, 1991).

Sartre, Jean-Paul. *Saint Genet: Actor and Martyr* (London, 1988).

Scanlon, Paul. '"Demon Dog" Has His Day', *GQ* (US) (October, 1992), 204–6.

Schechner, Richard. 'Acting as Incorporation', *The Drama Review*, vol. 37, no. 4 (1993), 63–4.

Schmid, David. 'Imagining Safe Urban Space: The Contribution of

Detective Fiction to Radical Geography', ·*Antipode*, vol. 27, no. 3 (1995), 242–69.

Schulberg, Budd. *What Makes Sammy Run?* (London, 1940).

Scott, Allen and Edward W. Soja (eds.). *The City: Los Angeles and Urban Theory at the End of the Twentieth Century* (Berkeley, 1996).

Scruggs, Charles. *Sweet Home: Invisible Cities in the Afro-American Novel* (London, 1993).

Sears, David O. 'Urban Rioting in Los Angeles: A Comparison of 1965 with 1992', in *The Los Angeles Riots: Lessons for the Urban Future*, edited by Mark Baldassare (Oxford, 1994), pp. 237–53.

See, Carolyn. *Making History* (New York, 1992).

Shelley, Jim. 'A Genre's Demon Dog', *The Guardian Weekend* (January 7, 1995), 16–19.

Siegle, Robert. *Suburban Ambush: Downtown Writing and the Fiction of Insurgency* (London, 1989).

Siver, Alan and Elizabeth Ward (eds.). *Film Noir* (London, 1980).

Smith, Anna Deavere. *Fires in the Mirror: Crown Heights, Brooklyn and Other Identities* (London, 1993).

Twilight: Los Angeles, 1992 (New York, 1994).

'Not So Special Vehicles', *Performing Arts Journal* 50/51 (1995), 77–89.

Smith, Neil. *Uneven Development: Nature, Capital and the Reproduction of Space* (Oxford, 1990).

Soja, Edward W. 'Taking Los Angeles Apart: Some Fragments of a Critical Human Geography', *Environment and Planning D: Society and Space* 4 (1986), 255–72.

Postmodern Geographies: The Reassertion of Space in Critical Social Theory (London, 1989).

'Postmodern Urbanization: The Six Restructurings of Los Angeles', in *Postmodern Cities and Spaces*, edited by S. Watson and K. Gibson (Oxford, 1995), pp. 125–37.

'Los Angeles, 1965–1992: From Crisis-Generated Restructuring to Restructuring-Generated Crisis', in *The City*, edited by Allen Scott and Edward W. Soja (Berkeley, 1996), pp. 426–62.

Thirdspace: Journeys to Los Angeles and Other Real-and-Imagined Places (Oxford, 1996).

'Six Discourses on the Postmetropolis', in *Imagining Cities: Scripts, Signs, Memories*, edited by Sallie Westwood and John Williams (London, 1997), pp. 19–30.

Soja, Edward W. and Allen J. Scott. 'Los Angeles: Capital of the Late Twentieth Century', *Environment and Planning D: Society and Space* 4 (1986), 249–54.

Sonenshein, R. J. *Politics in Black and White: Race and Power in Los Angeles* (Princeton, NJ, 1993).

Sorkin, Michael. *Exquisite Corpse: Writing on Buildings* (London, 1991).

Stallabrass, Julian. *Gargantua: Manufactured Mass Culture* (London, 1996).

Starr, Kevin. *Inventing the Dream* (Oxford, 1985).

Material Dreams (Oxford, 1990).

Steele, J. *Los Angeles Architecture: The Contemporary Condition* (London, 1993).

Bibliography

Stephenson, Neil. *Snow Crash* (London, 1993).

Steppling, J. 'Storyland' and 'Theory of Miracles', in *Best of the West: An Anthology of Plays from the 1989 and 1990 Padua Hills Playwrights Festival*, edited by Muray Mednick, Bill Raden and Cheryl Slean (Los Angeles, 1991), pp. 245–80.

Sun, W. H. and F. C. Fei. 'Masks or Faces Re-Visited: A Study of Four Theatrical Works Concerning Cultural Identity', *The Drama Review*, vol. 38, no. 4 (1994), 120–32.

Tani, Stefano. *The Doomed Detective: The Contribution of the Detective Novel to Postmodern American and Italian Fiction* (Carbondale, 1984).

Tervalon, Jervey. *Understand This* (New York, 1994).

Thomson, David. 'Uneasy Street', in *Sex, Death and God in LA*, edited by David Reid (London, 1994), pp. 321–33.

Thurschwell, Pamela. 'Elvis Costello as Cultural Icon and Cultural Critic', in Kevin Dettmar and Willliam Richey (eds.), *Reading Rock and Roll* (New York, 1999).

Timms, E. and D. Kelley (eds.). *Unreal City: Urban Experience in Modern European Literature and Art* (Manchester, 1985).

To Rebuild is Not Enough: Final Report and Recommendations of the Assembly Special Committee on the Los Angeles Crisis, California State Assembly, Assemblyman Curtis R. Tucker, Jr., Chair (September 28, 1992).

Todorov, Tzetevan. 'The Typology of Detective Fiction', translated by Richard Howard, in *Modern Criticism and Theory: A Reader*, edited by David Lodge (Burnt Mills, 1988), pp. 157–65.

Tyrnauer, Matthew. 'Who's Afraid of Bret Easton Ellis?' *Vanity Fair* (August, 1994), 94–7.

Viegener, Matias. 'Men Who Kill and the Boys Who Love Them', *Critical Quarterly*, vol. 36, no. 1 (1994).

Walker, D. (ed.). *Los Angeles: AD/USC Look at LA* (London, 1981).

Walker, Richard. 'California Rages Against the Dying of the Light', *New Left Review* (January–February 1995), 42–74.

Watson, Sophie and Katherine Gibson (eds.). *Postmodern Cities and Spaces* (Oxford, 1995).

West, Cornel. 'Foreword', in Anna Deavere Smith, *Fires in the Mirror: Crown Heights, Brooklyn and Other Identities* (London, 1993), pp. xiii–xix.

West, Nathanael. *Miss Lonelyhearts and The Day of the Locust* (New York, 1962).

Wilde, Oscar. 'The Soul of Man Under Socialism', in *Plays, Prose Writings, and Poems*, edited by Isobel Murray (London, 1980), pp. 257–88.

Willett, Ralph. *The Naked City: Urban Crime Fiction in the USA* (Manchester, 1996).

Williams, Raymond. 'The Metropolis and the Emergence of Modernism', in *Unreal City: Urban Experience in Modern European Literature and Art*, edited by E. Timms and D. Kelley (Manchester, 1985), pp. 13–24.

The Country and the City (London, 1993).

Williams, William Carlos. *Selected Essays* (New York, 1969).

Wilson, Edmund. 'The Boys in the Back Room', in *Classics and Commercials: A Literary Chronicle of the Forties* (New York, 1958).

Wirth-Nesher, Helen. *City Codes: Reading the Modern Urban Novel* (Cambridge, 1996).

Woetzel, J., M. McLaughlin, and C. Westphal (eds.). *The Southern California Anthology 1984*, introduction by John Rechy (Santa Barbara, 1984).

Wolverton, Terry and B. Weissman (eds.). *Harbinger: Poetry and Fiction by Los Angeles Writers* (Los Angeles, 1990).

Wolverton, Terry (ed.). *bloodWhispers: LA Writers on Aids* (Los Angeles, 1991).

Young, Elizabeth and Graham Caveney. *Shopping in Space: Essays on 'Blank Generation' Fiction* (London, 1993).

Žižek, Slavoj. *Looking Awry: An Introduction to Jacques Lacan through Popular Culture* (London, 1991).

'Multiculturalism, or, the Cultural Logic of Multinational Capitalism', in *New Left Review* 225 (September–October, 1997).

Zukin, Sharon. *Landscapes of Power: From Detroit to Disneyworld* (Oxford, 1991).

Index

Index

Kafka, Franz, 6, 141
Kaufman, Bob, 111
King, Rodney, 148, 157, 177n63
Kiss Me Deadly (Aldrich), 60
Klein, Norman M., 75, 176n6

LA 2000 Committee, 107
LA Confidential (Ellroy), 43, 52
'LA Quartet' (Ellroy), 34, 43–59
La Vida Loca (Rodriguez), 125
LA Weekly, 81–2
Lambert, Gavin, 32
Lapham, Lewis, 165, 167
Lautréamont, Conte de, 103
Lefebvre, Henri: production of space,
18–20, 28; representational theory
21–5, 39, 94, 155; everyday life, 25,
63; and the visual, 74–6, 95; and
contradictory space, 141–2, 183n3;
and rhythm analysis, 146
Lévi-Strauss, Claude, 174n63
Less Than Zero (Ellis), 35, 77, 79–81,
83–90
Limbaugh, Rush, 138
Lipsitz, George, 143
Little Caesar (magazine), 141
Little Yellow Dog, A (Mosley), 61
Locke, John, 31
Long Goodbye, The (Altman), 166
Los Angeles: as minoritized, 1–2, 6, 33,
35, 106–8, 132; its literary
community 3–6, 15; as 'real-and-
imagined', 8–16; exceptionalism of,
10; Board of Supervisors' plans for,
11; Culture Industry in, 12, 96, 99,
113, 165; as representation, 12–13,
75–6, 141, 159–69; segregation and
fragmentation, 13–14, 108–9, 157; as
test-case, 16; and production of
space, 20, 51–2, 68, 138–9, 167–8;
and *noir*, 21, 37–73; and amnesia, 23;
no pedestrians, 23; as cliché, 31,
48–9, 65, 164–5; and politics of
literary production, 33–4; and
working class, 35, 132; and crime
fiction, 41–3; Police Department,
43–59, 70, 116, 135, 148–9; as post-
Oedipal, 46, 51–4; city Hall, 47; Skid
Row, 48; freeways, 52, 79–80, 110;
Dodger Stadium, 52; Hollywood,
51–2, 53, 76, 106, 161; growth in
black population, 59–60, 109; Watts
and South Central ghettos, 63, 67–8,
109–25; Central Avenue nightlife,
69–70; visual character, 75–6, 95;
'sim-city', 76; and the disappearing
subject, 78; negative value of
literature in, 94–5; and rap music,
108; riots (1965), 109–10; ethnic
prehistory, 117–18; Third World in,
121–2; Mexican settlement in, 122–3;
riots (1992), 125, 134, 142–57; River,
126–7; post-industrial, 129–30; as
'un-American', 163–7
Lukács, George, 27

MacMurray, Fred, 60
Magistrale, Tony, 112
Manson, Charles, 31
Marshall, George, 60
Martin, Carol, 151
Marx, Karl, 172n20
Mason, Theodore O., 66
Matsuda, Sumio, 106
McBain, Ed, 42
McCoy, Horace, 37, 163
McNamara, Kevin R., 167
McWilliams, Carey, 13, 78
Melville, Herman, 105
Middlebrook, Diane Wood, 151
Montoya, José, 131
Moretti, Franco, 39, 40
Mosley, Walter, 4, 34, 39, 43, 59–73,
109, 159; and lateral realism,
61–5
My Dark Places (Ellroy), 43

naturalism, 14, 113
New York: as 'other' to LA, 4, 9
New York Times, 4, 146
Nietzsche, Friedrich, 5
noir, 21, 37–73

Odds Against Tomorrow (Wise), 60
Outsider, The (Camus), 86

Paredes, Amérigo, 131
Parker, Chief William, 43, 45–6, 48–9,
55, 56
Pearlstone, Zena, 123
Plato, 71, 89
Play It as It Lays (Didion), 80, 87–90
Poems Across the Pavement (Rodriguez),
125
Poetry LA, 106
Pollock, Jackson, 54
Postman Always Rings Twice, The
(Cain), 37, 87